Writing and Cinema

Crosscurrents

General Editors:

Professor J.B. Bullen, University of Reading
Dr Neil Sammells, Bath Spa University College
Dr Paul Hyland, Bath Spa University College

Titles in the series:

Writing and Cinema

Edited by Jonathan Bignell

Longman

Pearson Education Limited,
Edinburgh Gate,
Harlow,
Essex CM20 2JE,
United Kingdom
and Associated Companies throughout the world.

*Published in the United States of America
by Pearson Education Inc., New York*

© Pearson Education Limited 1999

First published 1999

ISBN 0–582–35758–6 CSD
ISBN 0–582–35757–8 PPR

Visit us on the world wide web at
http://www.awl-he.com

British Library Cataloguing-in-Publication Data
A catalogue record for this book is available
from the British Library

Library of Congress Cataloging-in-Publication Data
Writing and cinema / edited by Jonathan Bignell.
        p.   cm. — (Crosscurrents)
    Includes bibliographical references and index.
    ISBN 0–582–35758–6 (csd). — ISBN 0–582–35757–8
    1. Motion pictures and literature. 2. Film adaptations—History
and criticism. 3. Film criticism. I. Bignell, Jonathan.
    II. Series: Crosscurrents (London, England)
PN1995.3.W72 1999
791.43'6—dc21   98–32105
                                                                        CIP

Transferred to digital print on demand, 2005

Printed and bound by Antony Rowe Ltd, Eastbourne

Contents

Notes on contributors

Jonathan Bignell lectures in English and Media at the University of Reading. He is the author of *Media Semiotics: An Introduction* (1997), and has published on topics in film, media and cultural studies. He is currently writing a book on postmodern theory and the media, and is joint Project Director (with Stephen Lacey) of a four-year programme of research into British TV drama funded by the Arts and Humanities Research Board.

Mark Bould is Field Chair in Film, Media and Critical Studies at Buckinghamshire Chilterns University College. He is currently completing a Ph.D. on North American, British and Japanese science fiction since 1980.

Alain Cohen is Professor of Comparative Literature at the University of California, San Diego. He researches in semiotics, psychoanalysis, and the history and analysis of cinema. His recent publications have focused in detail on particular films by master directors, the rhetoric of filmic violence, and the poetics of painting in film. He is working on a book on the aesthetics of the film image, and a book on technical methods of film analysis.

Sean Cubitt is Reader in Video and Media Studies at Liverpool John Moores University. He is on the editorial board of the journals *Screen* and *Third Text*. He is the author of *Timeshift: On Video Culture* (1991) and *Videography: Video Media as Art and Culture* (1993).

Robert Giddings is Professor of Media Arts and Communications at Bournemouth University. He jointly wrote *Screening the Novel* (1990), and has published books on the poets of the First World

War and on Smollett. He is the editor of a forthcoming book on film and TV versions of literature for Manchester University Press, and co-author of a book on the history of radio and TV classic serials for Macmillan.

Leighton Grist lectures in Cultural Studies at King Alfred's University College, Winchester. He researches in Hollywood cinema, and has published on film noir and the Western.

Jim Hillier lectures in Film and Drama at the University of Reading. He has published widely on US cinema, including his book *The New Hollywood* (1992). He is also the editor of a collection of translated essays from the journal *Cahiers du Cinéma* (1996). He has recently completed an edited book on the films of Howard Hawks.

Reynold Humphries is Professor of Film Studies at the University of Lille, France. He is the author of *Fritz Lang: Genre and Representation in his American Films* (1993), and is currently writing a book on US horror films of the 1930s, and a book on the films of David Cronenberg. He teaches US cinema, Kenji Mizoguchi, and psychoanalytic film theory.

Ian Hunter lectures in Humanities at De Montfort University where he teaches Media Studies. He is a founding member of the Society for the Study of Popular British Cinema, is on the editorial board of its journal, and is a co-editor of Pluto Press's Film/Fiction series. He is co-editor of Routledge's Studies in Popular British Film series, for which he is preparing an edited book on British science fiction film. He also writes on horror films and American trash culture.

Stuart Laing is Assistant Director of the University of Brighton. He has published widely in media studies and cultural studies, including *Representations of Working Class Life 1957–64* (1986) and recent essays on Ken Loach and British television in the 1960s.

Stephen Lacey lectures in Film and Drama at the University of Reading. He is the author of *British Realist Theatre: The New Wave and its Context 1956–65* (1995), and has published articles on various aspects of British theatre. His research interests are in contemporary British theatre and television, and he is joint Project

Director (with Jonathan Bignell) of a four-year programme of research into British TV drama funded by the Arts and Humanities Research Board.

David Lusted is a freelance lecturer and writer. He is the author of *The Media Studies Book* (1992), co-editor of *The Television Studies Book* (1998) and has published widely on topics in popular film and cultural studies.

Kevin Moloney lectures in Media Arts and Communications at Bournemouth University. He is an ex-Fleet Street journalist and PR professional who now teaches public relations to undergraduates. He has published on the culture of professional lobbyists, and his study of the marketing of the BBC's *Pride and Prejudice* is forthcoming (1998).

Rona Munro is a screenwriter and playwright. She was the screenwriter of Ken Loach's film *Ladybird, Ladybird*, and has also written award-winning stage and television drama. She is currently working on an adaptation of Mrs Gaskell's *Mary Barton* for BBC television.

Douglas Pye lectures in Film and Drama at the University of Reading. He is a member of the editorial board of the film journal *Movie*, and has published widely on Hollywood cinema, especially the Western. He is the joint editor of *The Movie Book of the Western* (1996).

Lib Taylor lectures in Film and Drama at the University of Reading. She has published on women's theatre and performance, including British women dramatists 1956–68, and Deaf Sign Language as a language of the theatre. She is currently researching the relationships of Marguerite Duras's play *India Song* with the film and written text. She teaches theatre studies at undergraduate and postgraduate level.

John Tulloch is Professor of Media Communication at Cardiff University. He is the author of *Television Drama: Audience, Agency and Myth* (1990), co-author of *Science Fiction Audiences* (1995), and has published extensively on drama, television and film including the films of Ken Loach.

General editors' preface

Crosscurrents is an interdisciplinary series which explores simultaneously the new terrain revealed by recently developed methodologies while offering fresh insights into more familiar and established subject areas. In order to foster the cross-fertilization of the ideas and methods the topic broached by each volume is rich and substantial and ranges from issues developed in culture and gender studies to the re-examination of aspects of English studies, history and politics. Within each of the volumes, however, the sharpness of focus is provided by a series of essays which is directed to examine that topic from a variety of perspectives. There is no intention that these essays, either individually or collectively, should offer the last word on the subject – on the contrary. They are intended to be stimulating rather than definitive, open-ended rather than conclusive, and it is hoped that each of them will be pithy and thought-provoking.

Each volume has a general introduction setting out the scope of the topic, the various modes in which it has been developed and which places the volume as a whole in the context of other work in the field. Everywhere, from the introduction to the bibliographies, pointers will be given on how and where the ideas suggested in the volumes might be developed in different ways and different directions, and how the insights and methods of various disciplines might be brought to bear to yield new approaches to questions in hand. The stress throughout the books will be on crossing traditional boundaries, linking ideas and bringing together concepts in ways which offer a challenge to previously compartmentalized modes of thinking.

Some of the essays will deal with literary or visual texts which are well known and in general circulation. Most touch on primary material which is not easily accessible outside major library collections, and where appropriate, that material has been placed in a portfolio of documents collected at the end of each volume. Here again, it is hoped that this will provide a stimulus to discussion; it will give readers who are curious to explore further the implications of the arguments an opportunity to develop their own initiatives and to broaden the spectrum of their reading.

The authors of these essays range from international writers who are established in their respective fields to younger scholars who are bringing fresh ideas to the subjects. This means that the styles of the chapters are as various as their approaches, but in each case the essays have been selected by the general editors for their high level of critical acumen.

Professor J. B. Bullen
Dr Paul Hyland
Dr Neil Sammells

Acknowledgements

I thank the contributors to this book for their effort, patience and enthusiasm throughout the process of compiling and editing the essays. I am grateful both to the Crosscurrents Series Editors, and to the editorial team at Addison Wesley Longman, for their support and efficiency. I am also grateful to my friend David Sutcliffe, who created the original artwork on the cover of this book. The Departments of English and of Film and Drama at the University of Reading have, as always, been stimulating environments in which to think about writing and cinema, and I thank all of the people there and elsewhere who have helped in so many ways.

Introduction

Jonathan Bignell

The expansion of film and media studies in higher education, and the blurring of disciplinary boundaries between literary and media studies, have been evaluated either as a process of reinvigoration or decline.[1] In my view, as someone who began as a student of English literature and moved gradually into the field of film and media, the crosscurrents of influence between these areas are stimulating forces. This book, following the aims of the series in which it belongs, argues for the importance of the study of writing and cinema together, in the various ways in which this topic can be understood. I hope that the book will be interesting and useful to that growing constituency of students of English, film, media, communications, and cultural studies, whose concerns are, I believe, more shared than separate.

There are already many books which focus on adaptations of 'classic' literature into film and/or television.[2] There are also many books emerging from the recent cross-fertilisation between literary and cultural studies, focusing on the study of contemporary film and literary culture.[3] This collection of essays investigates the relationships between written and cinematic communication, and offers detailed studies of a wide range of writing and film including 'classic' and 'popular' examples. It reconsiders the topics of study already addressed in this area, questions some of their assumptions and opens new areas of debate. So the aim of this book is to present, in accessible form, a wide-ranging selection of work which addresses the various ways in which the topic 'writing and cinema' can be understood. When I began work on this project, I was concerned to exploit the ambiguity which the title *Writing and Cinema* possesses. It seemed to me that there were at least four ways in which the title could be interpreted, and these four meanings are the basis for the four sections in the book. First, 'writing and cinema' could refer to the kinds of writing which are produced prior to the release of a film. Films (the vast majority of fiction films, at least) have a written screenplay, which is the working template used in production. As a film moves towards its release date, further kinds of writing appear, like press releases, publicity packs for journalists, and advertising copy, aiming to shape the meaning of a film for its potential audience. The first section of the book, 'Writing for cinema', deals with these aspects of 'writing and cinema', and includes three essays which address them in rather different ways.[4]

The first essay, by John Tulloch and Rona Munro, focuses on the processes involved in scripting films. This essay arises out of a series of dialogues between the two writers, in which they work towards a shared understanding of their different writing experiences. Rona Munro is a professional writer, who explains and reflects on her work writing the film *Ladybird, Ladybird* (1994) for the acclaimed director Ken Loach. As a theatre and television writer, she also places that experience in relation to the problems, politics and aims of her writing in other contexts. John Tulloch is a senior academic who has experience of writing critically about Loach's film work, with particular attention to the process of production. Tulloch and Munro begin with different agendas and different writing backgrounds, and thus the essay takes a dialogic form in two senses. It is the product of a dialogue (much of the essay is presented in a dialogue format), and it is about the ways in which Loach and his work are 'written' or constructed in an ongoing dialogue between different 'voices' or discourses. The essay illuminates relationships between writing for the cinema and the finished film product, and also relationships between films and the kinds of writing which define, reflect on, and critique them.

The second essay in the section is my own contribution, which looks at the ways we might understand a film written by the distinguished literary writer, Samuel Beckett. The essay shows that although Beckett's *Film* (1964) has very often been discussed via a traditional literary focus on Beckett's authorship, there are other valid claims for 'authorship' and authority over the film. The written text for *Film* is not like a script, and the finished film omitted a significant section of the written scenario. The film's director (normally the key creative worker in cinema, rather than the screenwriter) downplayed his own role in the production. The main actor, Buster Keaton, was the apparent centre of its meaning for *Film*'s first audiences. By examining some of the ambiguities and paradoxes around *Film* in detail, my essay tries to destabilise our easy assumption that *Film* is Samuel Beckett's film. The question of how the meanings of a film are shaped by different kinds of writing provides a link with the third essay in this section, by Kevin Moloney. He analyses the work of film publicists, placing the activities of contemporary publicists in a historical context, and paralleling their work with publicity in other areas of the modern economy. Giving brief examples in the promotion of recent films, Moloney shows how writing and marketing in the world of cinema publicity attempt to set the terms for the reception of films by actual audiences. For Moloney, contemporary culture is characterised by the circulation of commodities (like films) and their pleasures. His particular interest is in how this circulation is facilitated and achieved by means of various discourses and processes.

The second section of the book, 'Writing in cinema', addresses a relatively neglected area in the academic study of cinema.[5] Here the meaning of 'writing and cinema' which the contributors have focused on is the presence of written language or other kinds of inscription on the cinema screen itself. The essays by Sean Cubitt and Jim Hillier each present a detailed and historically situated discussion of the relationships between reading and viewing, to stimulate new ways of thinking about writing on screen, while Lib Taylor's essay discusses issues of gender and power concretised by the meanings of writing and other forms of inscription.

Cubitt investigates how a rhetorical method can be developed for the study of writing in film. He discusses the forms of screened writing, drawing on a range of examples and distinguishing between them to develop a taxonomic system which provides the basis for their analysis. The essay proposes a rhetoric of screen writing, discussing writing and frame, typeface, scale and movement; writing in relation to image, voice and background; and writing in subtitles, credits, titles and intertitles. Writing on screen in this literal sense is also the subject of Hillier's essay, which focuses on a very different type of film. In Hillier's view, most narrative cinema has assumed that watching and listening do not need (or are even opposite to) the written word. In avant-garde cinema, especially since the 1960s, writing on screen has been extensively used, partly to point out the difference of writing from the image. The essay analyses *So Is This* (1982), made by the avant-garde film-maker Michael Snow, which consists entirely of words on screen, placing the film in the context of Snow's other films and films by other radical film-makers. The essay considers relationships between reading and viewing, especially the control over the temporal rhythms of comprehension which Snow's work emphasises. The third essay in this section takes up some of these concerns with writing which literally appears on the cinema screen, but also extends the meaning of 'writing' into other forms of inscription. In her essay, Lib Taylor analyses the intricate pattern of uses of writing or physical communication in *The Piano* (1993), showing how this approach extends our understanding of issues of gender, power and sexuality in the film and in culture more generally. The multiple modes of inscription in the film include written notes, writing carved onto piano keys, subtitled Maori language, Deaf Sign Language 'written' by the body, and piano-playing as a cinematic inscription of the emotional and thematic concerns of the film. The essay shows how these multiple communicative forms disrupt and disempower patriarchal and colonialist structures of meaning.

The third section, 'Writing into cinema', deals with examples of written texts adapted for the film medium. This has been a topic of academic study for many years, and the essays in this section focus on texts and films from a broad historical range and from different literary genres, from a nineteenth-century 'classic' to recent science fiction and theatre plays. Robert Giddings's essay is based around an analysis of the various versions of *Mutiny on the Bounty*, outlining the cultural and historical context of the original book, and discussing the 1935, 1962 and 1984 film versions of the story. The essay asks why this relatively insignificant event in naval history has been of so much interest to film-makers and film audiences. Each version had strong resonances at the times when the various retellings were produced, and the essay investigates the different emphases of each version in relation to their cultural and historical moments. This comparative approach also informs Alain Cohen's essay, though it draws on a different, semiotic approach. Cohen analyses the adaptations of Flaubert's novel *Madame Bovary* by Renoir (1934), Minelli (1958) and Chabrol (1991). The methods he uses include using shot-by-shot analysis, and work on narrative construction. The discussion of the three film versions, one from

Hollywood and two by French directors, enables him to compare film styles, to discuss visuality in literary writing, and to consider the cognitive work of the spectator in relation to the various interpretations of Flaubert's text. The essay focuses in particular on a short sequence containing the motif of dance, and Cohen also situates dance sequences in the history of cinema.

Stuart Laing's essay addresses the different capabilities of literary discourse and film narrative, showing how the emphases of novels are produced or changed in the films made of them, and placing the film versions of three novels in the cultural and political context at the specific time of their release around the General Election in Britain in 1997. The essay uses case-study analyses of three apparently very different films, *The English Patient* (1996), *Fever Pitch* (1997) and *Crash* (1996), drawing out their shared engagement with contemporary cultural themes and mythologies. Although the section deals mainly with the relationships between cinema and prose fiction, an important comparative note is struck in the essay by Stephen Lacey. For Lacey, one of the distinctive features of the explosion in theatre activity following *Look Back in Anger* in 1956 has been the willingness of dramatists to work in the electronic media, especially film. The reasons for this often involve the desire to experiment with narrative form and to reach a newer and wider audience than that available to the theatre. These desires have frequently been underpinned by a radical (or at least liberal humanist) politics. Film has seemed to guarantee a narrative freedom beyond the box set of the naturalist stage, and the ability to show a society in transition. The essay discusses the relationships between theatre and film in recent times by tracing these aims through the work of playwright and film writer David Hare, who has pursued the same or similar concerns in both film and theatre.

The remaining two essays in this section address science fiction texts and films, genres which have lately become increasingly of interest to academic analysts working in popular fiction, popular film and postmodernism.[6] Mark Bould's essay analyses the clusters of literary and cinematic texts which we know as *Blade Runner* (1982, 1991) and *Johnny Mnemonic* (1995). For Bould, they potentially decentre notions of authority and originality by supplementing, rewriting, interpreting and reconfiguring each other through the proliferation of alternative versions and sequels, each attempting to 'fix' the meaning of 'earlier' texts in the cluster. Both clusters enable an exploration of the discursive construction of identity and the body, questioning notions of subjectivity in an interplay of proliferating intertexts. From a related critical perspective, Ian Hunter's essay discusses relationships between literary science fiction and sci-fi films. The essay concentrates on an analysis of the film version of Robert Heinlein's novel *Starship Troopers*, directed by Paul Verhoeven (1997). The discussion is situated in the context of analytical approaches to 'pulp' literature and popular film in postmodern trash culture, including discussion of analytical approaches to contemporary science fiction. The film version of *Starship Troopers* is also placed in relation to the particular version of trash culture evident in Verhoeven's other film work.

The fourth section of the book, 'Writing about cinema', contains essays specifically addressing critical discourses on cinema,[7] although the other essays in the book also reflect on their own theoretical and analytical methods. Douglas Pye traces the shifting critical discourses on *The Searchers* (1956), one of the most celebrated post-war Hollywood films, widely regarded as one of John Ford's masterpieces, and endlessly referred to by contemporary directors. But before the 1970s the film's reputation was much more mixed, and it was held in low regard by influential writers on Ford such as Lindsay Anderson. Pye's essay restores the claims made for *The Searchers* to their historical contexts. He places these claims within the development of critical approaches to Hollywood, the Western and John Ford. The second essay in the section draws on the specific critical tradition of psychoanalytic approaches to cinema. Reynold Humphries's essay argues that writing about cinema should be primarily concerned with the specificity of film 'language', rather than themes, manifest concerns, creators or economic environment. For Humphries, the meaning of a film depends crucially on the use of the camera to enunciate point-of-view and to position spectators in relation to character and action so that their sympathies and interpretations are oriented by the use of these enunciative strategies. The task of the critic is then to pinpoint what effect a film has on audiences through the different points of view created by identifications with the camera and with characters.

The fourth section concludes with an essay jointly written by Leighton Grist and David Lusted, which reflects in a wide-ranging analysis on two dominant traditions in writing about film. One of the most significant contributions to film studies has been the concept of specularity, addressed particularly in Humphries's essay. This influential idea has generated much writing on the ideological power of the Hollywood film to construct gendered viewing positions for audiences, and has underpinned an important claim for popular cinema's role in the reproduction of patriarchy. In a separate development, cultural studies have examined the historical role of the Hollywood film in twentieth-century culture, noting the contiguity between women as key figures in the new sound film genres of the 1930s and the actively consuming women of modernity among the predominantly female cinema audiences. Grist and Lusted explore conflicts between these two modes of writing about cinema by analysing the MGM musical *Dancing Lady* (1932). In keeping with the modes of performance in film musicals, *Dancing Lady* centres on the body of the heroine (Joan Crawford) as the object of an erotic look. Yet, as in many musicals of this period, she is a socially mobile working-class woman who becomes a star through hard work and talent. The object of the specular look is also the subject of the narrative. The essay discusses whether Crawford can be both object and subject, whether a historical framework questions the significance of a formal reading, or whether an attention to film form can amend the empiricism of a historical reading. Thus the essay explores essential questions about how film has been written about and understood through ideas of specularity and modernity.

One of the distinctive features of books in the Crosscurrents series is the presence of a Documents section following the essays, where study materials are presented. In this book, the Documents section is replaced by a guide to audio-visual material (especially films on videotape) which may be useful in following up the topics and ideas presented in the essays. A short guide to relevant resources is provided for each essay.

Notes

1. See, for instance, Antony Easthope, *Literary into Cultural Studies* (London, 1991) for a discussion of this issue.
2. See the 'Writing into cinema' section of the Select Bibliography at the back of this book for a list of works on this subject.

3. See, for example, Deborah Cartmell, I.Q. Hunter, Heidi Kaye and Imelda Whelehan (eds), *Pulping Fictions: Consuming Culture across the Literature/Media Divide* (London, 1996).

4. See the 'Writing for cinema' section of the Select Bibliography at the back of this book for a list of works on these subjects.

5. See the 'Writing in cinema' section of the Select Bibliography at the back of this book for a list of works on this subject.

6. See, for example, Vivien Sobchack, *Screening Space: The American Science Fiction Film* (2nd edn, New York, 1987), Annette Kuhn (ed.), *Alien Zone: Cultural Theory and Contemporary Science Fiction Cinema* (London, 1990), and J.P. Telotte, *Replications: A Robotic History of the Science Fiction Film* (Urbana and Chicago, IL, 1995).

7. This vast area of scholarship obviously overlaps with the subjects of the other three sections of this book, but see the 'Writing about cinema' section of the Select Bibliography for a selection of books on the subject.

Part One
Writing for Cinema

1 'Whose stories you tell': writing 'Ken Loach'

John Tulloch in conversation with Rona Munro

> Bakhtin's concept of language [is] inherently dialogic . . . it's [about] discursive polyphony, its subtle and complex interweaving of various types of speech . . . and its carnivalesque irreverence towards all kinds of authoritarian, repressive, monologic ideologies.
>
> David Lodge, *After Bakhtin* (1990)[1]

This essay comes out of a series of dialogues between John Tulloch (JT), an academic who has written about Ken Loach in his book *Television Drama*,[2] and Rona Munro (RM), a screenwriter and playwright, who scripted Ken Loach's award-winning film *Ladybird, Ladybird* (1994). Both participants in the dialogue share an admiration for Loach's films and for his politics. Both, therefore, are *'fans'*. JT and RM also share another kind of fandom – of television science fiction. While JT published an ethnographic academic study of *Doctor Who*,[3] RM wrote the series' final British episode ('Survival', 1989). So, as they speak about Ken Loach – both as enthusiastic *audiences* of Ken Loach's work *and* as writers of 'Ken Loach' – many other narratives and genres from their various other writing activities and audience pleasures circulate in their talk.

This, of course, is the very nature of situated dialogue. As David Lodge (himself a TV writer and academic) points out (following Bakhtin), in situated, *active* talk, words 'come to us already imprinted with the meanings, intentions and accents of previous users, and any utterance we make is directed towards some real or hypothetical Other' (Lodge, p. 21). When JT and RM talk 'Ken Loach', their words are not only 'imprinted' with finding out what the other one likes in writing (for or about) Ken Loach, but also imprinted with the agendas in which their two different kinds of writing take place.

JT's is an academic agenda, going back to a series of influential articles about Loach by Colin MacCabe in the late 1970s.[4] Loach's subject matter may, MacCabe argued, have *pointed* to the Left and to issues of liberation from exploitation, but his film form did the opposite by imposing an 'imaginary unity' on the viewer. The 'classic realist text' – whether a nineteenth-century novel or Loach's 1973 television film *Days of Hope* – certainly consisted of many voices, representing all kinds, classes and genders of people. But while this gave the text a 'reality effect', for MacCabe the classic realist text had two further features which in fact curtailed this carnival of voices. First, it always established a 'hierarchy of discourses', with the author's voice positioning and evaluating all the others; second, the author's voice was the only one *not* in inverted commas: it pretended not to be a discursive construction but reality itself – and this was abetted in Loach's film by a naturalistic shooting style. For MacCabe, Loach's practice was the very opposite of the kind of anti-authoritarian 'discursive polyphony' that David Lodge, like Bakhtin, admires.

JT's second agenda comes from researching and writing about Loach's film *Fatherland* (1986) and its writer, Trevor Griffiths. Sharing Griffiths's own cultural materialist position, JT also shared his concern that Loach's naturalist directorial method repressed Griffiths's 'critical realism punctuated by . . . expressionist dreams'; as Griffiths said of his film writing, 'critical realism accepts that it is a convention, a literary convention, or a filmic convention; and naturalism on the whole doesn't allow its practitioners that degree of reflexivity and self-consciousness' (Tulloch, *Television Drama*, p. 161). And for Griffiths this is also true of film actors. '*Performance* . . . is absolutely key to my work. My texts cannot be done by non-actors. . . . Film acting is minimal acting . . . but it has to be *acting* for me, not . . . what naturalists are looking for, which is *being*' (Tulloch, *Television Drama*, p. 159).

These earlier academic Others are in JT's agenda as he discusses Loach with RM. Yet JT still admires Loach and uses this dialogue to continue asking himself 'why?'.

RM's agenda is as a professional writer, surrounded by other professional writers – newspaper reviewers, or well-known 'Loach' writers like Jim Allen (a co-author on the planned TV soap opera that Loach originally approached RM to write), or 'dead, white female' writers RM is commissioned to adapt for film, like Mrs

Gaskell. So whereas JT's agenda included 'Other' academic and screenwriter criticisms of Loach for his 'controlling' naturalism, RM's 'control' agenda related especially to the effect *on* Loach's films (and on her own writing) of 'Other' writers. This sense of 'Other' writers was especially strong in relation to the British media, who like to tell a potential audience that Loach's films are 'about' his Left politics, thus missing the European media's analysis of *Ladybird, Ladybird* as a film about emotional loss. RM's agenda includes, also, a political take on the difference between her own writing and these media 'Others'; the fact that the publicists at the Venice Film Festival liked to glamorise the director and the writer of a film about people assaulted by police and social workers, who live in a two-room flat with three kids. For RM the media's 'control' is over potential audiences, over the actual subjects of films like *Ladybird, Ladybird*, and over herself as writer. As a writer, RM lacks direct contact with her audience. What she is surrounded by instead is media reviews. So RM tries 'not to have anyone else's voice . . . what *The Observer* or *The Guardian* or *Kaleidoscope* thought about' when writing. When she writes in the author's note to her *Bold Girls* (the play which Loach read before first approaching her), 'in 1995, I realise that I do not know what it is like to be in West Belfast now, except as it is shown to me through the media', she is regretting the 'lost touch with my friends in Belfast' over five years in writing the play.[5] So being 'different and fresh and original' *does* mean listening to other voices, and for RM it is Loach's direct contact with the voices of his audience/subjects that makes his films so special. Loach seeks to liberate onto the big screen voices of people that are all too often repressed (in courts, in the media, and among professional surveillance 'experts' like police and social workers).

According to *both* their intertextual agendas, JT and RM believe that Loach has 'been criticised enough'. This essay is not a 'representative' account of writing and film. Both the authors in dialogue here reject the notion of the 'transparency' of authorship that MacCabe criticises – hence the reflexivity of this introduction. Lack of 'objectivity' is not, however, the same thing as lack of critical relevance. The chapter tries, via a case study of Ken Loach, to approach the issue of what it means for academics and film writers to *write* in a book about writing and cinema. It tries to avoid a position where the academics are 'experts', while the film writers are simply exotic 'Others'. Not least this means reflexivity about the Bakhtinian future answering words towards which this *particular* academic book is oriented. This is not only for teaching students, but also is part of several academics' research output. So this is not a happenstance discussion between JT and RM. JT's academic interests in intertextuality, genre, popular culture, audience theory etc., are undeniably guiding voices in the discussion that follows, and in the reflexive framework of this introduction. However, despite the 'interweaving of various types of speech' in their dialogue, JT and RM *do* come to a consensus about their pleasure in Ken Loach. And that consensus is *itself* about the dialogic possibility of writing and film. They admire Loach precisely because of *his* 'complex interweaving of various types of speech' in opposition 'towards all kinds of authoritarian . . . ideologies'.

'True stories': *Ladybird, Ladybird*

Early in their series of discussions, JT raised with RM the academic debate since the 1970s around Loach's 'transparency effect', the so-called camera 'truth' of his naturalism. RM responded to this with:

RM: Is he trying to tell the truth or is he telling a story?

So, in response to JT's academic 'history', RM, like Trevor Griffiths, began to talk about writing/filmic conventions and the telling of stories in *Ladybird, Ladybird*.

RM: That was a true story and it was a dramatisation of a true story as it was told to me by the real people involved.

Already the developing dialogue juxtaposed both 'truth or story?' and 'true story'. How might these be reconciled within a writer's sense of creativity?

JT: As a writer what sort of ethical or professional or creative considerations then come into play? Are you trying simply to reproduce that story in another form or are you trying to change it creatively to make some more general point?

RM: At the end of the day I have to get the *emotional* truth right. . . . From my point of view it was telling the story that I'd been told and then getting the feel of it as empathetically as I could.

JT: But did you think of that as an individual story or as a representative story, or both?

RM: I thought about it as an individual story. I don't think of representative things, as though there's some way you can generalise people's experience. . . . You can emphasise any story as part of a larger experience, but you can't say this is typical of this or typical of that.

JT: But a lot of people would have read that film as a critique of . . .

RM: Yeah, but that's to do with the way people see Ken, isn't it? . . . In Europe the film's seen as being this great emotional story about loss and how people deal with loss; and in Britain it's seen as being an attack on government.

JT: Is that a worry?

RM: No, because it doesn't really bother audiences. It only bothers people that write articles in newspapers. . . . The problem is that the people that write in the papers can then *limit* the audience you reach. But once it reaches an audience I think most people respond to the story, they either identify with it or they don't, or they get absorbed in it or they don't. It would have been naive if we hadn't expected some of the reaction that we got. But the film doesn't get that in Europe, and most of its continuing life has been abroad anyway.

JT, wanting to tease out further Griffiths's 'creative fiction/naturalism/truth' tension, led the dialogue to Loach's 'method'.

Production relations: 'the Method'

JT began his questions from Griffiths's concern over Loach's choice of actors/writers etc., who have 'experienced' this or that social 'truth'. RM resisted this, saying that while *Ladybird, Ladybird* certainly 'had strong female characters in it', like her play *Bold Girls* about four women in West Belfast in the late 1980s, otherwise the film was 'different emotional territory' from her own or her characters' experiences. JT followed up with Griffiths's view

of realism as a thing of crafting, selection, and showing the underlying, as against Loach's 'method'.

RM: Well . . . Ken's method . . . produces a particular result that's
       like nothing else. And when I first saw it, on set, and he
       basically was very quietly saying to the actors 'what's this
       scene about, give me some suggestions about what the emo-
       tions here might be', and the actors were saying nothing
       that was in my script, certainly I *was* going 'Oh my God!'.
       But then they would do it again, and after about seventeen
       takes, the remarkable thing was, somewhere in the process
       the actors would end up saying almost exactly what I had
       written, and if they didn't it was probably because they
       were the wrong lines. For me this was really educational as
       a writer, because I started to learn which lines had some-
       thing solid in them, and the ones that were maybe just
       patched together . . . and didn't hold *up* to that method. It
       meant that the ones that were left were really strong . . . so
       that you end up with this extraordinary thing . . . which
       isn't like other films. It's a Ken Loach film, and I was
       always very clear I was writing a Ken Loach film – that if it
       isn't real for the person saying the lines you can't do it.

Still unclear about the relationship between the written lines and
the actor's 'real' role, JT then made Griffiths's point about actors,
naturalism and 'being'.

RM: He didn't do that on *Ladybird*. . . . I don't think he does
       that nearly as much as people think – that idea that he
       doesn't work with real actors. We had Ray Winstanley and
       he's a *stunning* actor. . . . But I always knew that Ken was
       going to use his method. I did know that he's an auteur
       in the sense that it is one vision, it's not a collective film
       process. It *operates* as a collective because everyone's given
       equal status, but you're working as a collective to make a
       Ken Loach film, and I think that's fair enough because he's
       brilliant.

JT: But I think sometimes that can be a very controlling, ideo-
       logically closed device. . . . The reason in my view that it
       isn't with Ken Loach is that he is so open and honest with

accessing voices to the screen, voices that I never ever hear, and I think that's why his films are so powerful. These are not voices that we normally get in the visual media – or at least, not telling their own stories.... Ken, somehow, by working through his method – and I don't know enough about the method ... because I found it hard to get close to it – does access these voices. But ... is that something you actually felt as you were writing?

RM: I admire the guy exactly for that, plus the end result is strong enough ... and it's then very exciting to *complement* that method.... It's *incredibly* exciting – *that's* the team thing. With Ken it's not like you're a writer of a 'work' hoping that some director's going to be a completely empathetic mind reader and reproduce your inner vision.

JT: I wrote about Ken Loach's method in my *TV Drama* book, but some of that came from ... Trevor Griffiths ... who had problems with Ken's method on *Fatherland*. That's why I'm trying to probe with you as a *writer*. You said earlier that everybody who's seen Ken Loach's films knows what the method is. Well, I'm not sure that's true, and I'm not sure that we'd have the same way of describing it from our different professional writing positions anyway.... You said you learnt it as you were writing it – what for you then as a writer *is* the Ken Loach method?...

RM: You know the feel that you're going to end up with, and it's that thing of it's not fly-on-the-wall, but it's film and it's beautiful film because Barry's a great lighting cameraman. So it does have that big cinema feel ... which obviously in one way isn't real, but it's completely real in another way....

JT: Emotionally real – is that what you mean?

RM: *Yeah* – and in its detail and in its complications.... Sometimes it's messy and sometimes it's completely clear. And *of course* it's not naturalism, because if it was naturalism *Ladybird, Ladybird* would have been a film that lasted four years.... There's no such thing as naturalism in that sense, is there?

The two writer-fans of Ken Loach seemed to agree that Loach's films reached well beyond naturalism; and JT drew on an earlier comment of RM about the 'emotionally real' which also had some purchase in cultural studies.[6] But 'emotionally real' might mean different things in these two writers' agendas. RM's response that this was not naturalism because 'sometimes it's messy and sometimes it's clear' led to comparing film in this regard with other visual media in the *practice* of writing.

Practising plays, television, films

JT: So how would your film writing process in this context of Ken's method differ from one of your own plays, or doing a television piece?

RM: It's different, as in telly, if you don't know who the director is going to be, because then you write in some ways more tentatively and in other ways more personally and bolder – sometimes you are trying to protect things because you can't imagine how someone's going to realise them, so you have to write in a way that spells out what needs to happen. . . . Television's about will they . . . get the money to make it, what are we going to do with this scene when we don't get the budget for that? And if it survives all that, it's a beleaguered team, I think. . . . And that's why there's not much good television drama around because the whole process of doing it is so enervating for everybody. . . . It's all about money. . . . Film's got money pressures too, obviously, but . . . if anybody's mad enough to do film in the first place it's because they've got a certain reckless quality, whereas telly's full of people protecting what's basically a steady job. . . . It can infect the whole establishment. . . .

In contrast, in the theatre the writer and the director are a very close partnership, and you've got to find a way of making that work . . . as a team. . . . Theatre is a different medium, a writer's medium. . . . Whereas a film's made in the editing . . . basically they're going to decide where the audience's attention is going to be focused. In theatre it's still collaborative . . . but at the end of the day a theatre writer determines . . . what an audience's experience of a theatre play will be.

RM takes this question down her own track as a practising writer; JT, still searching for a way of clarifying the writer/film-maker collaboration around 'emotional truth', follows a familiar media studies agenda, into 'political economy' and 'resistance' approaches.

JT: In theatre, in television and in film, what are the differences in the ways in which the economy of that particular site determines what you do, makes you have to resist?

RM: I still have a kind of mental morality about it, which is if the school fees are due and the mortgage isn't getting paid, and they offer cash to you, you do it. And you do theatre for the love of it because it's such an exciting medium and it gives you such a strong and unique voice and that's incredibly important. . . . But the money is ridiculously less in theatre. . . . I'm now getting to love film a lot – telly less, because it is so much about compromises. . . . It is about what . . . the producer's expectation is of what will get . . . financed. . . . So for me it's always 'if I can't pay the rent, then maybe I can do *The Bill'*. . . . That's not a value judgement – that what I do is higher and better than *The Bill*. . . . It's the same as a *Star Trek* fan . . . a similar serial type of programme . . . that I enjoy so much partly because I *don't* write it. . . . I can relax with it.

Having himself written about science fiction and soap opera audiences,[7] JT began more 'populist' media studies questions about audience pleasure in popular culture. RM resisted this populism. She was still talking about emotional truth.

RM: A television soap audience may be bigger than any other, but it's *how* you reach them. I want to reach them in that particularly magical way that you only do in the theatre or film. . . . Soap opera isn't magic. It's cosy and friendly and it's part of your living room like your teapot – and that's gorgeous too, but I want to do the 'Wow', the biggy, I really like that. . . .

There's something that came up at the Berlin Festival . . . I remember I got quite teary because . . . we'd never seen *Ladybird* on the big screen, and when we saw it in Berlin it was on the *big* 35 mm screen . . . and it was seeing Chrissie Rock's face with that wonderful Barry Ackroyd lighting – *that* big on that screen at that particular moment and going '*Wow*'. It's that thing that the big screen does, so that it all becomes slightly larger than life. . . . And to see someone with that kind of *ordinary* face and yet saying 'look, that's beautiful too' was *so* moving. I remember saying this, and Ken was kind of like, 'Oh, *yes!*'

But what is that Loach big screen magic *for*? The two writers begin to clarify that point – and their particular pleasure in Ken Loach – as they go on to discuss RM's current film project for television, *Mary Barton*.

Genre: 'tampering' with the canonical

RM had already said she tried to avoid 'the idea of a genre to aim for'.

JT: But presumably this is going to be part of the wave of TV costume dramas?

RM: No, I don't think they want a costume drama. What is so different about *Mary Barton* is that it's about working people in Manchester in the 1840s, it's not about the big house people in the poke bonnets and the carriages. It's actually about the Chartists . . . about the weavers . . . that's what's lovely about it.

JT: Where you're doing a writing job on a famous writer, what's that process like? How does that compare with *Ladybird, Ladybird*?

RM: Well, it's already written, so you've got your plot, you've got your characters. And whereas with *Ladybird* you're trying to represent the emotional truth of real people, in something like *Mary Barton* you're trying to represent the atmosphere of what another writer created in a completely different medium. . . . And then you have to ask yourself how much can you *tamper*?

Here JT and RM were discussing the intertextual relation of the writer to 'source' texts. Griffiths, for example, had substantially

changed the ironic and reflexive 'polyphony of variations' of Milan
Kundera's novel *The Book of Laughter and Forgetting* (which was
the text Loach had originally brought to the writer for *Fatherland*),
finding Kundera's Bakhtin-style 'laughter of variation' too 'terminal'
(Tulloch, *Television Drama*, pp. 153–5). So how much would RM
'tamper'?

RM: It's actually parallel problems: . . . the problem of how do
      you turn a novel into a film, and the problem of how do
      you turn a novel into a film that the person who controls
      the money wants to make at this time. And the biggest
      problem is trying to make sure that you're really focusing
      on doing the first and not being influenced by doing the
      second when you've just got a new flat and you know
      you're going to have to pay the mortgage tomorrow. . . .
          I've changed the book quite radically in some ways to
      make it work filmically. Because it'll be a one-off film as
      opposed to a series, the story dynamic inevitably has to
      change. In fact, Mrs Gaskell wrote – quite like Dickens – in
      a way which would have lent itself very naturally to serial-
      isation: loads of peripheral 'characters' in capital letters.
      But a lot of that had to go to turn it into a ninety-minute
      possible BBC film feature. . . . I've had to kill a lot of char-
      acters – but the nice thing about that is that a lot of the
      Chartist stuff and the working-class politics that was getting
      shoved out sideways is able to come back centre stage.
          And then, of course, at the moment we're all expected to
      produce the next *Full Monty* or the next *Trainspotting*. . . .
      And Mary Barton is set in this gritty urban environment,
      has strikes, has a murder in it, and is against a background
      of drug-dependency, prostitution and poverty. So one could
      do a kind of '*Trainspotting* Manchester 1840s'. . . . And
      I think one of the reasons that I got the gig is because of
      Ladybird . . . that kind of wham-in-your-face 'naturalism' in
      inverted commas. . . . But I feel I've been taken on to do an
      adaptation of *Mrs Gaskell*, and she's another writer, and the
      fact that she's been dead for a hundred years doesn't mean
      that you can just whack her around to make *Trainspotting*
      in Manchester in the 1840s. . . . I think you've got a certain
      responsibility to the original author. . . .

JT: My next question is about 'emotional truth' and your politics . . . when you said to me 'it's great' *Mary Barton*'s about working-class weavers.

RM: I think my politics are very muddy and unclear and not a conscious part of my work. . . . But in as much as I do have a political angle in my work it is in consciously trying to make unheard voices or invisible experiences visible. I think particularly as a woman writer doing female characters that's largely what you're doing. It's not like you have to give a particular slant to them. . . . It's the fact that women's experience isn't seen or isn't portrayed honestly. And it's the same with working-class historical experience – it isn't seen. We know the history of the poke bonnet, we don't know the history of the working class. . . .

   If you start to redress that balance that's very exciting, because it has a resonance to now – in the sense that if those ordinary people then were centre stage, then so are we now.

JT: Well, that is a politics – it's a very clear politics without it being doctrinal.

RM: Exactly, yeah. . . . Yes, I'm a lefty feminist and that informs my work. . . . So, for example, with my episode of *Doctor Who* I wanted to have these cheetah people be basically incredibly wild, and very very sensual and very very sexual, and very outgoing. . . . And this was quite a *female* thing, so Ace really had this relationship with a cheetah woman as a kind of lesbian subtext. . . . But *nowhere, nowhere* did that appear on screen. . . . Instead, visually we got Puss in Boots.

JT: So there's a politics which flows through your work, despite your earlier comment?

RM: It's the difference between showing a strong female relationship as in *Bold Girls*, which is one kind of politics, and going: 'All women should be lesbians because men are shits', which is another politics. Yes, it's a politics, but it's not making any broader statement than humanity contains all of these, and we only ever see and hear these few others' voices. . . . It's not agit-prop and it's not doctrinal. *The politics depends on whose stories you tell*. That's what it comes down to, it's whose stories you tell. . . .

JT: And that explains to me why you would enjoy working with Ken because that's what he also does ... with the working class and with different 'marginal' groups. . . . And it also seems to relate to that point you were making about cinema and ordinary faces which are still beautiful faces on the big screen?

RM: Yes, that's right. . . . You were saying Ken opens himself to the voices, but he does more than that. . . . He opens himself to the real voices, the invisible voices, the ones that never get normally represented. And at the same time he sees within that the building blocks to make the story that you were talking about . . . the story going on underneath. I think what Ken does is see the other story, the one that's going on underneath, but he sees it in the real voices. Which is what you do when you are constructing a script – you would go for the real voices, the real experiences, but you would select the experience that demonstrates the story.

Via the discussion of *Mary Barton*, the two writers are beginning to see a resolution to their authorship/intertext/'true' story/'emotional truth' question. Loach's 'emotional truth' is in a particular cinematic 'magic' elevating 'ordinary faces' and 'invisible voices' to the 'larger than life' screen. RM's emphasis on 'emotional truth' in terms of the underlying aligns her with the materialist position of Trevor Griffiths (and indeed JT). But there is *also* the strongly feminist RM of *Bold Girls* who had tried (and more or less failed) to introduce these beautiful 'invisible' voices and faces to the popular television of *Doctor Who*. 'Emotional truth', in this feminist sense, clearly was as much a matter for RM of 'empathy' with other female writers, as with 'invisible' voices. RM herself had a significant pleasure in Mrs Gaskell as single-parent/writer.

RM: She kept a diary of her kids growing up, which is lovely – because of her writing routine. You go: 'Oh God, you had to do that too!' – you know, fit the routine round the kids' routine, and she's going: 'I should really be worrying about this [writing], but I'm not, I'm worrying about the fact that he's sick'. . . . Also I gather that she ended up living very separate from Mr Gaskell and being very independent.

JT: Would you nevertheless see hers as a particularly middle-class view of the working class?

RM: She's writing *for* the middle classes and that's the voice you hear all the way through. She's translating experiences, which is why you get all this detailed description of living rooms because she's going: 'I bet you've never been in a living room like this, I bet you've never seen into a kitchen like this', and with both the 'good' characters and the 'bad' ones she's going: 'This is what it's like'.

So in a way I've tried to keep . . . 'this is what *we* were like, this is what your great-great granny was like'. . . . In the same way as she was saying to the middle class of her own time, 'look how close we are', you can go to people of a different century, 'look how close we are'.

By now RM and JT have agreed on why they find pleasure in Ken Loach, and they have implicitly sorted out a lot of their underlying politics and epistemology. Each is now also drawing on the other's agendas to clarify their own stance. RM, for example, draws on JT's research interest in Chekhov[8] to explain just *why* Ken Loach is not the authoritarian 'imaginary unity' of Colin MacCabe's analysis. Loach, RM insists, empathises with a whole range of hidden and unhidden voices – and 'that's what's so wonderful'.

RM: If you can't empathise with a character I don't think you can write it. That is why I thank you for introducing me properly to Chekhov, because I think that's what he's so wonderful at. . . . Every single character on that stage you know he identifies with. And therefore you can too, and that's what's so wonderful.

Audiences

Throughout, RM has emphasised the importance of 'empathy' – as writer, as director, and as audience member. JT, as a media theorist, is also interested in audiences, and RM's reference to Mrs Gaskell writing about the working class for a middle-class audience gives him the opportunity to return to RM's audience.

JT: You've said to me that you don't write with an audience in
       mind, and yet there with *Mary Barton* you're saying she
       writes with an audience in mind. So what are you doing
       then? . . . Let's say you're writing *Doctor Who*, or you're
       writing Mrs Gaskell's *Mary Barton*, or you're writing *Lady-
       bird, Ladybird*. In *all* of those you're not thinking about a
       particular audience?

RM: Well I think of it as the same audience . . . a great big group
       of diverse people. In actual fact in the theatre I rarely get the
       audience that I anticipate because . . . I usually get a very
       small bunch of middle-class people over the age of fifty. But
       I don't write for any specific group – I always just assume
       I'm going to get a nice football stadium cross-section.

JT: So even when you're writing something as cultish as *Doctor
       Who*, you're still not . . . writing to the fact that these guys
       are into intra-textual continuity, etc.?

RM: No, but in that case I *should* have done. . . . You see I was
       not a good writer for *Doctor Who* because I didn't take
       them seriously enough. . . . Especially given it was the last
       one that the BBC did, I really think that was a real shame
       from the fans' point of view, because no, I didn't think
       about a specific audience.

JT: So is the reason that you don't think of a particular audi-
       ence to do with the fact that in the end you're not directly
       dependent on an audience, unlike a TV producer?

RM: Well, I am obviously, because if no one watches anything
       I do, no one's going to commission me to do anything. I
       think it's because if you start to have an imaginary audi-
       ence of any kind in your head, you start censoring yourself,
       or currying up to them or reacting to them. In other words
       you're not *writing* the thing, you're doing something else. . . .
            And I also think that there's the assumption around that
       the vast majority of people are too thick to understand any-
       thing subtle, complicated or really moving, and that you
       should have to go through some higher education process,
       or some other hurdle to attain these things. And I hate that.
       . . . So when I write *Mary Barton* I'm writing for the same
       audience that I was writing *Casualty* for. If you say that
       soap opera is the only good because it's what the majority
       of the people enjoy, love, watch regularly, and therefore if

you don't write soap opera you're not writing for the popular audience, it's like the inverted form of the high cultural
argument. I really dislike that with a vengeance. I think
that the soap opera audience doesn't get as ready access to
other stuff like Chekhov, but that's to do with cultural
controls, it's to do with producers' decisions, it's to do with
scheduling decisions, it's to do with cultural expectations
which have politics behind them. And every so often you do
get something like *Trainspotting* that goes 'whoosh' . . . and
thumbs its nose at all that. And the more that happens, the
more those barriers are broken down.

JT: But your *Mary Barton* will be totally dependent on its
scheduling.

RM: Yeah. But I can't afford to worry about that when I'm
writing it. I just have to write it as though it's an episode of
EastEnders or an episode of *The Bill*, as though it's for *all*
those people, and God willing, it'll get to them. Chances
are it won't, but maybe the next one will or the next one.
And the great thing about film is that if you do a low-
budget British film you can really sneak it by them. Because
nobody has any expectations of them. So when they explode,
they can do it in a really unexpected way. Which is why
film's exciting.

RM and JT agree, finally, with Ken Loach that 'cultural control' is
'out there' and *not* in the narratives of Loach's films.

Conclusion

Because JT and RM are contributing to an academic book on
writing and cinema, they have revisited a continuing theme in film
studies: Left politics, film form and Ken Loach, one of the internationally most visible and successful living exponents of this genre.
As writers with very different backgrounds but a common respect
for Loach, they have drawn attention to some of their different
professional formations (and thus constructions of 'Ken Loach').
Their dialogical 'interweaving of various types of speech' has been
presented here in different ways (RM's more expansively in response
to JT's agendas, JT's more often as 'media studies' questions and
in the framing introduction and conclusion). This has been one

way of responding to the 'story going on underneath' – in the real economy of this book. Yet this dialogic methodology has also revealed common ground theoretically in relation to Loach's accessing of the discursive polyphony of the invisible-real. Against MacCabe's accusation that Loach imposes an 'imaginary unity' on the viewer, they argue that Loach *foregrounds the dialogic* himself – and so releases more voices (and faces) in the cinema than normally occur there. Finally, many familiar media/cultural studies issues and themes have been woven through this discussion: text, production, intertextuality, audience, genre, economy, high culture/popular culture, reflexivity, carnival, pleasure. Hopefully this will add a broader relevance to the very particular focus on Ken Loach; and also draw attention to the need to embed each of these areas in the daily practice of writing.

Notes

1. David Lodge, *After Bakhtin: Essays on Fiction and Criticism* (London, 1990), p. 21.
2. John Tulloch, *Television Drama: Agency, Audience and Myth* (London, 1990).
3. John Tulloch, *Doctor Who: The Unfolding Text* (Basingstoke, 1984).
4. Colin MaCabe, 'Days of Hope – a Response to Colin McArthur', *Screen* vol. 17, no. 1 (Spring 1978); 'Memory, Phantasy, Identity: *Days of Hope* and the Politics of the Past', *Edinburgh '77 Magazine*; both reprinted in Tony Bennett, Susan Boyd-Bowman, Colin Mercer and Janet Woollacott (eds), *Popular Television and Film* (London, 1981), pp. 310–13, 314–18.
5. Rona Munro, *Bold Girls* (London, 1991). The award-winning *Bold Girls* was also published by Samuel French (London, 1995), by Hodder & Stoughton (London, 1995), and in the collection *First Run 3* by Nick Hern Books (London, 1991). Published texts of other theatre plays by Rona Munro include *The Maiden Stone, Fugue,* and *Your Turn to Clean the Stairs,* each published by Nick Hern Books (London, 1995). Further plays are *Saturday Night at the Commodore* (published in *New Scottish Writing,* London: Nick Hern Books, 1990) and *Piper's Cave* (in *Plays by Women* vol. 5, London: Methuen, 1986).
6. See Ien Ang, *Watching Dallas: Soap Opera and the Melodramatic Imagination* (London, 1985).
7. John Tulloch and Henry Jenkins, *Science Fiction Audiences: Watching Doctor Who and Star Trek* (London, 1995); John Tulloch and Albert Moran, *A Country Practice: 'Quality Soap'* (Sydney, 1985).

8. John Tulloch, *Chekhov: A Structuralist Study* (Basingstoke, 1980). For an analysis of the Richard Eyre/Trevor Griffiths production of Chekhov's *The Cherry Orchard*, see John Tulloch, Tom Burvill and Andrew Hood, 'Reinhabiting *The Cherry Orchard*: Class and History in Performing Chekhov', *New Theatre Quarterly* vol. 13, no. 52 (November 1997), pp. 318–28.

2 Questions of authorship: Samuel Beckett and Film

Jonathan Bignell

Critical discussion of Beckett's 22-minute black-and-white 1964 *Film*, directed by Alan Schneider and starring Buster Keaton, has tended to come from three analytical points of view: focusing on Beckett's authorship, the film's sources and influences, and the ways it might be read by audiences.[1] The first of these is a version of auteurism, which in film study usually refers to the analysis of the work of a director to reveal distinctive structures of meaning and thematic patterns which permit a fuller understanding of his or her work. But in the case of *Film* the role of the director as the source of meaning has been taken instead by Beckett, the author of the written screenplay. Beckett's text for *Film* has not been considered in the same framework as screenplays produced for commercial cinema, but instead in the context of avant-garde independent cinema, or work commissioned for subsidised theatre companies, or 'art television'. In commercial cinema, screenwriters do not enjoy high status, often finding their work changed significantly in the production process, and it is the director's name which appears most prominently in the film's credits. Auteurist interpretations of *Film* have involved discerning its 'Beckettian' qualities, by reference to the written material in Beckett's screenplay and notes, and by comparison between the film and his works in other media, particularly theatre and television.

The second critical approach involves discussion of *Film*'s intellectual sources, notably Beckett's use of Berkeley's philosophy. Here again, the focus is on Beckett's authorship, and the ways in which it is constituted by assimilations and reinterpretations of written texts. The third critical point of view stresses the use of the film medium, and the form of audience response determined by the cinematic methods used to realise the screenplay. This is an evaluative critical method, which compares the probable intentions evidenced in the screenplay with the effects of meaning generated by the film version. These three approaches are not mutually exclusive, and all contribute to our understanding of the work. Aspects of all three kinds of approach will appear in my discussion of *Film*, but I would like to problematise and interrelate the three points of view. I shall suggest that, by a series of paradoxes, the film, the criticism of the film and the reception of the film can be seen to destabilise Beckett's transcendent authority over his work.

Existing critical discussions revolve around the question of how to frame *Film*: where to position the limits between the film-text and the texts and authors which border it. Like any text, *Film* is not a self-sufficient entity. Its meaning is constituted by its position in relation to other texts, sources or origins of meaning outside its frame. Criticism of *Film* has tended to limit these origins to Beckett as author, to other written or visual works with which *Film* can be compared, or to a notional spectator who actualises *Film*'s meaning in viewing it. My aim is to extend and displace these origins and frames for *Film* by considering the multiplicity of critical frames it invokes. Part of this process involves discussing *Film* in relation to the history and criticism of cinema, an approach which has received little emphasis. But I shall also show that *Film*'s production history, the general problem of how a spectator might read the film, and information about the response of actual audiences, all invoke the impossibility of constructing a definitive origin for, and frame around, the meaning of the film. Even the title, *Film*, suggestively refers to a recording technology, a cultural form of representation, and less obviously to an obscuring veil, and a surface separating one medium from another. There are also two *Film*s, the film and the written text anterior to it and different from it. The title itself begins to suggest that our ability to designate a unitary object is already in question.

Film poses a question of reading, so that, finally, the meaning of *Film* is neither determinable nor absolutely relative, but exists in the tension of different frames, different points of view. The film is rarely shown in Britain, has never been screened on television, and access to a videotape version is difficult. I shall therefore give a very brief description of what we see in *Film*, but the need to describe the images must already involve the construction of different meanings in the shift from the medium of film to written language, and the shift from the film's narration to a description. Linda Ben-Zvi has remarked that by 'refusing to use words to explain images, Beckett forces audiences to respond directly to what they see and think about how they see', though she attributes this effect to Beckett's intention.[2] The discussion and criticism of *Film* raise issues of translation in relation to the movement from the screenplay's origins to Beckett's text, to the making of the film, to its final form, and the ways in which the film might be read. Like the practice of translation, all of these activities of reading and writing displace the notion of the work's self-sufficient identity. The issue of translation here is parallel to the familiar critical problem raised by Beckett's translations from one language to another (especially French to English) in his written texts, and the 'translation' of play texts to stage performance. So the problem of framing *Film* is not unique, but reflects back onto the discussion both of Beckett's other work and indeed textuality in general.

Film begins with a close-up of Buster Keaton's right eye, then cuts to Keaton as O, the object of the camera's look, hurrying along beside a high wall, always keeping the camera behind him at a maximum of 45° from directly behind his back. He bumps into an elderly couple. We see them mistily from O's point of view, then the camera eye, E, turns to observe them. They slowly register a look of terror, then the camera resumes its pursuit of O, who enters a dilapidated tenement. In the vestibule O's blurred point of view sees an old flower-seller, and while he shrinks away from her the camera confronts her. She too looks horrified and falls to the floor. O has rushed upstairs, and the camera follows him into a room. O covers the windows, door, mirror, parrot-cage, fishbowl, and ejects a dog and cat. O tears up a photograph on the wall, turns around an envelope and tears up seven photographs from inside it, which show a male figure at different stages of life. As O falls asleep in a rocking-chair whose headrest he has also covered, E circles the room twice, finally confronting O who awakes with a shocked look. From O's point of view we see that the intense face of E looks exactly like O. The film cuts back and forth between the two faces, until O lowers his head and is still. The camera slowly zooms in on E's face until only the eye is visible.

Beckett as author

Beckett's name seems to authenticate *Film*, in the manner of a signature, when it appears superimposed over the eye in the first shot, referring us to the eye and 'I' of Beckett as the originator outside the frame. The name marks the film as Beckett's property, and guarantees its authenticity. But the proper name is actually invoking Beckett's authority as the writer of the screenplay, and not as the director, the usual 'author' of a film. The screenplay is a text in a different medium which is not simply a blueprint for a translation into film, but a somewhat ambiguous collection of writing, diagrams and notes that are not reducible to the finished film itself. Even if we accept Beckett as the origin of *Film*, he is already at one remove from the images, and the written text which precedes the images is by no means imprinted with a clear authorial intention.

A further function of the caption showing Beckett's proper name and the film's title is to mark the physical limits of the film, and thus construct the frame within which the narrative proper is delivered. The frame we see on the screen is at once part of the film and also tells us that it is not part of the film. This enforces a border between the inside and outside of the film, separating the text as an object from the subject who authored it. This reinforces the meaning of the title *Film* as a surface separating one thing from another. But since the frame which performs this function reads 'Film by Samuel Beckett', it suggests that the separation is itself under the authority of the author. Therefore the title frame, as a bordering device, has a double status. It separates the work from the author, and paradoxically denies this separation.

The title frame must be one of the components of the film's meaning because it is part of the film, and announces the film to be a self-contained work. But the citation 'by Samuel Beckett' on the credits also prompts us to search for what is not unique and self-contained about the film, what is repeated from or consistent with his other work. Beckett's name is both inside the film, a sign among the other graphic and visual signs which compose it, and outside the film, offering a context of Beckett texts, including the published screenplay, into which to place it. We can therefore look for the traces of a Beckettian 'signature' in thematic or structural aspects of the film. However, the marks of style and theme left in the work by its author lead in two opposite directions. They prove the authentic uniqueness of the work as Beckett's. But they also deny the uniqueness of the film by showing how it derives from the intertextual field of his other work. Here again, Beckett's signature divides and fissures the film.

Some of the same paradoxes appear because of the title's reference to the film medium. *Film* is a unique work, but its very name refers us to what is generically filmic about it, what is not unique. Here the contextual frames offered by other films are significant. As far as the production of *Film* is concerned, the meanings of films cannot be said to derive only from their originator because of the collaborative nature of production in the film medium. This must be the case with *Film* even though the people involved in making it tried to emphasise Beckett's authority as author. After *Film* Beckett never again wrote for the film medium. Jonathan Kalb suggests that this was because the contained and controllable interior setting of the TV studio offered Beckett a more effective authority as director of the realisation of his work, more so even than in the theatre, and that film-making lacked this possibility of control.[3] While *Film* must be by Beckett in some sense, the film medium is not perhaps 'Beckettian' because it is not conducive to Beckett's mode of authorship.

But *Film* was produced at an auspicious time as far as authorship is concerned, because film was then being valued as an 'author's medium' despite the fact that 'author' in this context more usually means director. In the 1950s and 1960s the auteur approach to cinema was inaugurated around the film journal *Cahiers du Cinéma* in France. Its valuation of directors as auteurs gave the seriousness of literary evaluation to cinema directors. In the context of this 'literary cinema', in 1965 and 1966 *Film* began to receive awards at film festivals in New York, Venice, London, Oberhausen, Tours, Sydney and Krakow. But despite the emerging critical framework which valued directors as authors, Alan Schneider, the director of *Film*, considered himself a translator and not an author, because the author was seen to be Beckett. Schneider suppressed his role as an auteur in order to bring out Beckett's role as author of the written text which Schneider felt he was simply translating into the film medium.

Schneider had never directed a film before, though he had directed Beckett plays in the theatre. He saw *Film* as an investigation of the medium by an author who was properly a playwright. It was a film about film, and privileged the role of its author as a visionary artist. Schneider portrayed himself as the facilitator of Beckett's 'vision', consciously reversing the auteurist slippage from literary author to film director: 'With every new wavelet of contemporary cinema turning directors, in effect, into authors, it took the surprising author of *Film*, playwright Samuel Beckett, to become, not too surprisingly, its real director'.[4] As produced, the film is different from the screenplay, but even this, for Schneider, was due to Beckett's influence. Schneider saw the screenplay as an intermediate partial object, a transparent film through which the author's creativity had to be made visible, 'it was the special vision and tone set by Sam which all of us were dedicated to putting on film . . . acquiring "a dimension and validity of its own that are worth far more than any merely efficient translation of intention". But, in the process, it was exactly that faithful translation of intention we were all after' (Schneider, p. 63, quoting Beckett). Schneider claimed to be using the film medium and film production techniques purely as translation machines through which Beckett's authorship would pass.

The view of film technology as transparent derives from the ideologies surrounding the use of cinema and photography to represent subjectivity. Since it is the notion of subjective being which Beckett regarded as *Film*'s subject, the relationship between visual technologies and identity is obviously important both for investigating authorship and for interpreting *Film*.

Berkeley and the camera

The film which Beckett authored is in a sense a rewriting of someone else's text, George Berkeley's *A Treatise Concerning the Principles of Human Knowledge*.[5] There is no explicit citation of it in the film images themselves. However, this example of intertextuality complicates the notion of Beckett's role as author of the film, by suggesting that the unique Beckettian signature which we might discern in it is in part constituted by the rewriting of a text by someone else.

Berkeley's text is an interesting choice, since Berkeley's view was that it is God's perception which maintains existing creatures in the state of being. Not to be perceived by God, the sole author of being and the universal authority, would be by definition impossible. From this angle, God is and has the transcendent point of view: He is the author because He is a perceiver. In *Film* perception is split between subject and object of perception, between the eye E (the camera) and the object O (Buster Keaton), though it is revealed that E and O are one and the same being. There is no third point of view in *Film*, no unmarked camera shot which could correspond with a transcendent point of view. The film was originally to be titled *The Eye*, and while this eye could be interpreted as the camera eye, Keaton's eye, or the eye and 'I' of the author, it certainly could not refer to the transcendent eye of God. What is missing in this visual text about perception is an eye which could synthesise the dialectic of E's and O's points of view by providing an authorial and authoritative point of view, a controlling origin for vision. The lack of an unmarked third point of view disallows the spectator a God-like perception of both E and O like that of a novelistic third-person narrative. Instead the film fractures the viewer's point of view into two, denying authority to a visual synthesis of camera points of view and simultaneously denying it to the audience.

Beckett's written outline for the film begins: 'Esse est percipi. All extraneous perception suppressed, animal, human, divine, self-perception maintains in being. Search of non-being in flight from extraneous perception breaking down in inescapability of self-perception' (Beckett, p. 11). We can see the Latin quote from Berkeley ('to be is to be perceived') as the invocation of a textual authority for the remarks which follow, but Beckett's remarks involve a recasting of Berkeley without God's point of view. Furthermore, these remarks intended to explain the aims of the screenplay can be seen as Beckett's attempt to set limits to the interpretation of his outline for the film, to impose his own point of view. However, this authority is immediately withdrawn by the following sentence: 'No truth value attaches to above, regarded as of merely structural and dramatic convenience' (Beckett, p. 11). There is a repeated invocation of authority, which insistently erases itself.

Depictions of God do appear in *Film* but He is triply objectified. He is represented by a carved primitive mask with a beard and staring eyes, the subject of a photograph on the wall of O's room, and this in turn is observed by the film camera. This suggests that His image can be captured by the same photographic process of containment which has afflicted O, and thus denies the difference and authority of His point of view. O is not only observed by a camera, but also owns an envelope full of photographs. Photographs have always since their invention had the status of an evidence of the past, a truthful record of being in the world. They entail the mechanical remembering of lived identity for the individual. Photography therefore becomes a support and guarantee for subjectivity rather as God was for Berkeley. Photographic technology claimed to authenticate the being of the individual subject, and photographs seemed to have no style, no mark of an author, because they were seen as a direct transcription of the real. They appeared to be a pure moment of perception by a transcendent other, like the perception of God in Berkeley's account. Although O strokes his photographs as he examines them in *Film*, suggesting precisely the nostalgic construction of a history and identity, the photographs preserve the traces which authenticate being, so O tears them up.

Film's subject could be described as the effect of the lack of God's authority as perceiver, as author of Being, and thus *Film* works as a displacement of Berkeley. The notion of displacement appears in the structure of *Film*, since we see that without God to guarantee perception, the authority for being is displaced onto the individual O, and the visual technologies which represent him to himself. *Film* divides the individual into perceiver and perceived, but shows that self as subject and self as object must co-exist in the state of being. Being is inescapably split in itself, as Sylvie Debevec Henning's essay on *Film* points out: 'all perception requires two and this is true even of apperception. Hence there can never be full unity of the self, nor any perfect self-identity . . .' (Henning, p. 99). Kalb suggests that Beckett might have made *Film*, with its questioning of perceivedness as the validation of identity, because of his 'abhorrence of publicity and bloodhoundish critics', thus representing himself as a being split into a pursued Object as well as an authorial Eye.[6] But Kalb's view replaces Beckett as the controlling author, by paradoxically seeing *Film*'s thematic and structural focus on displacement as derived from his intention. This displaces the notion of origin again, while simultaneously reinforcing it.

Buster Keaton and *Film*'s generic frames

Once *Film* had been made, its early exhibition history reveals that it was Keaton's name around which the film revolved, rather than Beckett's or Schneider's. It was difficult to find an audience constituency for *Film*, since Beckett and Schneider lacked any track record in cinema, and the film was clearly not a commercial feature. Its star, however, was extremely well known, and the film's first notable screening was motivated by an interest in Buster Keaton, whose work was being rediscovered in the 1960s. Schneider remembered:

> Then, in the summer of 1965, came an unexpected offer from the New York Film Festival. Amos Vogel had seen a print somewhere and thought it was worth showing – as part of a Keaton revival series. Already the film was becoming Keaton's and not Beckett's. I fought another losing battle to keep it from getting sandwiched in between two Keaton shorts.
>
> (Schneider, p. 90)

This early history revolves around the questions of which generic frame *Film* might belong in, and whose name is used to organise its meaning. The film was a short, but not a commercial one. It featured Keaton, but was not a comedy, a 'Keaton film'. Schneider was promoting it, but as 'Beckett's' film rather than his own creative property. This mismatching of categories is essential to an understanding of the audience's reaction to *Film* at the New York Film Festival.

Keaton's face, his trademark, became fully visible in the final shots, while the first shot was a close-up of his eye which the audience recognised and found hilarious. Schneider wrote: 'All through the next twenty-two minutes they sat there, bored, annoyed, baffled, and cheated of the Keaton they had come to see. Who the hell was Beckett?' (Schneider, p. 93). The audience were then reacting to *Film* as a Keaton film, a short comic movie in black and white. The audience at a Keaton revival had come with expectations which provided an intertextual frame for *Film*, and the opening of the film reinforced these expectations though subsequently the film appeared to undercut them completely. Enoch Brater succinctly remarks: 'Enticed by farce and vaudeville, the audience gets a phenomenology of visual perception instead'.[7] The

questions of generic frame and audience interpretation are inseparable, and relate to whose film *Film* was perceived to be: Keaton's,
Beckett's or Schneider's. However, it seems from Beckett's screenplay that it was precisely the intertext of silent comedy which
Beckett had wanted to evoke. Beckett's notes read: 'Climate of
film comic and unreal. O should invite laughter throughout by his
way of moving' (Beckett, p. 12). Schneider reports that Keaton
'misread' the script as being in the genre of silent comedy, and
Keaton frequently suggested during shooting that he could make it
much funnier if he were allowed to depart from the script and do
some comic routines.

Although the casting of Keaton led to a confusion of frames for
Film's first audiences, Beckett's use of Keaton for the role of O, a
comic actor in a 'serious' work, corresponded to the critical view
of Keaton being developed at the time. Writing in 1964 about
Keaton's comic films, Jean-Patrick Lebel dismissed the critics who
had regarded Keaton's face as a comic trick: 'They felt obliged to
reduce his opaque mask to something they themselves could understand, and not accept it for the disquieting thing it was: a face
turned in upon itself, concentrating upon itself with a prolonged
and unbearable determination.'[8] This notion of the comic mask as
a surface which points to a concealed depth is remarkably similar
to the questions which *Film* poses. The transparency or concealment
of identity entailed in the media of film and photography are part
of its subject, and are marked by the title *Film* itself. Further, the
'disquiet' Lebel refers to is parallel to the questions of interpretation and framing which *Film* poses for its audience. Moreover, the
double point of view of Keaton's mask, appearing to look out but
also looking in at itself, is the structural logic of perception which
Film attempts to render via two points of view, the look at the face
and look out from the face. While Keaton's appearance in *Film* had
the effect of separating the film from Beckett as its author, Keaton
seems to be inherently 'Beckettian'. The appearance of Keaton in
Film reinforces the links between Beckett's work and silent cinema
comedy and vaudeville. This adds to the intertextual field which
Film draws on, and extends it from cinema to the theatre medium
via considerations of performance as well as theme. Keaton is
another of the candidates for the role of centre of meaning in
Film, another of its possible authors, and this is most especially
the case for the audience at the film's first public screenings.

Film's cinematic intertext

The audience's possible readings of *Film* can be further explored in relation to a range of cinematic forms and historical frames which it invokes. The casting of Keaton in *Film* links it to vaudeville and slapstick silent comedies. However, these silent comedies would make considerable use of wide shots through which the action moved, and a static camera in front of which the actor performed his routines. The moving camera E in *Film*, and the lack of wide shots to establish space, make this kind of comedy very difficult to achieve, so that there is a disjuncture between what the camera observes and the conventions of the observation. This is a further example of *Film*'s mixing of generic frames, and the resulting problem of the spectator's strategies for decoding the film.

It is not possible to call *Film* a 'silent film' in the sense of an imitation, throwback or pastiche of films made before synchronous sound was common. 'Silent films' was a phrase rarely used before the coming of sound in 1926, since films were not silent. Apart from the noise of the projection machines and the audience itself, there could be spoken commentary by a master of ceremonies, recorded phonograph music, sound effects, pit orchestras and singers, piano accompaniment, and dialogue spoken live by professional actors. These features were gradually introduced right from the beginning of commercial film exhibition. *Film* is very different from modern commercial cinema, but also from silent cinema, because of the lack of music, intertitles, or melodramatic gestural acting. Although Beckett's *Film* alludes to silent films by its lack of soundtrack except for one reflexive 'Ssh', it does not repeat the experience of viewing silent films in the pre-1926 period. This works against the comedy which Keaton's performance, and expectations deriving from previous silent movies, might arouse in the audience.

The opening street sequence described in Beckett's screenplay was omitted from *Film* as it finally became: 'Dead straight. No sidestreets or intersections. Period: about 1929. Early summer morning. Small factory district. Moderate animation of workers going unhurriedly to work. All going in same direction and all in couples. . . . All persons in opening scene to be shown in some way perceiving – one another, an object, a shop window, a poster, etc.' (Beckett, *Film*, p. 12). Problems of lighting, performance quality and continuity led to Beckett's suggestion to cut the opening street sequence, since, as Schneider explained, the extras seen moving about in wide shot 'gave it and the film a different texture, opened up another world' (Schneider, p. 77). The scene's omission makes the film narratively tighter, focusing on O more closely, but deprives it of its 'establishing shot', which would provide a coherent sense of place or time. Thus *Film* is further distanced from the conventions and structure of mainstream narrative cinema.

If we turn to avant-garde cinema, the unconventional cinematography in *Film* can be partially explained by an authorship approach. In 1935 Beckett was reading books by and about Eisenstein, Pudovkin and Arnheim, and the film journal *Close-Up*.[9] Unable to learn about cinematography in Dublin, he wrote to Eisenstein in 1936, offering to go to Moscow and work unpaid as his assistant. Eisenstein did not reply, but Beckett also wrote to Pudovkin about his interest in naturalistic silent cinema, which had by then been eclipsed by developments in sound and colour. Nothing came of this contact either, but both attempts show that Beckett was aware of and interested in modes of film-making which were different from the commercial cinema of the time. *Film* draws on this avant-garde tradition, as Enoch Brater has described, and Brater points out that *Film*'s short running-time and its juxtaposition of odd perspectives recall avant-garde dada-surrealist films of the late 1920s.[10] Beckett's American publisher had commissioned *Film* as part of a composite of three works, where the other two writers involved were the prominent avant-garde playwrights of the period, Eugene Ionesco and Harold Pinter.

Beckett's authorship functions less as a secure point of origin for meaning than as a location for the interaction of competing frames of reference. The issues of *Film*'s construction, its editing conventions and shot types, raise the question of how the cinema audience might read its film 'language'. *Film* breaks the rules by its lack of wide shots, and the absence of cuts back and forth between the characters until the last minute. The audience is forced to identify with E's look almost exclusively, and is deprived of sound or music cues with which to narrativise and understand the scenario. The audience's foremost problem is to understand the 45° rule whereby O can be safe from E's perception if the camera remains behind him at less than this angle. This rule is alien to the syntax of narrative cinema, and appears to allude to the impossibility of seeing oneself in a mirror if positioned beyond a 45° angle. Clas Zillacus conducted a survey at the January 1970 Bleecker Street, New York screening of *Film*, and his results 'amply confirmed that the two-vision idea did not work'.[11] To clarify the convention, the points of view of E and O were different in visual quality, with a misty 'film' over O's eye, so that the final confrontation between E and O would be comprehensible. Because of the scarcity of shot-reverse shot in *Film*, this special code was needed, but it is certainly questionable whether a viewer who hadn't read the screenplay would understand it.

Film both mixes conventions of spectatorship from a variety of cinematic forms and historical periods, and also introduces conventions of its own. This mixing demonstrates that the 'language' of film is not transparent and universal, and can be read as a critique of the assumptions about filmic 'language' which have been promoted since the technology was invented. The film medium was granted a unique authority to communicate above and beyond the Babel of spoken language, as a unique translation machine which could record life without the intervention of a distorting medium. As I have suggested, both 'internal' and 'external' features of *Film* militate against this ideology of cinema. The issue of the audience's positioning is inseparable from *Film*'s relationship to cinema history, and the conventions which that history has established. Aspects of Keaton's performance, the film's exhibition contexts, aspects of camera technique, and silence, all solicit audience knowledge about previous films. But *Film* cannot be simply aligned with particular genres of film, modes of spectatorship, or types of cinematic construction. These problems of finding a frame into which *Film* can be placed are paralleled and exacerbated by the issue of authorship. There is no one authorial signature which can hold *Film* in place, so that both its origins and its destinations remain multiple and paradoxical. Rather than being a pessimistic conclusion, this opens *Film* to the plurality of discourses with which it invites us to supplement it.

Notes

1. There are two versions of *Film*. The first was directed by Alan Schneider in 1964 and produced by Evergreen Theatre Inc. A colour version was made by David Clark in 1979 for the British Film Institute,

and included an opening scene from Beckett's written text (omitted in the 1964 version) and added sound. I refer only to the first version here. The published written version is Samuel Beckett, *Film* (London, 1972) (page references are cited in the text), and is also published in Samuel Beckett, *Collected Shorter Plays of Samuel Beckett* (London, 1984).

2. Linda Ben-Zvi, 'Samuel Beckett's Media Plays', *Modern Drama* vol. 28, no. 1 (March 1985), p. 32.
3. See Jonathan Kalb, *Beckett In Performance* (Cambridge, 1989).
4. Alan Schneider, 'On Directing *Film*', in Beckett, *Film*, p. 63. Further page references are cited in the text.
5. See George Berkeley, *The Works of George Berkeley, Bishop of Cloyne*, ed. A.A. Luce and T.E. Jessop (London, 1949). Several articles have considered the film's relationship to Berkeleyan ideas in more detail than I shall attempt here: Raymond Federman, 'Samuel Beckett's Film on the Agony of Perceivedness', *Film Quarterly* vol. 20, no. 2 (Winter 1966), pp. 46–51; Charles C. Hampton Jr, 'Samuel Beckett's *Film*', *Modern Drama* vol. 11, no. 3 (December 1968), pp. 299–305; Vincent J. Murphy, 'Being and Perception: Beckett's *Film*', *Modern Drama* vol. 18, no. 1 (March 1975), pp. 43–8; Sylvie Debevec Henning, ' "Film": A Dialogue Between Beckett and Berkeley', *Journal of Beckett Studies* no. 7 (Spring 1982), pp. 89–99 (page references to the latter are cited in the text).
6. Jonathan Kalb, 'The Mediated Quixote: The Radio and Television Plays, and *Film*' in John Pilling (ed.), *The Cambridge Companion to Beckett* (Cambridge, 1994), p. 137.
7. Enoch Brater, 'The Thinking Eye in Beckett's *Film*', *Modern Language Quarterly* vol. 36, no. 2 (1975), p. 173.
8. Jean-Patrick Lebel, *Buster Keaton*, trans. P.D. Stovin (London, 1967), p. 15 (first published Paris, 1964).
9. See Deirdre Bair, *Samuel Beckett: A Biography* (London, 1980), pp. 177–8.
10. See Brater, 'The Thinking Eye'.
11. Clas Zillacus, *Beckett And Broadcasting: A Study of the Works of Samuel Beckett for and in Radio and Television* (Abo, 1976), p. 186.

3 Publicists – distribution workers in the pleasure economy of the film industry

Kevin Moloney

Background

There are two historical contexts to the development of film publicity that place it inside larger themes of the late nineteenth and early twentieth centuries. The first is the combination of applied science and capital to create new industries. The film industry was the economic consequence of such a combination when finance capital was added to the technical development of photography from still to moving pictures. Other combinations based on technical advances such as electricity, the internal combustion engine and chemical compounds occasioned the rise of industries (household goods, motor cars and make-up for women) that have marked off this century from others.

These new industries offered for sale physical goods and emotional experiences that had to be mass consumed to be economically viable. Like electric lights, the telephone, the car and face make-up, the 'movies' needed persuasive communications if a populous, widely dispersed, homogeneous and effective market for this new form of working-class entertainment was to exist. As apparently naturally as car and lipstick advertisements, film publicity emerged as a hyphen connecting new producers of novel goods and services with new consumers. Thus, persuasive communications are the second historical context within which to place film publicity.

The origins of film publicity as a set of techniques are found in the immediate antecedents of the 'movies' as a form of popular, out-of-home entertainment (the circus and the nickelodeon) and these techniques were well developed by them.[1] The role of circus entrepreneur Phineas Taylor Barnum in the development of publicity for public entertainments is well recorded:[2] he employed a staff of press agents and was the first to use display advertising on a large scale for product promotion. The term 'publicity' was the common one used historically to describe generically all categories of persuasive communications for industrially produced goods, but inside the film industry now it has a narrower meaning. This narrowing began in the 1920s with the growth of advertising, merchandising and special events as separate activities one from the other. Now 'publicity' is the generally used title for the work of press agents who write up editorial matter and arrange 'free' exposure of it in the press. Their work is distinct from both paid advertising and 'exploitation', a miscellaneous category of other promotional work, such as merchandising and sponsorship. Gaines quotes Litivak in order to divide 'publicity' into the sub-categories of gaining news coverage, preparing packs of information for journalists, and arranging interviews and screenings for previews and reviews (Gaines, p. 148).[3]

Earlier, Gaines writes that the beginnings of film 'publicity' to catch media attention were found in incidents such as the 'Florence Lawrence stunt' where press agents planted stories rumouring her death in a streetcar accident in the city where her film was due to show (Gaines, p. 40). Other 'attention-attracting gags' attributed to them were the use of wild animals, church sermons, souped-up automobiles and suicide notes to create stories in newspapers. In this essay, 'publicity' will be the standard term to describe the work of those who deal with the press to promote films and who organise promotional activity and material other than advertising and merchandising. Another term (public relations) could be employed, but as film publicists generally do not use it, it will be largely eschewed here. These definitional distinctions and etiquettes are made for clarity and no more. For Cutlip, however, they make up the developing morphology of that form of persuasive communications known as public relations. He writes: 'Public relations has evolved in response to the growth of democratic freedoms and free markets' (Cutlip, p. 15).

Gaines agrees with others that the star system began evolving its current form between 1914 and the early 1920s when it took the earlier theme of a 'picture personality', around since 1902, and combined it with the parallel narrative of the 'private life' of the picture personality (Gaines, p. 37). The narrative often took one of two forms. The first involved the denial of actual behaviour by writing it into the script, as when Clara Bow's actual gambling at Lake Tahoe was portrayed in a film and its reality was scripted into the film as rumour. The second form was to deny the unedifying by transforming it into the wholesome, as when Fatty Arbuckle was portrayed as exemplary after the actual scandal of finding a woman dead in a bathtub at one of his parties.

Whatever the publicity narrative followed, it needed an essential consequence for success. Trent and Lawton sum this up: 'Newspaper copy has frequently created stars but it has always taken audience support at the box office to sustain their careers'.[4] This may be obvious but it is a powerful truth: it is not publicity which creates success for films but the reception given to the film, first by its media audience and then its audience of consumers. This is well understood by film professionals: the first question asked in the headquarters of the distribution companies on Monday mornings is 'how big were the weekend audiences?'.

Industry leaders did not doubt the importance of persuasive communications for the development of their markets, and Gaines, for example, reports that studios wanted film publicity people controlled by their producers, even licensed by them, and not controlled by stars (Gaines, p. 149). As other mass markets developed, the opportunities for cross promotion and selling became evident, and from the 1930s film increasingly joined up with consumer commodities in joint publicity. Gaines gives the example of Rita Hayworth in the 1942 production *You Were Never Lovelier* which was linked to Lustre Creme shampoo in 'a natural and spontaneous relationship' (Gaines, p. 149). He notes that the method of tying films and personal image products together was a novelty: but the goal was constant – more sales.

The history of film publicity offered so far has been American, but an English version was being developed. Betts was a journalist on the *Evening Standard*, the *Daily Express* and *Sunday Express*, as well as a film publicist for ten years.[5] He records a £150,000 budget which included £15,809 for 'artistes', £1,730 for story and script, and £1,579 for publicity salaries and expenses (Betts, p. 20). Moreover, persuasive communications were not exclusive tools for commercial, mass production industries. They were (and are in the form of spindoctoring) used by American and British politicians of most hues. The American government used public relations and advertising extensively to sell war bonds in the First World War. British governments used the former to promote the idea of Empire and the sale of British goods in the 1920s and 1930s, while the fascist and communist governments in Germany, Italy and Russia used the film medium as persuasive communication itself to increase home support and impress external publics. Box picked up on these interconnections between consumer goods, politics and film as a promotion channel in 1937.[6] He noted that 'other nations have not been slow to learn the lessons of Hollywood' and that 'In the adult use of the screen, Britain lags years behind the rest of the world' (Box, pp. 13, 17), giving as better examples Germany, Italy and Russia. He noted also that the British companies CWS and Cadbury were the earliest to use film for propaganda. His use of this word to cover the promotion of the Rochdale Pioneers, chocolate bars and dictatorships, without apostrophes or prior explanation, shows how susceptible meanings are to colouration by politics.

He could write the following in an unabashed, innocent and ahistorical way but we can read it only with recoil after knowing the work of Goebbels and Stalin: 'The Publicist who proposes to use the film as a means of propaganda is faced with almost exactly the same set of problems as when he decides to utilise the Press for the same purpose' (Box, p. 17). What is promoted often feeds back into a welcome or rejection of the means of its promotion: the messenger or message system is usually 'shot' if the content is unacceptable to the audience. 'Propaganda' was a common, positive and morally acceptable term in the 1920s and early 1930s and seen by communications theorists such as Bernays as a social engineering technique to steer public opinion away from ignorance and chaos.[7] After the Nazis and Stalin, the word was replaced with 'public relations' but only if you favoured the contents and source of the message; otherwise, the persuasive communication remained 'propaganda'. Labelling communications is the privilege of the message receiver. If you like a film, you are kind to its publicists.

The political economy of film publicity

Moran reminds us that film exists as an economic good and a cultural good and that before it 'can be considered as a cultural object, it must first be conceived as an industry'.[8] In this duality, the cultural good passes through the process cycle of industrial supply and demand – production, distribution and consumption. He places publicity inside the distribution function, notes that the latter 'is low not only on glamour but on contact with the public', but states that 'distribution is the key to the film industry' (Moran, p. 2). The argument in this essay is that publicists are the human agents for a classic function of distribution: the diffusion of a good to all its markets. They do not do this in a way which involves the physicality of film. They do not warehouse it nor drive the reels around the country to cinemas to link up with audiences. This is the system of direct, physical distribution. Rather publicists distribute their preferred meaning of films (cognitive and affective) via an independent agency (the mass media) to audiences and use a special form of language and visual representation for the transmission. This is the indirect and non-physical distribution of film to its consumers. Publicists are the metaphysical logistics experts of film.

Film publicists write (and produce photographs) about film but the discourse is always persuasive, non-critical and designed for mass consumption. They use the language of publicity/journalese to carry their preferred meanings. They will answer to being in the public relations industry but they will call themselves publicists – never propagandists. British film publicists are based in London and number some 40 working for distribution companies and a similar number working in five sizeable agencies and as individuals. There is some personnel overlap with television publicists but not much. The largest agency is the longest established and employs thirteen publicists with some seventeen support staff. Most publicists are women, as are most public relations executives in the USA and the UK. They have distinct sets of regularised relations with groups of co-workers inside the film industry (writers, market researchers, actors, directors, producers, schedulers, cinema mangers and accountants) and certain behaviours are expected of them by their principals. In particular, they work closely with marketing people who use the industry equivalent of focus groups (tester showings), where stratified, sample audiences are shown the film pre-release and their reactions are fed back into final editing. The data gained here helps publicists by defining the film audience and/or by showing reactions to themes, characters and incidents in the script.

Publicists are hired in the first instance on the bases of liking film and 'getting on with people'. This means not rankling with actors, producers and directors who may or may not be temperamental, and cooperating with the stable pool of fellow publicists whom they will regularly meet through the production and distribution cycle of the film. Relations with actors are crucial as they are the probably the single most potent promotional feature of the film distribution system, the one most appealing to audiences. Publicists will, for example, 'mushroom' a minor role in a production if it is played by an actor known to the press. They can say about their dealings generally: 'It's important to observe selling points in an actor. Though it might seem like you are treating them like a commodity, as a publicist you can instinctively feel where their target audience is, be it teen magazines, style magazines, tabloids, broadsheets or women's glossies.'[9] Publicists are also talent spotters and informal agents for those actors they favour. 'Forging a rapport with the acting talent is essential. Gaining their confidence means they'll give much more to publicity. It's even more important with rising stars as they are "green" when it comes to the press and interviews and need briefing and nurturing and to be constantly reassured.'

At the other side of publicists and outside the industry but in a symbiotic relationship are journalists (news story and feature writers and picture editors), and here productive, professional relations have two sides which mirror each other. For the publicist, journalists are the human agency for their indirect distribution system to audiences. Publicists need frequent, easy, direct access to them to try out promotional ideas, picture opportunities and 'angles', all to be expressed in publicity/journalese, about a new film. Ideas for pictures are particularly important for 'good pix mean good space'. Publicists seek to maximise their influence over journalists because, although the relationship involves the barter of mutual benefits, they do not control these media workers. The second side to relations centres on journalists. They need access to stars, actors and directors in order to produce 'copy' (the trade argot of publicity/journalese) to fill their columns. Apart from the development of mutually acceptable ideas, this access results in the passing of pre-prepared information to journalists by publicists. This material reduces the professional cost to the media of gathering it themselves.

These good relations are the lubricants for the stresses in the relationships. 'The hard sell is made easier by utilising your press contacts. Quite often with a difficult sell, you need to call in favours from the press. If you have a film with weak points, you do not lie to them: you merely pull out the positives; you can always find something to interest them.' In these contacts with journalists, the publicists are fulfilling an ideological role which Gandy identified as the supply of 'information subsidies':[10] information constructed in the interests of the publicists but accepted by the media contact to reduce the professional news-gathering costs of their work.

Publicists have group identity based on professional vicissitudes produced by working with these other groups. 'We often feel like poor relations. Always the ones sitting on the table near the kitchens or the loos at a flash dinner with a plate of half-eaten food because you are constantly jumping up and down making sure everyone else is OK.' Their working code says: 'always stay in the background as the fixer; never get more column inches than your client; always be one step ahead of everyone as the buck stops with you'. After first employment, the following abilities matter for advancement. They have to match the publicity tastes of the cast and the promotion policy of the film with media outlets (as some names rise, they grow to like or dislike, say, the *Sun* newspaper). There is organising actors for interviews and photographic sessions, recognising the publicity profile of a film which will maximise audience, and then persuading journalists of their version of the film's contents, cast and future popularity. In Britain, publicists deal with some 100 journalists who write mostly about films and the industry and another much smaller number who also write about television programmes. Most of the contact is by telephone. It is face-to-face at previews and on location.

Publicists in agencies work either for the production companies or, more likely, for the distributors, of which there are five major and half a dozen smaller ones in Britain. They often have to make competitive 'pitches' to get this work. Sometimes they are taken on only for the launch of a film. Most launches are in London with the traditional trimmings of a first night. If the reviews are favourable, the publicist is complimented for working up the fair wind of approval; if there is general criticism, publicists hunker down and think enviously of television publicists who have up to three or four instalments of a series to attempt to change opinions. But film, because of unsynchronised regional screenings, often has a longer product life than television programmes and books, both of which have a publicity window of opportunity of two to four weeks. This opportunity for film is lengthened by regional cinemas which will show a film for as long as the audience justifies it. Monday after the opening weekend is the critical day for it is then that the distribution companies tally up audiences and could utter the darkest words known to a publicist: 'It's a flop. Why should we keep it on for another week?' On average, a film moves from pre-production stage to regional publicity in nine months, but if demand in the regions is strong, publicists can stay with it for a year. Publicity contracts with production companies are worth around £4–8,000, and £12,000 with distribution houses. Publicists deny that their work is 'glamorous': few stars are heroes to their publicists. They add that their work is not a short road to wealth.

The above is the observable and demographic profile of the film publicist. They have also an ideological role, similar to fellow professionals in other sectors. Publicists and their fashionable counterparts in politics – the spindoctors – are a response to a dominant theme in the UK political economy today, the commodification and marketisation of culture and politics. They take a film or a policy and apply a reductionist technique to it, shaking down the complexities of its themes and language to the simpler structure of the popular folk story, and decoding the subtleties and nuances of its language to the level which attracts the largest number of voters or cinema-goers. For most films and policies, it is a straightforward task to apply the reductionist techniques of mass consumerism or mass voting. Not so in other cases where the populist card can be played too heavily. The film *William Shakespeare's Romeo and Juliet* (1996) has been critiqued for over-playing the dynastic rivalries in the play through a noisy and violent representation of Mafia-style gang warfare and so overshadowing the love affair. *Hamlet* (Kenneth Branagh 1996) was said to visually over-state its locations and interiors as a way of easing the digestion of iambic pentameters. Equally, political spindoctors are the reducers of the ideas and texts of political philosophers to the soundbite and photo-opportunity. Literally a soundbite when the Labour Party's 'bulldog' party political broadcast in April 1997 is remembered!

Film publicists and political spinners work for the cultural production and political party elite, crafting the easy tale and memorable slogan to attract mass audiences and mass electorates. Their principal channels are the press and television media, themselves engaged in an endless struggle for more audience. Publicists and spinners are the shelf-fillers and dressers of the cultural and political superstore where simplicity, explicitness and emotion are piled up prominently and promoted over nuance, irony and the cerebral. They are the distribution agents at the diffusion point of the cultural and political 'product', pushing their wares to the largest numbers of film-goers and voters. But always they promote on the terms of their principals – producers, directors, distributors, party leaders and ministers. It is plain and worthy work on the whole. It is unavoidable work in a mass society which is geared to individual self-fulfilment and self-improvement through mass demand, mass consumption and mass participation.

Doing film publicity

The basic professional act in the creation of publicity/journalese is to characterise the production in a way that is meaningful to the media gatekeepers who in turn make judgements about its appeal to the film-going public. What is needed is a memorable soundbite, tag line, headline, strap line – some slogan which integrates production values, media interest and audience demand. The development of this characterisation gives the film a 'publicity personality' which is based on the three factors above. One publicist puts the task as follows: 'Sparking interest in one line; giving a flavour of the genre and the story; pulling out the selling points – fun, intriguing, interesting, sexy, bizarre – which will ultimately pull in Joe Public'. But the seasoned professional knows that she or he cannot succeed alone: that publicity of itself does not make films successful. It is the first fair wind behind them; the second is the favourable opinion of the media; then it is take-up by a mass audience – or not. Publicists also know that there is one influential promotional network beyond their influence: word of mouth. It is particularly potent in large urban areas at the start of a film run. They listen for it and work with the grain when it is favourable by holding screenings for film industry staff and their families. But they cannot work against it.

An example of publicity personality is the film of the story *Waking Ned* by Pat Devine, which is in production with Tomboy Films for distribution in autumn 1998. It centres on two old men in an Irish village where there is an anonymous winner of the national lottery. It is aimed at a British, urban, national film audience in which the most numerous age segment is 25–35. So the title was nearly converted to *Old Men Behaving Badly*, with the supporting line 'they grew old but they did not grow up'. The tag line continued that the film 'hypes up the humour and is hip entertainment, not hip replacement'. Another example is *Shooting Fish* (1997), which is about 'two nineties scammers chasing their childhood dream: a million pounds and a mansion . . .'. *Keep the Aspidistra Flying* (1997) was promoted as about 'a quirky 1930s couple with very modern ideas of love, poetry and garden plants' and it involves a hero whose 'bizarre passion [is] to escape that dreaded symbol of middle-class "respectability" – the aspidistra'. *Donnie Brasco* (1997) was launched with the tag 'FBI agent, gangster, husband, father – how many identities can one man assume, how many families can one man be tied to, before they split him apart completely?'. The publicity personality does not necessarily lie inside some component of the film: it may be the film itself looked at from some exogenous perspective. An example is the branding in newspapers of *Titanic* (1998) as 'the world's most expensive film', with a budget of $250 million, just before its UK release. All these tag lines and supporting cast notes are written up in the style of newspaper copy ready for insertion into film columns: the package, complete with technical and financial details and full credits, is known as production notes or publicity information briefings. They are the publicity personality made journalese.

In their work, publicists are literate in the way of mass, persuasive communications. They seek words and visual images which will resonate with the youthful, multi-ethnic, changing tastes of popular culture. Their closest links are with journalists on the mainstream media: they make the same discourse. They are creative in the way of headline writers and picture editors. They seek immediate meanings, accessible references and easy understanding: they eschew the ironic, the esoteric, the ambiguous. There is no art in their work but there is artfulness: they are like copywriters for consumer goods advertisements except that the products are cultural.

This creation of a publicity personality goes through the five stages associated with TV programme publicity (the read-through of the script; location publicity; pre-transmission; transmission; and post-transmission), although in an amended form. For the classic novel adapted to the screen, the script is the embodiment of part of a literary canon and the publicity associated with the TV series or film has to fit in with the halo effect of the classic. If the script is not a classic, there is more room for the development of a personality profile. In the example above, *Waking Ned* can be portrayed as traditional stage 'Oirish' or as impoverished, rural, older males facing a modern development in fortune hunting, i.e. the lottery. It is difficult to see how the publicity personality of *Hamlet* can be as elastic as that. Hamlet as a mass murderer to gain a family fortune or Hamlet as a camp homosexual? It seems hardly likely.

Location publicity is the same as for TV programmes and is another source of characterising the publicity profile, this time through association with sites and cities. It is where the publicist is responsible 'for pin-pointing the look and feel of the film'. This is where the visual personality of the film is developed through physical linkage with landscape, period architecture or physical features such as battlefields. The pre-opening and the première showing stages rely heavily on actor and director interviews where personality traits and connections to current news and cultural themes are developed to link with the film and create an impression of modernity and relevance.

Film is different in the fifth and final stage, which is on-going, post-launch publicity. Here the time-spans and geographic reach are often more extreme. Work can last up to a year on a film, much more than with a television series, and can be international and national at the same time. If the film is failing to draw, the publicist can be hired for a month to try and turn the situation around. Film work can also be regional; for instance, a production such as *Hamlet* can be promoted more heavily in university towns than elsewhere. This regional aspect is demand-led in that the publicist has to respond to the needs of the cinema managers. Another difference from television is that along the five stages of the publicity process, the freelance publicist can work for both the production company and for the distributors. Supplementing these five stages are 'tie-ins' and 'cross-overs' where motor manufacturers, publishers, clothing companies, sunglasses makers, fast food chains and so forth run parallel promotions with those of the film industry. For example, *Titanic* (1998) increased sales for both Fox films and Tesco supermarkets when the video was the reward for 200 loyalty points earned at the stores; and the cinema release of *Mulan* (October 1998) was scheduled alongside a competition for 50 Packard Bell multimedia PCs and 100,000 interactive CDs wrapped in the packaging of Robinsons drinks.

The pleasure economy of film publicity

Grunig has categorised public relations into four types and film publicity is a classic example of the first, press agentry. He calls it 'propagandistic public relations' that seeks media attention in almost any way possible.[11] Grunig, an American, would call the work of Phineas Barnum, the circus entrepreneur mentioned at the start of this essay, press agentry. In the world of public relations theorists, this allocation is not meant as a compliment, for what is admired among them is communications which are two-way, responsible and negotiating amongst the parties. Film publicists, however, would not be concerned about their 'dumbing down' by this typology. Instead, they can build a conceptual justification for themselves in nineteenth-century philosophy. They start this by taking the word 'utility' away from modern economists and returning to it the meaning of 'pleasure' or 'happiness': the meaning which Bentham, the nineteenth-century philosopher, gave to the word. His aphorism that poetry was as good (pleasurable) as pushpin rested on the assumption that all pleasures are of equal value.[12] With this symmetry, Bentham provides the foundational value for the concept of a pleasure economy. In it, wealth is measured in quantities not of money but of pleasure, which is generated by the supply of cultural goods matching the demand for them.

Maximising pleasure (as an undifferentiated and unranked experience) from the highest level of consumption of their films via the distributional effects of promotion is the task of the publicist in this other economy. These are the words of one pleasure distribution worker: 'We should be pleased with what we do because we bring people pleasure. We might think it's a bit frivolous and it's not the cure for cancer; it's not saving lives. But we create the fun side and the escapism for people.' This is a testimonial to the

needs met by film and their conversion through film production
and consumption (seeing) into pleasure. As with all mass consumption industries, film professionals know the shape of the demand
curve for their products: the supply of some actors, roles, plots,
locations and scripts regularly increases demand. Publicists know
that most of the pleasure demand for their films by journalists and
audiences is stereotypical with a few basic themes, such as 'chase
and catch', 'attack and defend', 'true love will out' and 'fame is
fickle', acted by 'stars' in popular language. Publicity/journalese is
a conventional and limited language.

Film publicists do service in the cultural production sector of a
market, liberal democracy. They agree with Bentham that it does
not matter whether the greatest happiness of the greatest number
comes from poetry or pushpin. In markets and democracies, it is
unwise and elitist to rank cultural pleasures. One said,

> if you've got a free rein to promote the film of a classic novel or
> play and you want to bring in people who wouldn't normally be
> interested in it, you have to bring out the sex and the romance and
> the glamour and the actors in it. You've got to bring it to the man
> in the street; bring it to their level.

Film publicists use the practices of the modern publicist –
selection, sensationalism, exaggeration and repetition. Their task
is to match the supply and demand for pleasure-through-film. They
may be media journeymen of uncertain status but why should
those who stand and spin not be hailed as members of a creative
team producing new work? For their precise role is a potent one,
characteristic of twentieth-century culture (and politics): the injec-
tion of persuasive communications into marketplaces (and ballot
boxes). Modern politics needs spindoctors. Can't the film industry
have theirs? They are publicity craftsmen and women, introducing
and re-introducing us to ephemera and classics. In contemporary
terms, they are agents for mass engagement with Cool Britannia
as film. They do their work well. They and their creative principals
fashion and re-fashion new and classic talent to modern, mass
taste. Their distributional skills are essential for the attraction of
audiences measured in millions by the British Film Institute (£426
million and 123.8 million people in 1996).[13] Very few screenings
ignore their skills (the exceptions are those productions which the
big distributors have no faith in).

They ply their trade in a contemporary cultural climate which is politically sympathetic to their industry. It is a climate which allows these media journeymen and women to be viewed as contributors to the politically powerful and fashionable part of the UK's contemporary political economy: as a group they are the publicists for a resurgent British industry making cultural goods which are expressive of 'modern', 'stylish', 'creative', 'new' Britain.

The author thanks the following for discussion, debate and time in the preparation of this chapter: Ginger Corbett, Julie Jones and Peter Mares. The opinions expressed and the statement of facts are, of course, entirely his.

Notes

1. J. Gaines, *Contested Culture: The Image, The Voice and The Law* (London, 1992), p. 39. Further page references are cited in the text.
2. See S. Cutlip, 'The Unseen Power: A Brief History of Public Relations' in *The Handbook of Strategic Public Relations and Integrated Communications* (London, 1997). Page references are cited in the text.
3. L. Litivak, *Reel Power* (New York, 1986).
4. P. Trent, *The Image Makers: Sixty Years of Hollywood Glamour* (London, 1973), p. 9.
5. E. Betts, *Inside Pictures* (London, 1960). Page references are cited in the text.
6. S. Box, *Film Publicity: A Handbook on the Production and Distribution of Propaganda Films* (London, 1937). Page references are cited in the text.
7. E. Bernays, *Crystallising Public Opinion* (New York, 1923).
8. A. Moran (ed.), *Film Policy* (London, 1996), p. 1. Further page references are cited in the text.
9. Unattributed quotations in the essay, like this one, are taken from dialogues between film publicists and the author, carried out as part of his research into this subject.
10. O. Gandy, *Beyond Agenda Setting: Information Subsidies and Public Policy* (Norwood, 1982).
11. J. Grunig, 'Symmetrical Presuppositions as a Framework for Public Relations Theory' in C. Botan and V. Hazleton (eds), *Public Relations Theory* (Hove, 1989), p. 17.
12. For an introductory account of Bentham's thought, see for instance T. Honderich (ed.), *The Oxford Companion to Philosophy* (Oxford, 1993).
13. See E. Dyja (ed.), *BFI Film and Television Handbook 1998* (London, 1998).

Part Two
Writing in Cinema

4 *Preliminaries for a taxonomy and rhetoric of on-screen writing*

Sean Cubitt

The relation between image and text has rarely been so important as today. Internet and CD-ROM drag them together into a hybrid form which in many ways dominates current network communications. Photography and text have shared the pages of print for almost 150 years, and their interaction has provided the grounds for some of the most challenging and theoretically sophisticated photographic art of recent decades. For one of the leading practitioners of this photo-text art, Victor Burgin, 'the use of photo-text was a way of establishing continuity of languages between the cultured tones of "high art" and the vernacular of the "mass media"'.[1] As both artist and essayist, Burgin points us towards the gulf that exists between the realm of pure media (the fine arts of painting and sculpture, for example) and that of impure, mixed and hybrid media that characterise the popular cultures of everyday life (billboards, TV, computer games and magazines).

Although cinema has in some ways lost the dominant position it held in the early and middle years of the twentieth century, it is nonetheless still a major element of popular or 'vernacular' culture, not least as a major, indeed essential, marketing tool for videos, merchandising and the industry of celebrity. In their historical development, films began as images accompanied by music and words, and very soon the words entered the space of the screen. Some of the earliest on-screen writing was there simply to identify ownership of the print (rather like contemporary videos, where each copy has a specific number marked on the image track in order to identify pirate copies). Méliès began putting his Star logo on the print (and occasionally painted it into the sets of his films) in an effort to curtail the illicit copying of his films in the USA during the late 1890s. Writing rapidly expanded to include film titles, credits for the production companies and later for their stars and crew. Intertitles were employed to help guide audiences through the more complex narratives of the emergent feature film, reaching an early high-point in the films of D.W. Griffith. Alfred Hitchcock began his career painting intertitles for Famous Players-Lasky's London studio. You might expect that, with sound, the intertitle would have disappeared: far from it. Even the advent of recorded dialogue could not loosen the grip of the written word, which still instructs us as to where and when the action takes place: Los Angeles 2019, in the case of *Blade Runner* (1982) for example.

One of the beauties of writing is that it is, in a sense, invisible. We read all day long: we see street signs, hoardings, and the names of shops, registering what they say without being aware of the fact that we are reading. Words are embedded in the contemporary landscape, communicating constantly with us, yet we are by and large aware, to use the language of information science, only of their message, not their channel. Film makes use of this 'invisibility' to deliver both legal data (credit lists and copyright information) as well as narrative information without disrupting our engagement with the photographic and sound elements which otherwise dominate our perception of a film. Yet writing is a visual medium, and in some ways also, because of its unique and complex relationship with speech, a medium with a special relationship to the world of sound. After all, before sound recording, writing was the only tool for recording what had been said in the past, or what should be said in the future (as in scripts for plays). Something of the complex and confusing relationship between writing and cinema can be caught in Fiona Banner's artworks, in which she laboriously transcribes the stories of Vietnam movies from screen to paper, stretching out the time of viewing into the far longer time of writing.[2] Yet on-screen writing is as ephemeral as speech.

We will need a few terms to help us deal with this most critically underrepresented of film codes. We can begin with an elementary listing of types of writing, vocabularies for describing them, and places in films where writing appears on screen. The question of rhetoric, to which we then turn, concerns the relationship between writing and image (and occasionally sound) according to general headings of hierarchy (for example, illustration), space and time (is writing in front of the screen, on the screen or in the image? Does writing occupy the same time as the image, or does it predict, or look back towards the time of the image?), and finally of hybridity. This last category will bring us back to the opening of this essay, and confront, in slightly new terms, Rudolf Arnheim's criticism of the talkies, first voiced in the 1930s, a criticism based in what he perceived as the failure of talking pictures to create the necessary unity of elements proper to a mature art form.[3] But it will also bring us to the question of picture writing, of the hieroglyph, and the contradictions that inhere in the concept of a universal language combining image and word.

Elements for a typology of on-screen writing

In the interests of space, I want to concentrate here on writing presented as a graphic element of cinema, that is to say the kind of writing which is separated from the fictional world of the film, the diegesis. Diegetic writing appears photographically, as letters, newspaper headlines, storefronts, advertisements, calendar pages, maps inspected by characters, or introduced in montage sequences. With the phrase 'on-screen writing', I want to isolate those letters and words which appear as if written or painted or printed onto the surface of the film directly, without the benefit of cameras. Of course, most such lettering requires optical equipment – rostrum cameras and optical printers in the old days, digital edit suites nowadays. But it is distinguishable from diegetic writing by the sense we have that on-screen writing is not just invisible to the characters in the story world: it occupies an entirely different universe. So we would not expect the character sitting on the fountain portrayed in the title sequence of *I Was a Male War Bride* (1943) to be able to see the letters superimposed on the image, or the car on the left to crash into them. As we will see, there are some uses of on-screen writing which can be rather ambiguous in this sense. A certain kind of film exploits just this ambiguity, which we will investigate in the second part of this essay when we come to consider the rhetoric of on-screen writing. But first, we must isolate some types of writing, and the places where they occur in films.

Let's start with types of lettering. One large scale-division in almost all written languages is that between handwriting and printing. Orthography – letters clearly made by handwriting with pen or brush – is relatively rare in western films, although it features quite strongly in the Chinese and Japanese traditions. European and North American films do however sometimes use cursive letters, designed for printing but made to resemble the flowing style of handwriting, as in *Monotype Corsiva*. More common are typographic letters, clearly derived from families of lettering or fonts which have been created for the print industries. Alphabetic fonts can also be very broadly distinguished between serif and sans serif families: the serif being the little flags attached to the extremities of letters, as in the classic typeface Palatino, and sans serif the style of lettering without these little serifs, as in Avant Garde. So we can see that the lettering in *I Was a Male War Bride* is serif, even if we might need the services of a type designer to identify the specific typeface used (many production companies will commission specialist letterface designers to provide original fonts for films: a well-known example is the rather beautiful Bajoran typeface designed for Paramount's *Star Trek*). Of course there are many other distinctions that might be added: bold, italic and oblique are common ones.

We should also note the use of ornamental styles of lettering, especially in title sequences, which can be used to locate the film's genre, period and tone. Also useful is the distinction between upper and lower case, otherwise known as capital and small letters. Many films use upper case throughout; many more use upper and lower. Relatively few use lower case throughout, a notable exception being *sex, lies and videotape* (1989). Similarly, it is worth observing the size of the lettering. In print, point size is the unit of measurement of the width (and therefore the height) of letters; in film analysis, of course, there is no absolute size for the letters, because that depends on the size of the screen image. But we need to be aware of the size of the lettering relative to the dimensions of the frame, and the relative dimensions of particular words: in *I Was a Male War Bride*, for example, the film's title is much larger than the name of its director. Likewise, it is often useful to be able to note the spatial position of writing on-screen: ranged left or right (that is, with a straight margin on the left or right side, and a ragged one on the opposite side), centred or justified (that is, with straight margins on both sides). And finally, we should distinguish between letters which are solid, and those which are present as outlines, especially those which are transparent, so that the action of the film is visible inside the masks formed by the shape of the letters, reversing the normal pattern in which letters hide whatever is behind them.

These tools of analysis come from the print media. Of course, in the cinema, we are also dealing with movement. The commonest form of movement in cinematic lettering is probably to remain static. The title of *I Was a Male War Bride* is flashed up, held on screen, and then replaced by a further title after a short gap. It doesn't move relative to the edges of the frame. End titles very frequently move up the screen, a vertical scroll imitating the familiar scan down a page when we read. Some title sequences and other lettering scrolls sideways, the commonest being a lateral scroll from right to left, imitating the left-to-right movement of the eye in alphabetic reading. One of the most famous examples of this is in the opening titles of *Gone with the Wind* (1939). Here the lettering combines a right-to-left scroll with an upper case, serif typeface given both ornaments to suggest the nineteenth-century USA and decorative flashes to suggest a wind blowing across the letters from left to right, the opposite direction to the movement of the letters themselves. This in turn suggests that the title is having to struggle against the storm, so establishing the theme of striving against the elements, and in a sense too of striving against history, which give the film its epic theme.

The third dimension of movement open to titling is the axis of projection running from the projector to the centre of the screen, so linking the spaces of the audience, the screen and the diegetic world of the picture itself. Movement along this axis of projection is perhaps most famously employed in the introductory sequence to *Star Wars* (1977), where the sans serif, upper and lower case, justified and centred text rises from the bottom of the screen and disappears towards a vanishing point just below the top of the frame at an angle of approximately 30° to the axis of projection. Clearly there is a suggestion of infinite space, a generic attraction of science fiction. But there is also the sense that, because the lettering appears from below, we are witnessing an episode in a

far longer conflict, an impression emphasised in more recent release prints of *Star Wars* which introduce the film as 'Episode
Four'. But it is also important to the film as a stand-alone product
that the audience are invited to understand the importance of the
past in the unfolding of the plot in the present movie. The suggestion then is of not only infinite space, but infinite time. Moreover,
the stately pace of the scroll, and the use of the modern, somewhat
anonymous sans serif style combined with the symmetry of centring and justification, give us a sense of an ordered universe, one
in which our own narratives will take their allotted place. The axis
of projection can also be used to have a title rush towards the
spectator from the depths of the image, or to have the letters
appear to arrive on the screen from the auditorium, beginning
usually with the central letter of the title coming into frame first,
followed by the rest.

Letters may also be animated, and arrive bouncing onto the
screen, for example in comedies, or arrive one by one to form the
title as a kind of enigma which the audience are invited to solve
before the process is completed. In this instance, the rules of animation can be brought to bear, so that the letters can become objects
to be manipulated by animated characters. In one variant, animated
letters may bring a certain ambiguity to the status of the writing,
when a title is seen in the process of being generated on screen, for
example on a typewriter. I will return to this ambiguous case later
in the essay.

These basic tools of analysis need to be supplemented with two
other groups of categories consequent on cinematic movement,
categories of time and space. Spatially, lettering can appear to us
as lying in front of the image, as in our examples from *I Was a
Male War Bride* and *Gone with the Wind*. In other cases, like the
Star Wars example, the words appear to exist inside the image. In
some cases, for example when a title is shown being obscured by
sand or smoke, the title may appear to be behind the image. This
last case, once again, brings us to that ambiguous line between
the diegetic and the extra-diegetic, the story-world and the world
beyond it. Each of these spatial variants brings with it, in general
terms, a temporal connotation. The title for *I Was a Male War
Bride* is clearly added to the image, that is, it has been made after
the image. In the case of a title obscured by diegetic smoke or
sand, the implication is that the title existed before the image.

Titles which appear to be generated inside the image will then give a sense that they are being generated at the same time as the image, which would explain why the *Star Wars* exposition is couched in the present tense. One further example needs to be raised here, that of titles which appear, for example, as the cover pages of a book which is being opened to introduce us to the narrative. One function of this type of title is to suggest that a book pre-exists the film, perhaps a famous novel, or perhaps a family album. Here, once again, we are in the ambiguous space between on-screen writing and diegetic writing.

Towards a rhetoric of on-screen writing

This brief survey of some analytical tools gives us some chance of being able to describe what we see, and in describing, to begin to analyse the relationships that can exist between on-screen writing, the photographic image and recorded sound. To begin to study these relationships, I propose to start with the places where we find writing in films. We have already looked at the beginning of films. Here we normally expect to find at least the following:

- the distributor
- the production company
- the name of the film
- the stars' names
- the name of the director
- the names of key production staff, including but not restricted to producers, director of photography, set, costume and sound designers.

In addition we may find some kind of exposition. This may take the form it has in *Star Wars*, where quite a lot of information is passed on to the audience. Or it may be a simple title card: Beirut 1984. We also expect to find a full credit roll at the end of the film, containing all sorts of creative, technical and production credits, information about songs and locations, and frequently in Hollywood films the logos of unions which have worked on the film, along with copyright information and the date of the production. The beginning and end of a film are marked by writing, as if to tell us that we are passing over a threshold from the ordinary world to the cinematic. It is then doubly intriguing to note that these boundary markers should be so interested in legal information about copyright matters, which generally appear as the very first and very last written elements of the film. Enclosed within them – the second and the penultimate items – we find a level of production information, data which, in ordinary circumstances, the film narrative will invite us to forget while we engross ourselves in the action. These forms of writing form the borders of the cinematic, and like any border zone, are of immense interest for contemporary film criticism.

But there are a number of other places where writing will appear. In silent films, or films which parody them, we can expect to find intertitles which may contain either dialogue or plot information ('You!!', 'Meanwhile, back at the ranch . . .'). Here another question will arise, about the status of the quotation of speech in intertitles: do intertitles transcribe dialogue? Or do they quote it? Behind this lies a further question: who 'speaks' the narrative information in intertitles like 'Little did she know . . .'? The question is important for assessing the kinds of narration involved in intertitles, whether restricted to the kinds of knowledge the characters have, or sharing the omniscience of a disembodied narrator. This question returns in another common site for writing, subtitles. We can expect that many films whose dialogue is in languages other than English will be distributed in English-speaking territories with subtitles, and even some mainstream movies give subtitles for dialogue in languages other than English, as in the Russian sequence at the beginning of Dreamworks' *The Peacemaker* (1997). Further issues arise in subtitling: reading subtitles for a film whose language you know can be an entertaining if distracting exercise in bowdlerisation and mistakes; and many of us have caught an English movie with foreign subtitles while on holiday, and found our eyes drawn to the bottom of the screen. Hong Kong films were often exported during the 1980s with subtitles in both English and Chinese (to allow translation between Cantonese and Mandarin), often in such copious quantities you wondered how anyone ever had the chance to decipher them.

Finally, there are those multiple points in films, especially where the scene changes to a new location, or to events some years earlier or later, where the shift is signalled to the audience with on-screen writing, as with the title 'One Year Earlier' which appears after the opening sequence of Verhoeven's *Starship Troopers* (1997), a film overburdened with titles. An increasing number of films, especially in the US independent scene, use intertitles to introduce sequences, not by overprinting onto photographic footage, but by interrupting the film with a title card, as happens in *Pulp Fiction* (1992), though the practice was common enough in classical cinema, as witness the inordinate number of title cards in *Clive of India* (1934). If *Pulp Fiction* gives us the impression of a puppetmaster pulling the strings of the narrative, *Clive of India* suggests the godlike voice of posterity announcing the historical justice of imperialism. But both films raise again the question of who is giving this information, and of its place in the narration of the film. In fact, this is the same question that arises in the intertitles of silent film, and it is to this aspect of the rhetoric of on-screen writing that we turn first.

One of the most insightful analyses of silent screen intertitles comes in Miriam Hansen's book on D.W. Griffith, where she analyses the use of pictorial writing in the intertitles for *Intolerance* (1916).[4] The film covers four historical periods – Babylonian, Biblical, seventeenth-century France and early twentieth-century USA. Titles associated with the earlier periods tend to use decorative symbols – heraldry for the Huguenot story, hieroglyphs for the Babylonian. Hansen points out that Griffith substitutes for the abstract marks of Babylonian cuneiform a vaguely Egyptian pictographic writing which in some ways parallels his belief that cinema would produce a new, universal and pictorial language. At the same time, however, she argues that the attempt to unite picture and writing produces a certain kind of disturbance, and that instead of unifying image and text, the pictograph produces a self-contradictory hybrid. One way of thinking about this is to look at the temporal relationships between writing and image. After a title showing a stone slab carved with small figures of men and animals, over which are superimposed the words 'The Mountain Girl from a distance watches the priest's arrival', we see first the priests' arrival followed by a shot of the Mountain Girl watching them, standing in front of a richly painted wall.

The intertitle is carrying a heavy load. It is telling us in advance what we will see. And it is helping to explain to the audience the spatial relationships of Griffith's novel editing techniques. At the same time, the combination of phonetic script with pictograms in the intertitles echoes firstly the combination of writing and image in the edit from intertitle to image, and then introduces us to the combination of photograph and painting in the shot of the Mountain Girl where painted or ceramic bulls adorn the walls behind her. As a mode of storytelling, then, Griffith's subtitles have already explained the action to us, leaving the images merely to illustrate the text. Such, it could be argued, is the case with many film titles: films with names like *Greed* (1924) or *Fury* (1936) have already told us what they are about; the film that follows the title can only illustrate it. In this sense, writing can pre-empt the work of the film, as it does in Griffith, and make it redundant. Yet this is not what happens. Instead, we find ourselves working out where we are in the film, what aspect of the title is being explored when, collating the ramifications of the specific ways in which the images interpret what was written. In other words, there is no simply illustrative relation. Instead, images interpret words, and by the same token, when words succeed (rather than precede) the image, as at the close of Griffith's film, when the intertitles allude to a future of peace and universal love, the words do more than point up a moral: they lead us out from the theatre with as firm a hand as the very final title: 'The End'.

For it is one of writing's functions to signal the end of the film and to tell us when to exit from the cinema, just as it is to introduce us to the film, before we decide to buy a ticket, and as a kind of overture to the film narrative. Curiously enough, in the UK the first sign we have of the film beginning is the censor's certificate. Overseas visitors may be perplexed by the cheer that often greets this apparent symbol of our oppression. The cheer is not for the censor, but for the end of the preliminary business of trailers and adverts, the moment when we turn away from our conversations and engage our attention on the screen. The logos and fanfares of distributors and producers allow us enough time to get comfortable before the title sequence comes up, and we begin our involvement in the story. This introductory moment, this edge of the film experience, mirrored as it is at the end of the film, this marginal space of writing, frames the film by giving us visual symbols of beginning and end. But as Tom Conley indicates,[5] drawing on the work of philosopher Jacques Derrida, far from unifying the film by giving it a discrete existence between the enclosing brackets of credits and titles, this opens it up to the external world, and more specifically to the external discourses which we bring with us to the cinema, or which the fiction film itself trails in with it.

Radical cinema has taken advantage of this uncertainty at the opening of the film by the insertion of writing since Vertov's *Man with a Movie Camera* (1928). One of the most vivid examples comes from the Latin American Third Cinema,[6] in the epic, revolutionary documentary *La Hora de los Hornos* (*The Hour of the Furnaces*) (1966–68).[7] Solanas and Getino's film, especially in the first of its three segments, hurls text up on the screen using all the movements we have described, accompanied by ominous and gradually more complex and violent drumming with which it is roughly synchronised, and intercut with black screens and brief snatches of clandestinely shot footage of insurrection and bloody police reprisals. Here the texts function as slogans, and graphic design techniques increase the potency of the anti-colonial quotations. In their 1976 manifesto, Solanas and Getino call for cinema as weapon, cinema by, for, and with the people, against their masters and the entertainment (First) and bourgeois psychological (Second) cinemas' ideological violence against justice and liberation. The film-makers clearly share with Conley a belief that making the written word visible on screen, as a vital part of the film, is a challenge to the normative workings of the cinema of oppression, and as such is a radical technique, much as Eisenstein's followers had argued of montage.

But what is radical in one generation becomes the staple fodder of the next. The revolution happened, but it happened in print design and titling, and was picked up by the emergent engineers of television titling, especially to become the mobile graphics we are perhaps most familiar with in sports coverage, where the statistics of the game are constantly superimposed on the image, and provide a third information channel alongside camera coverage and voice-over commentary. The technique of provocation in *La Hora* becomes the technique of totalitarianism in those films which attempt an epic bourgeois account of history. In *Clive of India*, the scope of the action exceeds the budget, just as the mass of events exceeds the ability of Hollywood's simplistic and triumphalist historiography. Intertitles are an admission of defeat, at the same time as they proclaim the victory of Empire and imperial narrative. In *Starship Troopers*, budget is no problem, but the excess of narrative detail leads the production towards titling as an authoritarian mode of delivering story information and even (in this unlike the similarly title-heavy *Dune* (1984)) the ideological account that is intended to direct the audiences' sympathies. Perhaps a critic with sympathies at the opposite end of the political spectrum to mine would find *La Hora* equally propagandistic, authoritarian and clumsy. My point is, however, that there is no struggle between images and on-screen writing that can be 'won'. Instead, we must understand that the processes by which films produce meanings include all the technical means open to the medium, and we must understand their relation, not as a struggle over domination of the meaning, but as the terms of a dialectic.

It is by now a truism to say that a film can never have a single meaning. But neither can a film be said to generate meanings at random. The plurality of meanings arises from internal dialectics at work within the film, one among which is the dialectical relation between on-screen writing and image, on-screen writing and sound. That this is a systematic capacity of cinematic writing can be seen by looking at the relatively uncontrolled addition of subtitles to a film, where there can be little sense of the directorial voice or even the original production company having much say in the affair.

It is clear that neither Monsieur Lange nor the actor playing him are aware of the subtitles which intrude into the scene in export versions of Renoir's *Le Crime de M. Lange* (1936). The subtitles give the rough meaning of Lange's dialogue, which the English audience cannot be presumed to understand otherwise: in this sense, the subtitles are free of the soundtrack, adding the dialogue in written form, while the voice provides the intonation and emotional parameters of our reading. Lange is a writer, and in one shot the camera roams through Lange's room while he enthusiastically speaks aloud the adventures of Arizona Jim which he is busy writing. In one frame we can see the speaker behind the subtitles. But in a later frame the camera has moved on, so that the frame makes almost no sense on its own, and requires the whole of the film's action to make sense. The subtitles translate Lange's voice into writing, and Lange's voice is speaking the words which he is writing. So the subtitles are not even anchored to the speaker's image, no more so than the soundtrack itself, which continues as Lange whips up the action in his fantasy world. Only the chaps hanging on the wall above the bed, and the circle around Arizona on the map of the USA to the right, anchor the subtitles and Lange's voice to the image. What we hear is Lange reciting as he writes, which is then translated for us in the subtitles. In a sense, we are privileged with a direct translation from writing to writing, without the detour of sound which is necessary in the French dialogue track. In fact, you could argue that both recorded voice and image are redundant, and that this writing-to-writing translation is the only essential element of the scene.

But of course, sound and image are not redundant. The shot plays on the gulf separating Lange's fantasy Arizona and his actual one-room apartment, a theme the film will develop in the clash between harsh reality and the utopian cooperative at the heart of the plot. And the roaming camera resonates with the complex and fluid camera movements, culminating in a famous 360° pan, which stitch the little community together throughout the movie. Meanwhile Lange's increasingly flamboyant enactment of the story he is writing, including slapping his haunches like a boy playing horses, not only situates the childlike Lange's character, but swells with the humanism of Renoir and the visionary anarchism of scriptwriter Jacques Prévert. In some sense, reading the subtitles allows us to listen more acutely to the dialogue, to hear not its semantic message, but the enthusiasm of its delivery. Likewise, we can see more clearly the little room, and the movement of the camera, because we do not need to listen for narrative information. So the written element helps to separate the visual and auditory codes of the film, to allow each the room to breathe, and so gives back to the text the space which more monolinear narration denies it, and so denies to the audience too.

When Arnheim claimed that the talking film failed the artistic test of unity, he was drawing on a Romantic ideology of art as organic. Renoir's film, so profoundly in and of its time, is not an organic unity. On the contrary, it revels in the dispersal of its elements. Arnheim calls for hierarchy, like that of opera, where the music governs acting and libretto. Renoir refuses, and in some sense that refusal is typical of film. Arnheim's observation is flawless: the talking film (and he might have added, the titled film) lacks both unity and hierarchy. What it offers instead is an open and permeable network of activities, and one in which the resolution of dialectical contradictions is a mark not of artistic success but of totalitarian ideology. It is the great achievement of the cinema as a hybrid art that it enables, almost demands, such dialectical openness, such movement within and between its elements, that even its least gifted auteurs (the Richard Boleslawski of *Clive of India* for example) are forced to accept the impossibility of completing a purely authoritarian movie; while those whose gifts are only enough to tame the medium, but not to liberate it (the Paul Verhoeven of *Starship Troopers* springs to mind) are alone in producing those stultified spectacles of fascist pomp which plummet so instantly into the maw of forgetfulness, becoming events as they fail to be cinema.

Notes

1. Victor Burgin, *Between* (London and Oxford, 1986), p. 181.
2. Fiona Banner's work is documented in the catalogue for *Spellbound* at the Hayward Gallery (London, 1996). Her book, *The Nam*, reproduces works from the Vietnam film series (London, 1998).
3. Rudolf Arnheim, 'A New Laocoön: Artistic Composites and the talking Film' in *Film as Art* (London, 1958), pp. 164–89, originally published in 1938, argues that 'up to now, artists have shown little capacity or inclination to produce work based on more than one medium' (p. 183), but where they do, as in opera, ballet or theatre, one of the media involved – poetry, music, dance – takes the lead over all subsidiary media. Arnheim accuses the talking film of failing to develop such a hierarchy, and in the process, destroying an art form, the silent film, which had already achieved major artistic works.
4. Miriam Hansen, *Babel and Babylon: Spectatorship in American Silent Cinema* (Cambridge, MA, 1991). See also Miriam Hansen, 'The Hieroglyph and the Whore: DW Griffith's *Intolerance*' in Jane Gaines (ed.), *Classical Hollywood Narrative: The Paradigm Wars* (Durham, NC, 1992).
5. Tom Conley, *Film Hieroglyphs: Ruptures in Classical Cinema* (Minneapolis, 1991).
6. See Fernando Solanas and Octavio Getino, 'Towards a Third Cinema' (no translation credited) in Bill Nichols (ed.), *Movies and Methods*, vol. 1 (Berkeley, CA, 1976); revised translation by Julianne Burton and Michael Chanan in Michael Chanan (ed.), *25 Years of Latin American Cinema* (London, 1984).
7. Fernando Getino and Octavio Solanas write: 'The man of the third cinema . . . above all counters the film industry of a cinema of characters with one of themes, that of the individual with that of masses, that

of the author with that of the operative group, one of neo-colonial misinformation with one of information, one of escape with one that recaptures the truth, that of passivity with that of aggression'. Cited in Charles Musser, 'Cinéma-Vérité and the New Documentary' in Geoffrey Nowell-Smith (ed.), *The Oxford History of World Cinema* (Oxford, 1996), p. 532.

5 Writing, cinema and the avant-garde: Michael Snow and So Is This

Jim Hillier

For something like a quarter of its history, film lived very happily with the written word as an integral part of the possibilities, even the nature, of the medium. Nevertheless, for its first ten years or so, the new medium worked on the basis that it did not need the written word, that in some senses it made itself distinctive by eschewing writing and that part of its supposed universality stemmed from this fact. It was, in a sense, an admission of failure when the evolving complexity of filmic narration in the period roughly 1907–12 seemed to imply the necessity of recourse to written text.

In some ways, this might have seemed inevitable. Dialogue was always present in that the spectator could see characters opening their mouths and 'speaking'. Given the greater complexity of narrative organisation, and the increasing use of closer shots of actors' faces, it was perhaps unsurprising that the audience wanted to know what the characters were saying. While it may have been relatively unproblematic for titles to provide dialogue which was, after all, present – mouthed, but 'unvoiced' – a very different kind of relationship between word and image confronted spectators with some of the title cards in a later film like D.W. Griffith's *Broken Blossoms* (1919). Although almost any film of roughly the same period would serve as example here, *Broken Blossoms* may be particularly appropriate, as a film with one foot in an earlier, more 'theatrical' (and literary) approach to both film space and film dramaturgy, and the other in a more 'filmic' approach closer to what became regarded as 'classical'. Intertitles here range from straight transcriptions of dialogue to the narratively explanatory

('The manager's protest against Burrows's dissipation sends him home in another rage'), to the clearly interpretative ('Poor Lucy, never having cause to smile, uses this pitiful excuse instead'), to general moralising ('In every group there is one, weaker than the rest – the butt of uncouth wit or ill-temper. Poor Lucy is one of these') and the frankly literary ('Blue and yellow silk caressing white skin – her beauty so long hidden shines out like a poem'). Clearly, the film's construction of narrative point of view owes a great deal to intertitles such as these, to the point that the film could not be read in the way Griffith intends without them.

In the sense that 'silent' cinema – though never really silent – came to depend extensively on the written title card, and was therefore a very upfront combination of image and written text, should we see the coming of sound as a major change? Some writers on film history – notably André Bazin in 'The Evolution of the Language of Cinema'[1] – have argued that it was not. But Bazin's argument was very much a response to an established view of the history and aesthetics of cinema which had seen its specificity in the process of editing and its history culminating in, in many ways, Soviet montage and German expressionism. Bazin wanted to argue for a different aesthetic and history (represented by Robert Flaherty and F.W. Murnau, for example). Despite such attempts to play down the 'break' in film history brought about by the coming of sound (more properly the coming of 'talkies', despite the warnings and polemics of film-makers like Sergei Eisenstein or René Clair who argued for a very different approach to sound[2]), generally speaking the coming of the sound film re-asserted a kind of taboo on the written word on the screen, except in the highly conventionalised form of credits and the occasional explanatory title. Such titles occur usually at the start of a film, after which the more or less naturalistically spoken word and visual narration were considered able to 'carry' the narrative.[3] From this point we can posit that whatever dominant film form owed to theatrical and literary novelistic forms, or to some kind of synthesis of the two,[4] illusionist film, like illusionist theatre, did put a kind of taboo on the written word, certainly in the sense that 'reading' the visual image, in all its apparent plenitude, was considered as a wholly different mental activity from reading the written word.

Outside the main developments of the fictional feature film during the 'silent' period, there existed counter currents of thinking and practice. In one such current, film was taken to be somehow 'purer' by doing without written text. Certainly, this was the aim of several more or less experimental (though industrially produced) works of the 1920s, such as Murnau's *Der Letzte Mann* (*The Last Laugh*, 1924), which aspired to tell a complex story in wholly visual terms. Much Soviet work of the 1920s, like Eisenstein's, worked in the opposite direction, aspiring to a more dynamic, and more immediately political, relationship between image and text in which the written text had a greater equality with the image, rather than the usual very subservient role. At roughly the same time, avant-garde film-makers in France were incorporating written text in innovative ways. Works such as Clair's *Entr'acte* and Fernand Léger's and Dudley Murphy's *Le Ballet mécanique* (both 1924), for example, incorporated written text into montages of images, precisely as heterogeneous materials, in much the same way as early twentieth-century modernist painting, particularly Cubism, had.[5]

Certainly, it is to avant-garde work, like that in France and the Soviet Union in the 1920s, that we need to look for any concerted exploration of the function(s) or the problematic of writing or written text in cinema. Even so, there was very little such exploration, even in avant-garde film, until the explosion of experimental and counter cinema in the 1960s. Peter Wollen divided the 1960s–1970s 'avant-garde' into two main strands – a 'political' avant-garde, mainly European, connected with the industrial processes of the 'art film', manifest in the work of film-makers such as Jean-Luc Godard in France, Jean-Marie Straub in Germany and Dusan Makavejev in Yugoslavia, and a more 'formal' avant-garde, mainly North American, exemplified by the work (in very different registers) of Stan Brakhage, Hollis Frampton, George Landow, Paul Sharits, Malcolm LeGrice and Michael Snow.[6] Leaving aside some of the inevitable over-simplifications which Wollen's division produces, but taking advantage of its boldness and its broad historical usefulness, we can begin to think through some of the different ways in which writing was foregrounded in these different kinds of work.

The broad, overall strategy of the 'counter cinema' film-makers like Godard (in films like *Vivre sa vie* (1962), *Pierrot le fou* (1965) *Masculin féminin* and *Deux ou trois choses que je sais d'elle* (both 1966), and into the more obviously political and politicised period of *Le Gai savoir* and *Vent d'Est* (both 1969) and *Tout va bien* (1972)) and Makavejev (in films like *Switchboard Operator/Love*

Dossier, or the Tragedy of a Switchboard Operator (1967), or WR – *Mysteries of the Organism*, (1971)) was to problematise, and make more conscious, the generally unproblematic, relatively unconscious relationship between spectator and the fictional, usually illusionist, narrative text. The purpose was a political, 'Brechtian' one (we should remember that most of Bertolt Brecht's writings were translated into French and English only in the late 1950s and 1960s): to point, via their various deconstructions, to the constructedness of the text and the constructedness of its ideological formulations and to create an active, politically conscious spectator. The use of written text on the screen was part of this process, drawing attention to the fundamental differences between the way we read the film image and the way we read written text (whether on screen or not). Since the written texts which are introduced into the (already leaky) fictional worlds of the films are typically non-diegetic, materials such as book covers, captions, poems, and so on, serve to further destabilise the apparent solidity and naturalness of the films. The point is very clearly made that language needs to be 'read', and that reading needs a knowledge of language systems and principles of combination, while the visual image seems to be 'natural', self-explanatory. Written language then appears as a critical activity which can break down the illusion of the image.

The films of the more 'formalist' avant-garde cannot be considered Brechtian in these same ways, although one reason for qualifying them as 'formalist' is that they, too, are 'deconstructive', though in a different register, pointing to conventional uses of film form and conventional assumptions about the nature of the medium. A film like Hollis Frampton's *(nostalgia)* (1971), for instance, plays with, among other things, images and voice-over descriptions of them which are deliberately out of synch, so that the spectator, once adjusted to the film's system, needs to remember the present description, so as to apply it to an image yet to come, while also trying to remember the previous description in order to relate it to the present image. Here there is a clear interest in the relationship of spoken language/description and the image, as well as an attempt to find a structure which demands of the spectator both retrospection and projection, a structure consciously reminiscent, despite its somewhat abstract quality, of the demands a narrative makes on a spectator.[7]

Not surprisingly, though – given the often 'formal' interest in language since the 1960s – it has been left to this avant-garde to undertake some of the most direct and focused exploration of the problems around writing and cinema. Martha Haslanger's *Syntax* (1974), for example, directly confronts the 'syntactical' relationships between images on screen and the syntactical relationships of words, also on screen. Paul Sharits's work had been characterised by an interest in flicker, perceptual thresholds and colour fields (what he modestly refers to as 'working towards a completely new conception of cinema'[8]) with some interest in the written word on screen, but the image track of *Word Movie* (1972), despite retaining the concern with physical perception and colour, consists entirely of constantly changing words on screen: while some letters remain in place for several seconds, others constantly change, evoking in a startlingly direct way the paradigm–syntagm relationship in language; the sound track throughout features a male and a female voice reading, alternately, single words from a text, the combination of which pushes reading and aural competence to, and beyond, its limits.[9]

However, no avant-garde film addresses the problematic of writing and cinema more systematically and directly than Canadian film-maker Michael Snow's *So Is This* (1982), which consists entirely of words on the screen. Cinema, since the 1920s, has always attracted fine artists, like Snow, from other art media by the possibilities of play with time and duration, taking 'narrative' as just one kind of structure in time. In many ways, this should have come as no surprise since, on the one hand, writing/the written word is one of the medium's established elements and, on the other, Snow's previous work had single-mindedly addressed and explored the isolated elements which make up the 'vocabulary' of film. Snow explored the zoom in *Wavelength* (1966–67), the 360° circular pan in *Standard Time* (1967), the static camera in *One Second in Montreal* (1969), lateral panning in ←——→ (1969) (also known as *Back and Forth*, though because of the limitations of language in rendering visual phenomena, Snow prefers the original 'title'), all kinds of circular 360° panning in spherical space in *La Région centrale* (1971) ('"orchestrating" all the possibilities of camera movement and the various relationships between it and what is being photographed'[10]), recorded sound in *Rameau's Nephew by Diderot (Thanx to Denis Young) by Wilma Schoen* (1974) ('an attempt to make a genuine talking picture' (Snow, p. 17)) and the apparent three-dimensionality but actual flatness of the screen in the installation/film *Two Sides to Every Story* (1974) ('an involvement in the mystery of light really as much as it is a reduction of the illusion of depth'[11]).

To summarise these films as being about, or exploring, the zoom or the pan is misleading. In that they focus single-mindedly on one element in film's vocabulary to the apparent exclusion of others, and in that they are experimental in the almost scientific sense of asking, for example in the case of ←——→, what happens to the photographic image and the spectator's perception of it if we pan the camera from side to side at increasing speed ('a kind of demonstration or lesson in perception'[12]), Snow's films can perhaps justifiably be regarded as examples of 'minimalism' (though they are often monumentally minimal: *Rameau's Nephew* lasts 285 minutes). However, although *Wavelength* is, at one level, a 45-minute zoom across a room, it is also about light and hence about the nature of the photographic image and its ontological status (or otherwise). Further, it raises questions about narrative and narrative structure, by offering elements of a 'narrative' which is largely 'absent' and simultaneously offering a much more abstract 'structure' which nevertheless, like a narrative, involves the viewer in both expectation and retrospection.[13] All these considerations of Snow's work are relevant to the way *So Is This* works, and despite their apparently forbiddingly austere concerns and approach, Snow's films can also be very funny.

So Is This consists entirely of individual words and occasionally numerals, presented on the screen one at a time. Crucially, the words remain on screen for varying lengths of time: like *One Second in Montreal*, *So Is This* is 'literally made with lengths of time',[14] varying from one frame (one 24th of a second, which is, of course, subliminal in effect) to almost one minute. The words are all centred within the film frame, which of course remains constant, which means that word and letter sizes change constantly, and dramatically, from word to word in order to fit into the frame. The words are usually white, and the background usually black, but varying on occasions: in a 'flashback' near the end words are 'faded' (a good example of the film's knowing humour) and the background is sometimes more green than black (and sometimes other colours). The actual typographical qualities are also not absolutely consistent – some letters, intentionally or not, are a little imperfect, as if the type had crumbled away.

We can get a pretty good sense of what Snow would be interested in exploring about the written word on screen from his account of what he wanted to explore about sound and (recorded) spoken language in *Rameau's Nephew*:

> to use spoken language to any deeper effect in film, I think one ought to be involved in provoking differences of hearing and listening counterpointed with those of seeing, watching, looking and making possible raw or concrete understandings. Meaning is a constituent not only of the words used but, even more than in real speech, of qualities possible only with film sound: a conscious use of the differences between actual speech and recorded speech . . . click.[15]

Not surprisingly, *So Is This* is interested, as Scott MacDonald puts it, in 'essential elements of reading texts and experiencing films'[16] and, vitally, making them able to be experienced by the film viewer. The interviewers of Hollis Frampton once put to him that his films were 'about the consciousness of the people who are looking at them', one commenting, 'I can see the way I project my thoughts into the film . . . it's a sort of feedback system'.[17] This is precisely what Snow seeks to demonstrate here, even more than in his other works.[18]

It is immediately clear that reading this kind of writing on the screen is both like and very unlike reading conventional written text on the page. For a start, the text itself does not render itself in a sense invisible by its extreme conventionality (much as the classical conventions of film tend to render themselves transparent to the film viewer). The constant variation in the size of words necessitated by the constant frame demands constant re-adjustment by the reader/viewer, unlike words on the printed page, which tend to extreme uniformity. The hierarchy in normal reading between form and content is here reversed: the reader/viewer's first consciousness is of form – typographical design – rather than of content. More important, and more fundamental, the reader/viewer is clearly not able to exercise the kind of control he/she is used to exercising over the printed page. The pace of reading the printed page is normally wholly controlled by the reader. Here, on the contrary, Snow's film is in control, and can speed up or slow down the pace at which reading is required. The mental experiences of 'watching' *So Is This* involve hypothesising what will come next and 'waiting' for structure and sense to be accomplished, 'keeping up' with the text, and so on. As James Peterson puts it, Snow's procedure 'lays bare the viewer's cycle of hypothesis generation and testing', providing 'explicit answers to what we would normally hypothesise and gradually confirm' (Peterson, p. 124) (in some of the same way that Frampton's *(nostalgia)* does). All this makes for a very active, aware reader, very unlike the relatively 'passive' reader of most written text (and most film). And this is true even before the film makes its procedures absolutely explicit: having presented a sentence so quickly that it is 'almost/ impossible/ to/ read',[19] the text speculates about reading speeds and preferences and then offers, 'in/ an/ attempt/ to/ please/ everybody', the same sentence in four different speeds and rhythm patterns. (This is also a passage of the film when the colours of words and background change very rapidly, creating some similar effects to those in Sharits's *Word Movie*.)

In reading the printed word on the page, syntactical sense is almost a given, more or less 'invisible' in the sense that it is expected, and is only problematic when absent. Once we can read and speak fluently, we take syntactical and grammatical rules for granted, but they remain crucial to comprehension. We expect written and spoken language to conform to the rules – particularly written language. *So Is This* does not *not* conform to syntactical and grammatical rules but, by making them strange, it foregrounds these rules and their essential functions by getting in the way of comprehension – the opposite of their usual function. Meaning then needs to be 'struggled' for – though 'struggle' need not imply a lack of pleasure. If the primary drive in reading the printed word on the page is towards 'meaning', the semantic dimension of language, one interesting effect of *So Is This* is to draw attention to the degree to which we depend on syntactical sense in arriving at 'meaning'. Here, that meaning which is the primary objective of reading text on the page becomes almost secondary to the act of reading itself: the main struggle in which the reader/viewer is involved is imposing syntactical sense, and in the course of this struggle, meaning frequently slips to secondary importance.

As a very obvious example of the way in which Snow achieves these effects, as MacDonald puts it, 'prepositions, conjunctions, and articles often become the most powerful, visible words' (Macdonald, p. 35), and cease playing the more or less invisible but facilitating function they play in 'normal' writing: in a sense they are here the *opposite* of facilitating, obstructing the imposition of meaning by taking on an importance equal to that of more obviously semantically loaded words. This process is exacerbated by the control of pace and rhythm already mentioned: even if the presentation of one word at a time – in accord with the way we watch one film image at a time but not quite in accord with the way in which we read the written word on the page – were not off-putting, the changing speeds of delivery appear wholly unrelated to the semantic dimension of the 'content' of the text, and thus 'throw' the reader/viewer even more. Similarly, a pause – as necessary to reading as to speaking, but generally naturalised – is represented in the film sometimes as simply a black screen held for a certain duration, sometimes as a full stop held for a certain duration, but sometimes as, for example, /Pause./ held, say, for 88 frames.

By its very nature, it is impossible to 'quote' adequately from *So Is This*. However, it may help to convey some of its effects to 'transcribe' in more detail a typical passage. Here, the figure in brackets after each word which appears separately, represents the number of frames for which the word is held on screen (the duration can be calculated from the normal running time of film: 24 frames per second). The figures in brackets following these brackets – normally, in this example, six – represent the interval between words on the screen, during which the screen is blank.

> One (10)(6) of (8)(6) the (10)(6) interests (12)(6) of (10)(6) this (14)(6) system (10)(6) is (8)(6) that (10)(6) each (20)(6) word (40)(12) can (10)(6) be (20)(6) held (56)(12) on (10)(6) the (20)(6) screen (100)(18) for (10)(6) a (8)(6) specific (12)(6) length (240)(6) of (8)(6) time (2)(48)

The combination here of an apparent system, with sometimes motivated but sometimes arbitrary breaks from the system, and with jokiness, goes some way to explaining the frustrations and the pleasures of this teasing, instructional text.

Another of the differences between reading printed text and watching film which *So Is This* foregrounds involves questions of personal and collective reading/spectatorship. The film's spectator is made very aware of the differences between the usually very *individual* act of reading printed text on the page and the more *collective* act of watching film. This produces at times a consciousness on the spectator's part of shared, simultaneous mental reading activity, a consciousness, in other words, that every other individual in the collective audience is performing the same (or similar) mental operations, every bit as vivid (and as precisely manipulated) as the collective gasp at certain moments of, say, *Jaws* (1975) – except that here the viewer/reader is, naturally, much more actively conscious. It is typical of Snow that this process of consciousness-raising should be rendered in primarily humorous terms. Early on, the film warns us that: 'This/ film/ may/ be/ especially/ unsatisfying/ for/ those/ who/ dislike/ having/ others/ read/ over/ their/ shoulders', while later commenting 'But/ look/ at/ the/ bright/ side/ of/ it/ :/ Sharing!/ When/ was/ the/ last/ time/ you/ and/ your/ neighbour/ read/ together?', before forging community with an 'optical/ cranial/ sing-song' of an 'old/ favourite':

Let's (14)(4) all (16)(4) raise (16)(4) our (12)(4) mental (18)(4) voices (16)(4) mutely, (18)(8) mutually (18)(4) in (12)(4) song (18)(4) (please (6)(3) don't (6)(3) move (6)(3) your (6)(3) lips) (6)(20) Ready? (96)(6) 1 (36)(2) 2 (36)(2) 3 (36)(2) 4: (36)(2) 'Some (35)(0) where (36)(2) o (12)(0) ver (24)(2) the (12)(2) rain (24)(0) bow (36)(2) skies (36)(2) are (36)(2) blue . . .' (46)(2)

The teasing and pleasurably confusing aspects of *So Is This* are complemented in other ways. In another comment on the nature of language and texts, the film frequently lies to us, or misleads us – with crucial consequences for our perception of system. The film is very open about this: 'This/ film/ will/ be/ about/ 2/ hours/ long./ Does/ that/ seem/ like/ a/ frightening/ prospect/ ?/ Well,/ look/ at/ it/ this/ way:/ how/ do/ you/ know/ this/ isn't/ lying/ ?/' In fact, it *is* lying: the film runs for about 46 minutes. Elsewhere, for example, what the film refers to as its 'third/ paragraph' is in fact the fourth, the 'sixth' the seventh, and the 'fifth', which comes after the 'sixth', is the eighth. Near the end, the film says it is going to present 'ten/ solo/ words' and proceeds to offer twenty. When, in another reference to film's distinctive capacity to organise time, *So Is This* offers a kind of 'flashback' – 'For/ those/ who've/ arrived/ late/ here/ is/ a/ brief/ resumé' – what follows is a rather inaccurate account of what has preceded (though in suitably faded style). Peterson puts very well the way this uncertainty principle informs the end of the film:

> As the film ends, we are once again reminded of the dilemma that arises from the lack of global schemata. The film's last sentence is: 'This film will seem to stop'. Even after a minute without a word on the screen, as the projectionist lets the tail of the film run through the projector in accordance with Snow's projection instructions, we are so unsure what will happen next that we are likely to remain in our seats until the house lights come on. Whether we react with humor or anxiety, what we respond to is the overt and self-conscious frustration of our viewing strategies for the minimal strain of the American avant-garde film.
>
> (Peterson, p. 124)

Sitney places his discussion of the relationship between photographic image and written text in 1920s Surrealist and Soviet cinema under the rubric of 'image and title' – written captions were referred to as 'titles'. Snow has this nomenclature in mind in *So Is This*, whose 'images', of course, consist entirely of 'titles', but there is also some dizzyingly punning play on 'title' and the actual title of this film (for example, 'long/ title/ isn't/ it?'). Although we know from external evidence that the title of the film is *So Is This*, internal evidence is not at all so clear, and *This* could equally well be the title (see MacDonald, p. 35).

So Is This also takes on a number of the still current debates about film and its responsibilities, in particular critiques of the 'formal' or 'structural' film and its reflexivity as somehow sterile. Thus, 'In/ case/ you/ are/ getting/ restless/ this/ film/ (long/ title/ isn't/ it?)/ won't/ discuss/ itself/ all/ the/ time/ ./ It's/ going/ to/ get/ into/ some/ real/ human/ stuff/ that/ will/ make/ you/ laugh/ and/ cry/ and/ change/ society'. As for politics: 'There'll/ be/ not/ one/ word/ about/ El/ Salvador,/ no/ mention/ of/ Trudeau/ and/ no/ political/ commitment/ whatsoever/ ./ So/ relax/ and/ enjoy/ yourself/', after which a specifically Canadian political reference – 'yes/ of/ course/ there/ will/ be/ a/ French/ version' (the author is applying to the Quebec Ministry of Culture for help), some sentences in French 'just/ for/ now' and 'Back/ to/ English./ If/ you/ don't/ read/ French/ you/ should/ learn./ Canada/ is/ a/ bilingual/ country'. Even gender debates feature: 'A/ good/ thing/ about/ reading/ words/

like/ this/ and/ not/ hearing/ a/ voice/ is/ that/ you/ can't/ accuse/ it/ of/ being/ male/ or/ female'. And there are comments addressed, with single frame subliminal inserts, to the Ontario Board of Censors and its decision to censor experimental films: 'Since (30)(41) this (30)(41) film (30)(41) was (30)(20) tits (1)(20) originally (30)(41) composed (30)(20) ass (1)(20)', and so on.

The so-called 'structural film' movement, of which Snow's films are generally considered a vital part,[20] was often thought to be primarily concerned with its own material specificity (particularly in its 'structural/materialist' incarnation of Peter Gidal).[21] *So Is This* is not reflexive in quite the same way that much of *Wavelength* is, say. Although there are moments in *So Is This* when we are reminded of the specificity of the medium, these are moments where the reflexive impulse interacts with our reception and perception of written text. For example, Snow leaves in the end-of-roll flaring – normally simply junked as unusable – during which 'image' (here, written text) is progressively unable to be registered. It is a very forceful reminder of the very precise filmic conditions necessary for image/text to be registered on celluloid, and another facet of the film's interplay between written text and cinema.

Since *So Is This* was made in a period of fevered work on semiology and cinema, Snow has some comments in this direction too. Having begun the film with 'The/ film/ will/ consist/ of/ single/ words/ presented/ one/ after/ another/ to/ construct/ sentences/ and/ hopefully/ (this/ is/ where/ you/ come/ in)/ to/ convey/ meanings./ This,/ as/ they/ say, /is/ the/ signifier', Snow later remarks that 'Some/ of/ the/ more/ cultivated/ members/ of/ the/ audience/ may/ regret/ the/ lack/ of/ in-depth/ semiological/ analysis/ in/ this/ film/ and/ note/ that/ the/ vocabulary/ used/ is/ quite/ basic', as a prelude to comments about appealing to elite intellectual audiences ('Is/ there/ anybody/ reading/ this/ right/ now?').

This is, in many ways, an appropriate point to conclude. Though Snow may seem to be making fun of semiology, he does engage in questions central to it and he engages with them in a way which makes accessible and experienceable ideas which would otherwise remain abstrusely theoretical. Snow's comments in the film about the anger and displeasure his films can arouse must be seen in this light: such reactions owe more to the in-built laziness and conformity of the average – even educated – film spectator, than to the films themselves. Snow himself sees his work as epistemological in nature and purpose, capable of confronting complex aesthetic and theoretical issues in an accessible – and pleasurable – way. And he is clearly right.

Notes

1. André Bazin 'The Evolution of the Language of Cinema' in A. Bazin *What is Cinema?*, vol. 1, ed. Hugh Gray (Berkeley and Los Angeles, 1967) (translation of Bazin, *Qu'est-ce que le Cinéma?* vol. 1, Paris, 1958). The essay is reprinted in many anthologies, e.g. Gerald Mast, Marshall Cohen and Leo Braudy (eds), *Film Theory and Criticism* (4th edn, New York and Oxford, 1992).
2. See, for example, David Cook, 'The Theoretical Debate Over Sound' in D. Cook, *A History of Narrative Film* (4th edn, New York, 1996), pp. 265–8.
3. Silent cinema has become an increasingly crucial area of film studies, partly because the critical and theoretical focus on the conventions of 'classical' sound cinema prompted enquiry into how these conventions had evolved, and why. See Thomas Elsaesser, *Early Cinema: Space, Frame, Narrative* (London, 1990), and Richard Abel, *Silent Film* (London, 1996).
4. See, for example, John Sayles, 'Thinking in Pictures' in J. Sayles, *Thinking in Pictures* (Boston, MA, 1987), pp. 3–8.
5. See P. Adams Sitney, 'The Instant of Love: Image and Title in Surrealist Cinema' and 'Revolutionary Time: Image and Title in Soviet Cinema', both in P.A. Sitney, *Modernist Montage: The Obscurity of Vision in Cinema and Literature* (New York and Oxford, 1990).
6. Peter Wollen, 'The Two Avant-Gardes', *Studio International* (December 1975), reprinted in P. Wollen, *Readings and Writings* (London, 1982). The best single introduction to North American avant-garde film is probably P. Adams Sitney, *Visionary Film: The American Avant-Garde 1943–1978* (2nd edn, Oxford and New York, 1979) but an important more recent reflective and corrective text is James Peterson, *Dreams of Chaos, Visions of Order: Understanding the American Avant-Garde Cinema* (Detroit, MI, 1994). Page references to this book are cited in the text. On Makavejev's work, see Ian Cameron (ed.), *Second Wave* (London, 1970) and Roy Armes, *The Ambiguous Image* (London, 1976). On Godard, see Ian Cameron (ed.), *The Films of Jean-Luc Godard* (2nd edn, London, 1969), Toby Mussman (ed.), *Jean-Luc Godard* (New York, 1968), Royal S. Brown (ed.), *Focus on Godard* (Englewood Cliffs, 1972), and Colin MacCabe, *Godard: Images, Sounds, Politics* (London and Basingstoke, 1980).

Godard's earlier work has elicited most critical debate, but a more recent collection, with essays on some of his later work, is Wheeler Winston Dixon, *The Films of Jean-Luc Godard* (Albany, NY, 1997).

7. See Jim Hillier, *'(nostalgia)'*, *Movie* nos. 34–5 (Winter 1990).

8. Paul Sharits, 'General Statement: 4th International Film Festival, Knokke Le Zoute' in Peter Gidal (ed.), *Structural Film Anthology* (London, 1976), p. 90.

9. See Peter Gidal, 'Notes on *Word Movie*' in Gidal (ed.), *Structural Film Anthology*, p. 94.

10. Michael Snow, 'Proposal to the Canadian Film Development Corporation, March 1969', *Afterimage* no. 11 (Winter 1982–83), p. 14. Further page references are cited in the text.

11. Michael Snow, quoted in Pierre Théberge, 'Conversation with Michael Snow' in P. Théberge, *Michael Snow* (Luzern, 1979), reprinted in *Afterimage* no. 11 (Winter 1982–83), p. 18.

12. Jonas Mekas and P. Adams Sitney, 'Conversation with Michael Snow and a Letter', *Film Culture* no. 46 (October 1968), reprinted in *Afterimage* no. 11 (Winter 1982–83), p. 9.

13. See, for example, Annette Michelson, 'Toward Snow', *Artforum* (June 1971), reprinted in, for example, P. Adams Sitney (ed.), *The Avant-Garde Film* (New York, 1978), and Gidal (ed.), *Structural Film Anthology*.

14. Michael Snow, 'On *One Second in Montreal*', *Afterimage* no. 11 (Winter 1982–83), p. 10.

15. Michael Snow, 'Edinburgh, 1979' in M. Snow, *The Collected Writings of Michael Snow* (Waterloo, Ontario, 1994), p. 207.

16. Scott MacDonald, '*So Is This*', *Film Quarterly* vol. 39, no. 1 (Fall 1985), p. 34. Further page references are cited in the text.

17. Simon Field and Peter Sainsbury, 'Interview with Hollis Frampton', *Afterimage* no. 4 (Autumn 1972), p. 53.

18. This closeness between Snow's and Frampton's thinking should not be surprising, since Snow and Frampton were very close collaborators, Frampton appearing as the 'dying' figure in Snow's *Wavelength* and Snow reading the 'first-person' voice-over in Frampton's *(nostalgia)*.

19. 'Quotes' and transcriptions from *So Is This* are taken from Snow, *The Collected Writings of Michael Snow*, p. 207. Quotes from the film's text are represented with a caesura between each word as a reminder that each appears separately on the screen.

20. See, for example, the chapter on 'Structural Film' in Sitney, *Visionary Film: The American Avant-Garde*.

21. See Peter Gidal, 'Theory and Definition of Structural/Materialist Film' in Gidal, *Structural Film Anthology*.

6 *Inscription in* The Piano

Lib Taylor

At the beginning of Jane Campion's film *The Piano* (1993) Ada McGrath (Holly Hunter), its central character, is brought from Scotland to New Zealand in the mid-nineteenth century in order to marry a white colonial landowner, Stewart (Sam Neill), a man she has not previously met.[1] She brings with her her ten-year-old daughter Flora (Anna Paquin), her trunks and baggage, and her baby-grand piano. In an opening voice-over delivered by Ada, we learn paradoxically that she has not spoken since the age of six. She is an elective mute who, for no reason apparent to herself or her family, has taken it into her head not to utter a word. Rather than becoming a symbol of the disempowerment and dispossession often associated with the absence of speech, Ada's silence becomes an expression of strength and resistance. It is an assertion of defiance, a refusal to cooperate with patriarchal regulation or to participate in the masculine linguistic economy which circumscribes women. Ada can hear and respond to the speech of others but refuses to engage in verbal dialogue or exchange. Her own expressive communication systems are a complex blend of types of inscription or 'writings'. It is these issues of sound and silence, speech and muteness, writing and erasure that I want to address in this essay in relation to feminist debates around gender and identity.

Although the film is framed by Ada's voice-overs at the beginning and the end, the central narrative is concerned with non-verbal forms of communication apparent particularly in the music of the piano and the physical resources of the actors. While the opening and closing voice-overs mark the film as Ada's story, focusing on her point of view, the emphasis on visual codes reinforces the film's dependence on the spectator's ability to read ocular cues. *The Piano* employs a range of different systems of representation some of which are familiar to the spectator and some of which are not. Deaf Sign Language, the language in which Ada communicates with Flora, is a visual and physical form of language which is interwoven into the linguistic text throughout the film. In recent years Deaf Sign Language has been recognised as a precise and fully developed syntactical language, but it is a language in which the majority of the film's spectators would not be fluent. In the film, Ada also uses handwritten messages, mostly for communicating with those who do not understand Sign Language. These are more accessible to the viewer, although her notes are very condensed and frustratingly terse in form. Traditional writing for Ada is used only as a last resort. Arguably, the primary system of communication used by Ada is her piano-playing, which pervades and circumscribes the majority of the film. The music is not merely an expression of her mood or emotional state, nor is it used to entertain or divert. Rather the spectator is asked to 'read' the music as a privileged self-revelation. In the absence of speech, the piano becomes the vehicle by which Ada 'speaks' most eloquently.

Deaf Sign Language, piano-playing and handwriting are very differently encoded and deciphered, but they are language systems which all depend upon the body, more particularly upon the use of the hands, in their inscription. Furthermore, Ada's communication extends to encompass the highly disciplined corporeal movements, gestures and glances which are so significant for interpreting her. In this way, her entire body becomes a site of and a resource for encoded messages. Liberated from oral communication, a language which marginalises her, Ada's multiple linguistic mode both exhibits her refusal to comply with her oppression and alludes to her self-possession and potency. Her visual and physical 'voice' imprints the language of the film with a materiality and with a poetic visual aesthetic. It discloses Ada's potential to be coerced while becoming her means of defiance; it reveals her enforced silence as a woman while exposing a will of her own.

Ada disengages from language in order to engage with the possibility of her own subjectivity and desire. Feminist theory maintains that man-made language, with its focus upon rationality and masculine values, has excluded women from dominant forms of representation and consigned them to the margins of power. In the Lacanian model of the development of the child, at the point at which the child acquires language, he or she takes up their allotted place in what is termed the Symbolic Order, a linguistic and social order commanded by the Law of the Father. The Symbolic Order is dominated by the principal signifier the phallus, which privileges the masculine, while the feminine is consigned to a subordinate position. Thus the woman is denied access to an equivalent subjectivity through language and denied expression of her desire.[2] Luce Irigaray challenges Lacan's assertions and claims that masculine discourse positions women outside representation, proposing that the only way that women can speak is to appropriate the language of man which positions them as negative, Other and without subjectivity. She insists that if woman is to claim identity she must find ways of subverting dominant forms of language. She states that, 'Woman's desire would not be expected to speak the same language as man's; woman's desire has doubtless been submerged by the logic that has dominated the West since the time of the Greeks'.[3] Feminist practice has taken up the challenge to experiment with linguistic formations, signifying systems and discourses in seeking to represent woman. This project has involved invoking the body as a site of, and resistance to, patriarchal forms of language, speech and writing and as a location for 'a "poetry" which is necessarily innovative and evocative'.[4] The body, with its potential for disruption and a plurality of signification, can disturb and fracture the monolith of language, challenging its claims to stability and unproblematic, transparent meaning. For women the body offers a space for alternative forms of representation or, in the terms of French feminist criticism, an *écriture* (a form of inscription or writing) for inscribing feminine subjectivity.

In *The Piano* the spectator is alerted to the significance of corporeal inscription, or *écriture*, through the *mise-en-scène* of the film. It is infused with visual imprints and markings on or by the body which signify writing but which evade the secure meaning assumed by a written language and speech. The marks indicate presence, desire and identity but resist rational interpretation. As Flora and Ada leave the beach on which they arrive for the first time, Ada looks down at her piano left on the edge of the sea and sees it surrounded by a clean sheet of sand. Their loneliness is signalled by the emptiness of the landscape and their isolation by the solitary piano, but it is also quite apparent that they have left no imprint on the place despite their stay on the seashore. Their footprints and the marks of their recent habitation have been erased, washed away by the sea; their physical presence is unacknowledged and their identity unsecured. Shortly afterwards, Ada and Flora return to the beached piano with Baines (Harvey Keitel), Stewart's neighbour and rival for the affections of Ada. While Flora tumbles and dances on the beach, Ada plays her piano, elated to be reconciled with the instrument. The two women inscribe the location with a kind of *jouissance* enacted through the body, Ada's playing set against Flora's movement.[5] As they leave the beach on this occasion the empty sand is seen to be marked out with the delightful picture of a decorated seahorse, the kind a child might create while playing with its mother on the beach, and the imprint of their feet. They leave the place marked by their pleasure and their bodies.

The significant relationship of the body to inscription is also foregrounded by the character of Baines, a white colonial figure who is nevertheless aligned with the Maori characters in the film. Baines's sympathies for the indigenous population are signalled predominantly through visual signs as his face is marked by coloured lines similar to those apparent on the faces of the Maoris. Baines also occasionally speaks in the Maori language but his identification with and compassion for the colonised group is most clearly inscribed through the marks on his face which link him to them. These marks are never erased, even when Baines finally leaves the bush for the town of Nelson, and his body is read as a site of resistance, stamped with the signs of his opposition to colonial hegemony.

The piano functions in the film as a way of representing Ada more emphatically than any other signifying system. The symbolic connection between the piano and Ada in *The Piano* is plain. Not only does she 'speak' through its tunes but there is an equivalence between the instrument and Ada's physical appearance. Ada is dressed in hooped, voluminous skirts and is tightly corseted in excessively elaborate and inappropriate clothing amid the muddy wilderness of New Zealand. The piano is securely packaged in wooden boxing and deposited on a wild and windswept beach, a completely unsuitable place for a sensitive and valuable musical instrument. Both Ada and the piano endure the indignity of being carried precariously across wet and swampy terrain into the barely tame, alien bush where they stand determinedly as a symbol of civilisation amid the surrounding wasteland. The physical correlation of Ada and the piano is most clearly apparent in the moment when Baines trangressively explores Ada's body while she plays.

As he crawls under the piano we see not only Ada's hooped under-skirt but also the working mechanisms of the piano and as he explores her body he not only violates Ada's exposed body but also trespasses on the hidden space beneath the keys.

Unrestricted by the intervention of an interpreter or an inter-mediary, the piano music emanates from Ada's body as her hands manipulate the notes of the piano. The music she plays (composed for the film by Michael Nyman) is somewhat baroque in style, ordered, disciplined and harmonic, but its relentless impulsion is disrupted by a certain dissonance and syncopation. The music expresses the tension in the film between discipline and passion, between order and fragmentation. Nyman exploits the polyphonic, contrapuntal characteristic of the piano as an instrument to under-score the plurality of Ada's 'voice' and the contradictions which circumscribe her. Ada's playing becomes a form of writing, an *écriture*, infused with a sense of confinement disrupted by a resist-ing desire. The minimalist composition for the film emphasises formal structures and repetitions fractured by melodic elaborations, echoing Ada's resistance to the social bonds that define and re-strict her.

The visual presence of the piano can be read as an index of these tensions and contradictions. More than any other musical instrument, the piano is emblematic of Victorian society and its values. No respectable, middle-class, nineteenth-century household was complete without one, albeit an upright, in the parlour. It represented the social and cultural centre of the Victorian family. Popular myth has members collected ritualistically around the piano at moments of celebration, while all cultivated young women learned to play the instrument as one of the accomplishments required for marriage, motherhood and their civilising role at the centre of family life. A non-orchestral polyphonic instrument, the piano was perfect for the solitary female musician denied access to the public and social space of the orchestra and restricted to the confines of the house. Decorated with family photographs and valued ornaments, embellished with carvings or marquetry, and with its legs modestly covered, the feminised piano might be seen as an icon of the tradi-tional Victorian home. It occupied a sanctified place.

Ada's determination to take her piano to the other side of the world reflects both her Victorian sensibilities and her desire to transcend them. In moving to New Zealand she shifts to the antipode of her homeland, Scotland. New Zealand is both a reflection of her home and is its binary opposite; a place that is both familiar and alien. The physical presence of the piano provides a connection with the past and the familiar but it also functions as a sign of a potentially civilising agent in the savage land into which Ada has been projected. It connotes the values of Victorian Britain in a New Zealand eager to maintain its colonial links. For Stewart it reflects his wife's accomplishments and by extension his own good taste, and for Baines mere contact with it brings him closer to Ada and to the culture she represents. But Ada's piano is not the upright instrument of the Victorian parlour, it is the sophisticated instrument of the public recital room – a baby-grand piano, an altogether more eloquent and refined instrument. While Ada does not play in public her aspirations reach beyond the limitations of the home and hearth.

As a cultural sign, the upright piano signifies mediocrity; it functions mainly as an accompaniment to family or community entertainment. An example of this is seen in *The Piano* where the upright piano is part of the children's concert, an event in which Ada does not participate, despite being a more accomplished pianist than Nessie (Geneviève Lemon). The baby-grand piano, on the other hand, signifies elegance, dignity and grace. It is an instrument played by virtuoso soloists and connotes the skill, distinction, display of public performance. Ada chooses not the parochial upright piano, she reaches beyond the parlour and the home, preferring to express herself with the 'voice' of the more authoritative grand. As Aunt Morag (Kerry Walker) says, 'You know, I am thinking of the piano. She does not play the piano as we do Nessie. . . . No, she is a strange creature and her playing is strange, like a mood that passes into you. You cannot teach that, Nessie, one may like to learn, but that could not be taught.'

For Ada, the piano is also a repository of secret messages. Not only are its tunes unknown and ambiguous, disguised and elusive, but also it conceals the secrets of an unknown past within its body. As spectators we know virtually nothing of Ada's history except that the presence of Flora raises tantalising questions around her parentage. Flora herself tells a fantastical and unreliable tale of her father but we are never offered any secure information about him or his role in Ada's life. At one point in the film, as Ada caresses the keyboard we glimpse a small heart with an arrow through it and the letters 'A' and 'D' around it drawn onto the side of one of the keys, hinting at a possible previous clandestine relationship. Ada's mysterious history and her secret passions are quite literally inscribed upon the piano and hidden in its recesses. Later in the film, Ada writes in words the message 'DEAR GEORGE YOU HAVE MY HEART ADA MCGRATH' to Baines on the side of another key. Ada continues to use the piano as her confidante, marking it with the signs of her secret desires and ardours.

The semiotics of Ada's expressive language draw attention to the codification of writing in the film. Throughout the film, the written word functions as a significant part of the text, woven into the overall fabric of linguistic codes, operating at several levels of communication. Ada herself carries around her neck a little notebook on which she writes short messages which are passed from her to her husband and to Baines. The physical position of the book forces her to write just under her chin near her neck and in front of her voice box. At these moments, the connection between the writing and Ada's absent speech is palpable, although the writings she produces from this book are no more than short notes, reduced to their most concise form. She only uses the book when other forms of communication are impossible, or to assert her immediate demands. The notebook with its ornate cover resembles a decorative silver locket. Traditionally a locket is not only an heirloom, passed on from generation to generation through the female line, but is also a receptacle for some of the most precious and personal keepsakes, particularly curls of hair or photographs of those most dear to the wearer. Embedded in this 'locket', however, are blank sheets of paper. Ada's history and personal secrets are secured within the piano and her locket notebook yields nothing of herself.

One significant element of the written information presented by the film is the subtitles, not as an additional channel of meaning imposed on the film by the international market but as an integral part of the signifying systems of the film. All the information conveyed in *The Piano* in the Maori language is translated into subtitles. Subtitling is one of the most familiar ways in which we are made aware that we are watching a foreign-language film. While dubbing erases difference, in subtitles the process of translation is materialised through the presence of both languages (one generally spoken, the other written) within the filmic text and questions of difference are foregrounded. Ada's marginalisation and dispossession are underscored by the presence of the Maoris and more particularly by the encounter with their language. Both Ada and the Maoris are alienated, Ada by her femininity and resistance to conformity and the Maoris by the process of colonialisation. Neither group participate in the linguistic economy of the dominant culture. Both speak a language which requires an interpreter, an additional channel of communication through which meaning is filtered, both inside and outside the diegesis of the film. A combination of interpretative systems function in a complex way throughout the film: sometimes Flora interprets her mother's Deaf Sign Language while at other times their Signed exchanges are subtitled; Baines acts as an intermediary between the Maoris and the English speakers, functioning alongside the subtitling of the Maori language. Although lack of linguistic authority disempowers both Ada and the Maoris within colonial New Zealand society, within the film the multiple linguistic resources destabilise the supremacy of the spoken English word. The significant difference between the Maoris and Ada is that within the film Ada's plural language systems function to govern her own representation while the Maoris are completely marginalised. As Stella Bruzzi maintains: 'Although functioning in relation to patriarchal laws Ada is not subsumed by them and, despite all the potential for restriction, oppression and unhappiness, she is the controlling force of both the narrative and how the film is to be perceived'.[6]

The key to Ada's discourse is her hands. Without them she is unable to communicate. In the first shot of Ada in the film she is seen looking through her hands and she continues throughout the narrative to interpret the world through her hands. Not only does she use them to write on her notepad and tap out the notes on her piano, but, in her most precise form of communication, Deaf Sign Language, her fingers become the pen with which she sketches signs into the air. Deaf Sign Language is a highly codified and sophisticated language, most commonly used by those who cannot hear. Dependent upon the shape, position and movement of the hands in space, it traces in the air Signs representing letters, words and, sometimes, full phrases. The hands constantly move as one Sign or word blends into the next, creating an evanescent form of writing, disappearing or erased almost before it is fully apprehended. Despite its pictorial, visual patterning and its apparent resemblance to theatrical mime, it, in fact, yields meaning no more effortlessly than complex spoken or written languages. Without very specific knowledge of its systems of signification, it remains inaccessible. What makes the use of Deaf Sign Language so significant for the film, however, is its visual impact and its physicality so that the body becomes a material site for writing. For Ada, Deaf Sign Language is an alternative form of linguistic expression which is articulate and yet exclusive, precise and yet corporeal. It gives her access to a highly developed and eloquent form of communication from which her husband and his domain are barred.

Furthermore, it is in the dynamic use of hands that Ada expresses her fascinations and desires. Her hands caress the piano, the body of Baines (and indeed the body of Stewart), and the sea in which the piano is finally deposited. It is through the hands and the sense of touch that she investigates territory which compels her as well as that which is transgressive and repellent. Ada is physically drawn to and aches for her piano, which she strokes and fondles at every opportunity: she plays it when it is prohibited and parcelled up; she plays it in her sleep. In cutting off a finger from Ada's hand, Stewart attempts to destroy her means of representation, to disempower her and silence her. He reasserts his damaged authority by re-enacting the patriarchal denial of a female voice. In psychoanalytic terms, he castrates her by cutting off her 'pen', her device for writing, and reassigns her to the margins of representation.

It is through Deaf Sign Language that Ada communicates with her daughter and this is partly seen as a private language shared by the two women. This exclusivity is seen most clearly at moments of close intimacy when they slip totally into the Signing register, for example when Ada Signs stories for Flora, telling her of her past. As a pictorial language system, Sign Language is a dynamic form of expression. It is captivating not only for Flora, caught up in the pleasure of the narrative, but also for the spectator, intrigued by the visual display. Just as the stories Ada tells take Flora into the fluid world of the imagination, so their shared knowledge of Sign Language gives them access to a vivid space beyond the spoken word.

In the wider social space, Flora interprets for her mother. She is the only other character in the film who understands Deaf Sign Language and, consequently, she speaks for her mother, interpreting not only her words but the tone and emphasis of her messages. The complex and shifting relationship of Ada and Flora is central to the film and strong connections between the two women underscore this dyadic, symbiotic relationship. These are made evident both visually through their costume, demeanour and physical proximity, and through their shared discourse (particularly in the first part of the film). They mirror movements and play piano duets, one plays the piano while the other dances, and one sings the notes played by the other on the imitation keyboard scratched onto the table. However, while at points in the film they seem to reflect each other exactly, with matching scowling faces framed by similar bonnets, there are times when Flora's voicing goes beyond the interpretation of Ada's Sign. She extends Ada's messages by elaborating upon them. What is more, when Flora speaks for Ada she never does so in the first person, as many interpreters of Deaf Sign Language would. Her deployment of the third person 'she', as in, for example, 'She says "thank you"', or, 'She says, "No". She says she'd rather be boiled alive by natives than get back in your tub', indicates division, splitting and a lack of coherence in subjectivity, manifested in the separation of body and voice. Together, the body of the mother and the voice of the daughter create a kind of plural language in which the inscriptions and messages of one are filtered through the other. Ada's manual language is deciphered and re-encoded by Flora, while Flora's spoken language is inflected by the body of Ada.

The symbiosis of Ada and Flora creates unstable mother and daughter roles which shift fluidly between the two women. While Ada is Flora's biological mother, at points in the film Flora takes over the maternal function; she not only interprets Ada, she plays at house and she castigates Ada for disobeying Stewart. Ada repudiates her role as homemaker and does not participate in the schooling of Flora in her social role. In Lacanian psychoanalysis the child inhabits an Imaginary realm in which there is union with the mother prior to an entry into language and the Symbolic Order, dominated by the father. The intervention of the father at the Oedipal stage demands the repression of the mother and the plenitude she represents, in favour of an acceptance of the Law of the Father and symbolic representation through language. Suppressed into the unconscious the mother, for Lacan, takes up the position of the Lack or absence associated with the Real. In *The Piano*, on the one hand, Ada refuses to become the repressed maternal figure demanded by the Law of the Father. On the other, Flora undergoes a traumatic Oedipal crisis in which Stewart's intervention in the dyadic relationship of Ada and Flora forces a separation of mother and daughter and causes Flora to take up her allotted position in the Symbolic Order, under patriarchal dominance. Disconnected from her mother and the realm of the maternal, Flora's identity becomes dependent upon Stewart and the masculine order, culminating in her watching her mother's finger chopped off (in an act of castration) and a capitulation to Stewart's command.

Luce Irigaray recognises that if women are to have access to forms of representation of their own, they must subvert Lacan's phallic version of the Symbolic. She proposes a form of language that would leave space for the feminine:

> Its function would . . . be to *cast phallocentrism, phallocratism,* loose from its moorings in order to return the masculine to its own language, leaving open the possibility of a different language. Which means that the masculine would no longer be 'everything'. That it could no longer, all by itself, define, circumvent, circumscribe, the properties of any thing and everything. That the right to define every value – including the abusive privilege of appropriation – would no longer belong to it.
>
> (Irigaray, pp. 79–80)

Ada's rejection of rational, causal speech in favour of a rhythmic, physical and gestural patterning and forms of inscription can be seen as attempts to put into practice Irigaray's plea to find 'a space for the feminine' by thwarting masculine discourse.

Julia Kristeva in *Revolution in Poetic Language* refers to what Lacan calls the Imaginary, as the Semiotic. Her notion of the Semiotic is clearly associated with the maternal, for the Semiotic is equated with a kind of feminine *chora*. Kristeva draws on Plato's definition of the *chora* as 'nourishing and maternal', in likening it to the unrepresentable place of the mother.[7] She says the *chora* 'denote[s] an essentially mobile and extremely provisional articulation constituted by movements and their ephemeral stases' (Kristeva, p. 93). As Kristeva defines it, 'Semiotic language' takes on a poetic materiality rather than functioning as the discharging of messages. Sound, tone, colour and rhythm take precedence over any rational meaning. 'Indifferent to language, enigmatic and feminine, this space underlying the written is rhythmic, unfettered, irreducible to its intelligible verbal translation; it is musical, anterior to judgement' (Kristeva, p. 97). A woman passed from her father to her husband and defined by shared convictions is denied representation in language other than the language of the father. She is not allowed to make her own mark upon the world. Ada resists traditional linguistic forms and is represented through rhythmic music and visual gesture, in ways which recall Kristeva's theory. This disrupts the patriarchal linguistic economy and proposes a feminine alternative, which relates directly to the body of the mother and her desire for self-expression.

What for Irigaray is an impulse towards feminine disruption of masculine discourse is clearly located in this pre-symbolic domain of the maternal, the *chora*, for Kristeva. The process of breaking up the masculine, and its valorisation of the father, resides in a reappraisal of the function of the maternal and the reclamation of the mother. Lacanian theory insists upon the suppression of the maternal at the point of the child's entry into the Symbolic Order, but in *The Piano* Ada refuses to comply with this. She represents wholeheartedly the realm of the maternal, an imaginary field not circumscribed by man-made language and values. She is both a mother and a daughter and her refusal to conform to the Law of the Father functions at two levels. As a mother she refuses to comply with Stewart's efforts to regulate Flora under his patriarchal authority. Like a daughter refusing to relinquish her mother in order to take up her place in the Symbolic Order, Ada remains in the maternal realm of music, gesture and the body.

Towards the end of the film Ada leaves Stewart for Baines and they, together with Flora, set out by boat for the town of Nelson taking the piano with them. On the journey, Ada suddenly decides to throw the piano overboard and, despite Baines's objections, the piano is tipped into the ocean and consigned to its depths. As the piano sinks into the sea, at the last moment Ada deliberately places her foot in the rope attached to it and is dragged under the water along with the instrument. The potent image of Ada floating above her piano, attached to it by a rope, is resonant of an unborn child attached to its mother by the umbilical cord. The piano is the mother, and Ada the child. Projected across the film, this notion gains currency; it is the piano that has sustained and nurtured

Ada, it has given her comfort and solace, she has leant on it, cherished it and spoken through it. The image, however, proposes Ada as the daughter who must disconnect from her mother if she is to survive. She must separate herself from the piano if she is not to die; in psychoanalytic terms she must detach herself from the piano/mother and submit to the Law of the Father if she is to become a fully socialised woman.

The end of the film represents a struggle. Dragged into the water by the weight of the piano Ada is forced then to make a choice; either she must drown in the illusionary world of the Imaginary and her maternal piano, or she must kick herself free of the grip of the instrument in order to embrace a place in the Symbolic Order and take up a speaking, albeit compromised, position. She chooses the latter, consciously deciding to separate herself from the love object which is her piano. There is a serenity in the image of Ada with the piano underwater which is compelling and satisfying, even though it implies the death of Ada. Her surprise decision to choose life, or for her 'will' to choose life, means a disruption of that tranquil equanimity within the maternal space. Her journey through the water to the surface becomes a kind of rebirth. We see her gasp her first breath as she is pulled out of the sea almost as a baby would be dragged from the womb of its mother. It is only after this literal separation from the body of the piano that Ada accepts the Law of the Father and the masculine linguistic system. She shifts from the Semiotic and the *chora* to symbolisation through language. At the same time she moves away from the bush and the territory beyond civilisation to Nelson, a cultivated and refined town.

As Baines's wife in Nelson, slowly she learns to speak; she sees the light as, quite literally in the final scene, he lifts a black veil from her face. But for all her apparent contentment, Ada experiences compromise and lack in her rejection of her instrument. She continues to play a piano but her tunes are marked by the click of her prosthetic finger, made for her by Baines. She now taps the piano with a man-made 'pen'. The final image of the film is not of Ada's fulfilment with Baines but of her attached to her piano in its underwater grave. Her experience of loss is played out in her dreams and in this way the realm of the maternal continues to comfort her.

Notes

1. *The Piano*, written and directed by Jane Campion (Entertainment/Ciby 2000, Australia, 1992). A screenplay of the film including notes, extra dialogue and an interview with Campion is published as Jane Campion, *The Piano* (London, 1993).
2. See Jacques Lacan, *Ecrits: A Selection*, trans. Alan Sheridan (London, 1977).
3. Luce Irigaray, 'This Sex Which Is Not One' in L. Irigaray, *This Sex Which Is Not One*, trans. Catherine Porter with Carolyn Burke (Ithaca, NY, 1985), p. 25. Further page references are cited in the text.
4. Elizabeth Grosz, *Sexual Subversions, Three French Feminists: Julia Kristeva, Luce Irigaray, Michèle Le Doeuff* (Sydney, 1989), p. 101.
5. Hélène Cixous, Julia Kristeva and Luce Irigaray all use the notion *jouissance* in slightly different ways but for all of them it signifies a form of libidinal feminine pleasure. Jane Gallop says, '*Jouissance* is frequently cited by translators as an untranslatable word. It means enjoyment, also orgasm, and tends to be linked to a loss of control, a more primitive experience than the words "plaisir" (pleasure) and "orgasme".' Jane Gallop, *Feminism and Psychoanalysis: The Daughter's Seduction* (London, 1982), p. 29.
6. Stella Bruzzi, 'Tempestuous Petticoats: Costume and Desire in *The Piano*', *Screen* vol. 36, no. 3 (Autumn 1995), p. 265.
7. Julia Kristeva, 'Revolution in Poetic Language' in J. Kristeva, *The Kristeva Reader*, ed. Toril Moi (Oxford, 1986), p. 94. Further page references are cited in the text.

Part Three
Writing into Cinema

7 The mutinies on HMS Bounty

Robert Giddings

I can only conjecture that they have ideally assured themselves of a
more happy life among the Otaheitans than they could possibly
have in England, which joined to some female connections has most
likely been the leading cause of the whole business . . .

Lieutenant William Bligh, *The Log of HMS Bounty 1787–1789*[1]

the pursuit of the Inner Child has taken over just at the moment
when Americans ought to be figuring out where their Inner Adult
is, and how that disregarded oldster got buried under the rubble of
pop psychology and specious short term gratification. We imagine a
Tahiti inside ourselves, and seek its prelapsarian inhabitant: everyone his own Noble Savage.

Robert Hughes, *Culture of Complaint* (1993)[2]

Breadfruit and mutiny

The *Bounty*, a vessel of 215 tons with a crew of 44 commanded
by Lieutenant William Bligh, left Spithead on 23 December 1787
for the South Seas. It was not a large ship: 90 by 23 feet. Its
accommodation was restricted by having to make room for its
return cargo of breadfruit plants and botanical specimens. Breadfruit was proposed for use as cheap food for the slaves who worked
the West Indies sugar trade. Bligh was an experienced seaman of
33, who had earned his commission on merit, not by social advantage or patronage. He had accompanied Cook as sailing master in
his second voyage round the world in 1772–74. Tensions already
existed between Bligh and his first mate, Fletcher Christian, who
had sailed with Bligh on three previous occasions. There may also
have been class tensions between them: Christian had been educated at the same grammar school as William Wordsworth, and
his brother Edward was a Cambridge University professor. Bligh

was the only commissioned officer on board, and *Bounty* did not carry the usual body of marines to police the ship. Some of the crew might well have had a high opinion of their own seamanship, as Christian and two others had sailed with Bligh before, and two had been with Bligh on voyages with Cook.

Tahiti was reached and breadfruit samples taken. The *Bounty* left for its return voyage. The mutiny led by Fletcher Christian occurred on 28 April 1789, near Tonga. Bligh had maintained discipline by harsh measures, but although the details of floggings, strict rationing and putting seamen in irons seem harsh to us, Bligh's command and his disciplinary measures were no better or worse than was to be expected in the British navy at this period. Bligh and eighteen loyal men were set adrift in the longboat. They reached Timor after an incredible journey of 4,000 miles. The details of this event, and of the extraordinary feat of navigation under Bligh from Tofua to Timor which saved the lives of most of the crew of the 23-foot launch, were given by Bligh in a journal.[3] The stark details of events hardly foreshadow the importance the mutiny and its aftermath were to assume:

> 28 April 1789
> Just before Sun Rise the People Mutinied seized me while asleep in my Cabbin [sic] tied my Hands behind my back – carried me on Deck in my Shirt – Put 18 of the Crew into the Launch & me after them and set us a drift – Tofoa bearing NE to 10 leag – Ship steered to the WNW – Four cutlasses were thrown into the Boat.
> (Bligh, *Notebook*, p. 43)

The mutineers went back to Tahiti, where a few were later captured. Another group escaped, taking Polynesian men and women with them, to establish a colony at Pitcairn's Island. The island commune was not wholly successful. In 1819 two British warships, the *Tagus* and the *Briton*, arrived at Pitcairn and found the one remaining surviving mutineer, John Adams, ruling the roost as a rather saintly patriarch.

The mutiny on the *Bounty* of April 1789 has little or no importance in naval history, certainly when compared with the far more significant and dangerous mutinies at the Nore and Spithead in 1797 which threatened a greater possibility of breakdown in the service. But the story has something in it which continues to fascinate generation after generation. The version of the myth which has come down to us, with William Bligh the disciplinarian tyrant and arch villain, is a fairly recent variant. After Bligh's return to England several of the mutineers were brought back, tried and hanged. Bligh successfully completed the task of bringing breadfruit to the West Indies, but again his crew mutinied and he was put ashore. But he received several honours subsequent to the events in the South Seas, including a Society of Arts Medal in 1794, he was made a Fellow of the Royal Society in 1801, and became Governor General of New South Wales. His subjects objected to his rule, but the government supported him. He was made Rear-Admiral in 1811 and Vice-Admiral of Blue in 1814. He died in 1817.

The myth begins

The mutiny on the *Bounty* was initially made famous by Bligh's own account: *A Narrative of the Mutiny on Board His Majesty's Ship the Bounty and subsequent voyage of part of the crew in the ship's boat from Tofoa, one of the Friendly Islands, to Timor, a Dutch settlement in the East Indies, illustrated with charts*, published in 1790. The story of the *Bounty* mutiny and the settlement at Pitcairn and its aftermath attracted considerable attention, especially in Britain. Newspapers and periodicals spread the story: the *Gentleman's Magazine* and the *European Magazine* published extracts from Bligh's account. Relics were brought back, purporting to have been salvaged from the wreck of the *Bounty*. The most stirring scenes of the story were enacted on stage, including a spectacular called *The Pirates* at the Royalty Theatre. Rumours circulated that Fletcher Christian had, in fact, come back to England and there were reported sightings during 1809. In 1816 the Theatre Royal, Drury Lane, put on a ballet which enacted the story of the discovery of the Pitcairn colony, formed by and descended from the *Bounty* mutineers.

In June 1823 Byron published *The Island, or, Christian and his Comrades,* which rehearsed the *Bounty* story and the life of the mutineers on their island paradise. Byron was considerably influenced by his reading of William Bligh's *Narrative of the Mutiny of the Bounty* and William Mariner's *Account of the Natives of the Tonga Islands* (1817). Bligh is the hero of Byron's poem. In 1835 Captain Frederick Chamier published *Jack Adams the Mutineer,* an intriguing mixture of fact and fiction which drew upon and contributed to that enduring vogue for romances of seafaring life set in remote islands, in which exotic locations seldom turn out to be the hoped-for Paradise. Often these tales featured guilt-tortured protagonists, remote communities and men pitted in conflict with elemental nature or struggling with their own consciences: from 'The Rime of the Ancient Mariner', through the novels of Frederick Marryat, R.M. Ballantyne, R.L. Stevenson, Joseph Conrad and numerous serials in the *Boy's Own Paper*. William Golding's novel *The Lord of the Flies* (1954) revamps a version of the same configuration of experiences.

The movies get the story

The value of the *Bounty* story was early recognised by film-makers. In 1916 Raymond Longford, an Australian pioneer of silent cinema, produced *The Mutiny on the Bounty*, of which little survives. In 1933 Charles Chauvel directed a documentary-like version, *In the Wake of the Bounty*. This was another Australian release. In this film the Tasmanian actor Errol Flynn made his debut as Fletcher Christian. Little of this film survives. It was bought up by MGM to clear the way for their 1935 release *Mutiny on the Bounty*, though they used edited sections of it as publicity.[4] The first major *Bounty* film, MGM's 1935 release, was based on the collaborative work of Charles Nordhoff and James Hall, two former US Army flyers of the Great War. It was initially their intention to collaborate on a history of their unit in the War, but they went to live in Tahiti to write about Polynesian life. They had varying success in an assortment of enterprises including travel, adventure and books for boys, and eventually produced a number of bestsellers between 1929 and 1945. Several of these were successfully filmed.[5]

Nordhoff was the grandson of the American radical author and journalist, Charles Nordhoff, who served in the US Navy and wrote several seafaring books.[6] His later works on current affairs and politics are clearly written from the position of the radical-liberal, fuelled by the vision of the USA as mankind's last best hope for a better society. Some of this idealism may well have brushed off onto his grandson. James Hall intended to write up his wartime experiences but when the collaboration with Nordhoff began he found the magnetic pull of the *Bounty* story irresistible. He was very much attracted by the work of Edwin Arlington

Robinson (1869–1935), the New England poet, who concentrated particularly on the individual's moral choice. Robinson's view of human behaviour – the integrity of the isolated person – is closely related to themes in the *Bounty* story.[7] One thinks of the conflict in the choices Christian has to make, of the struggle in William Bligh against the elements in the open boat, and his need to save his companions, of Adams's personal visionary faith and resolve to ensure the survival of the Pitcairn community.

In the early 1930s they produced the influential *Bounty* novels: *Mutiny on the Bounty* (1932), *Men Against the Sea* (1934) and *Pitcairn's Island* (1934). The books divide the great story into three narratives: the voyage and the mutiny; Bligh's epic voyage in the open boat, returning to recount the mutiny to authorities; and finally the mutineers' attempt to create a settlement on the uninhabited island. *Mutiny on the Bounty* was wildly received and was a Book-of-the-Month Club selection. Nordhoff and Hall's *Bounty* books and the MGM film aroused considerable interest in the story and prompted other books on the topic.[8] There are three major surviving film versions of the *Bounty* story. All three films retell the same story, each in its own way. There are some important recurring moments, but the emphasis in each case is significantly different. The central relationship, between Bligh and Christian, is consistent. Whether the conflict is between Charles Laughton and Clark Gable, Trevor Howard and Marlon Brando or Anthony Hopkins and Mel Gibson, it is that recognisable movie archetype, the wicked and corrupt Old World attempting tyrannically to intimidate and thwart the New World. That theme is central and permanent in these narratives, and finds its echoes in Hollywood biblical epics, where Roman tyrants are invariably British actors and the repressed heroes always Americans. Yet each film carries the unmistakable fingerprints of its historic moment.

Into the big time

Mutiny on the Bounty, released by MGM in 1935, was closely based on Nordhoff and Hall. Its wholly unhistoric optimism about improvements in the Royal Navy is true to the optimistic spirit of Roosevelt's New Deal, to which MGM was overtly pledged. A film historian of the period recorded how the film struck a resounding chord in the 1930s:

The great appeal of the picture was that it was presented as a simple conflict between good and evil, between the champion of the underdog ... and the oppressive martinet. ... In the Depression, many people felt forced into virtual servitude by ruthless bosses, reminded constantly that others were waiting in line for their positions. Strikes were in the air; millions could identify with this story of rebellion against tyranny.[9]

By establishing the fact that the crew were press-ganged, the mutiny is seen as a manifestation of democracy. Nordhoff and Hall's version was that the seamen petitioned the *Bounty*'s Captain for the honour to serve on the ship.

Although the historic Bligh actually rose professionally from the ranks, the Bligh created by Charles Laughton represents the old-fashioned brutal British upper classes, thus making it a much more 'American' revolutionary story, contrasting the European way and the American way. This conflict would be heightened by the fact that Clark Gable was already an established star, personifying the virtues of the all-American hero, as he explained:

The things a man has to have are hope and confidence in himself against odds. ... He's got to have some inner standards worth fighting for or there won't be any way to bring him into conflict. And he must be ready to choose death before dishonour without making too much song and dance about it.[10]

These are exactly the wholesome qualities he brings to the role of Christian, and it is interesting to note that Gable deliberately declined the services of a voice coach offered by MGM in order to adopt a 'convincing British accent' (Higham, p. 233). Gable's homophobia additionally increased the tension between him and the homosexual Laughton.

Irving Thalberg, the MGM executive who produced the film, was an Anglophile. He had recently returned from convalescence in Germany, following a heart attack. Here he had witnessed the true nature of modern Germany's political revolution and the beginnings of Hitler's effect on Germany, including violent public demonstrations against Jews. The collective resistance to Bligh's power mania might be read as presaging the struggle between Fascism and Communism. Hitler, Mussolini and tensions in Europe filled the pages of the newspapers for several years preceding the release of *Mutiny on the Bounty*. Although the Laughton/Gable conflict doubtless echoed the historic British/American collision of 1776, audiences must have recognised contemporary political tensions in MGM's version of the *Bounty* mutiny. This version of the events is vastly important in placing them in our modern awareness of the past and highlighting these characters and incidents in our consciousness. This acclaimed release ensured everyone was aware of Bligh, Christian and the mutiny. A particular debt is due to Laughton's creation of William Bligh. Its survival in our awareness has been enormously aided by parodies and imitations. The Laughton-Bligh is immediately recognisable. As he himself said: 'It's got so that every time I walk into a restaurant, I get not only soup but an impersonation of Captain Bligh'.[11] The comedian Tony Hancock was doing Laughton's Bligh some three decades after the film.

MGM released a second version in 1962. This was in Technicolor and lasted over three hours. Laughton's 1935 performance had by this time apparently become the definitive model. Charles Lederer's screenplay was also based on Nordhoff and Hall. The original director was Carol Reed, whose first film, *Midshipman Easy*, released the same year as the Laughton/Gable *Mutiny*, was also a naval costumer. He had an international reputation for high drama: *Odd Man Out* (1948), *The Fallen Idol* (1949) and *The Third Man* (1951). He also demonstrated a sound touch with exotic subjects, such as *The Outcast of the Islands* (1953). Filming started on location in Tahiti even before a finished script had been approved. As Reed's intentions to make Bligh (Trevor Howard) the real hero became obvious, MGM fired him. He was replaced by Lewis Milestone. Milestone had earned fame as the director of *All Quiet on the Western Front* (1930). This gave him a reputation for spectacular action sequences. He also deftly handled properties which presented character conflict, both in comedy and dramatic contexts, such as *The Front Page* (1932), *Rain* (1933) and *Of Mice and Men* (1940). During the 1940s and 1950s he directed a series of adequate flagwavers and battle movies: *The Purple Heart* (1944), *A Walk in the Sun* (1946) and *Halls of Montezuma* (1952).

The MGM 1962 film was part of the fashion for blockbusters, started by King Vidor's *War and Peace* (1956). The aim was to give punters something they couldn't get on their domestic monochrome TV sets: big budget films exploiting the visual magnitude of the wide screen and stereophonic sound, and thus scoop the box office. This was the age of *Around the World in Eighty Days* (cost $6,000,000, grossed $22,000,000) and *The Ten Commandments* (cost $13,500,000, grossed $43,000,000), and other blockbusters of this period were *South Pacific* (1958), *Ben-Hur* (1959) and *Spartacus* (1960). *Mutiny on the Bounty* (1962) gave much greater emphasis to the Tahitian episodes and the mutineers' attempts at a return to the simple life, which now seem typical 1960s hedonism. This gave scope for exotic location material, scantily clad tropical maidens, vast crowd scenes and high drama in Technicolor and wide screen. Trevor Howard played Bligh as an arrogant martinet, and Brando's Christian is an insufferable fop, for which he deployed a caricatured upper-class English accent.

Ray Connolly, attempting to characterise the 1960s, singled out a pervading sense that things could, should and would change; that fairness and opportunity would prevail and that conformity was on the decline. Key movements he detected were changes in sexual morality resulting from the Pill, the creation of the Peace Corps and the emergence of Flower Power.[12] *Mutiny on the Bounty* (1962) presaged much of the Swinging Sixties. A striking feature of this version is the glamorous portrayal of the blissful, carefree Polynesian life offered the *Bounty*'s crew, and their subsequent attempt to make this alternative way of life permanent. This is signalled to us in the manner the *Bounty* is greeted: with a belly dance by sexy Polynesians scantily clothed in flowers. Trevor Howard (Bligh) warns the crew that the natives have 'absolutely no concept of ordinary morality. You will no doubt take full advantage of their ignorance.' Bligh attempts to intervene in Christian's wooing of the king's naively sensual daughter, only to find he has offended Polynesian hospitality. They tell him, if King Hitihi's daughter is not good enough for England, then breadfruit is not good enough for England. Bligh then finds himself obliged to order Christian to make love to her.

Motives for the mutiny are fully presented. Not only is Bligh's tyranny more explicit – verbal abuse, short rations, sadistic punishment – but additionally this Bligh is responsible for several deaths. The class tensions between Bligh and Christian are clear. The cue for the mutiny is Bligh's kicking a ladle from Christian's hand as he is attempts to succour a dying man. After Bligh and his companions have been set adrift, this film version goes on to detail the subsequent events on Pitcairn. This may be seen as the apotheosis of a theme constantly reiterated in the 1950s and early 1960s: exotic Pacific or Far Eastern locations offering Europeans and North Americans a cure for the anxieties and torments of their civilisation. Trevor Howard is shocked at the possibility that his expedition for breadfruit may fail: 'I dislike failure. I dislike failure as much as the Admiralty does.' Brando consoles him by pointing out how unfair and unworthy civilisation actually is: 'The Admiralty will blame you anyway, sir. It's an unjust world.'

The crew's settlement foreshadows the affectation of rejecting western industrial civilisation in favour of the East. In comic or serious treatment the theme is clear in such films as *Our Girl Friday* (1953), *Teahouse of the August Moon* (1956), *The Admirable Crichton* (1957) and *South Pacific* (1958). The decade also featured attempts to bring collective action to bear in finding solutions to social and political problems: the civil rights movement, sexual liberation, women's rights, politics in France and industrial problems in the UK. *The Caine Mutiny* (1954) was followed by *I'm Alright Jack* (1959) and *The Angry Silence* (1960). The ancient Roman setting should not disguise the fact that *Spartacus* (1960) was an epic portrayal of rebellion against authority. The presence of Charles Laughton as a Roman authority figure could not make the issue clearer. One of the most extraordinarily redolent films of this period, *Paths of Glory* (1957), explored the fate of the rank and file when caught up in the incompetent ambitions of the traditional officer class. Watching Brando as Fletcher Christian in 1962 one could scarcely be unaware of his numerous previous portrayals of rebellious young men, in *Viva Zapata* (1952), *The Wild One* (1953), *On the Waterfront* (1954) and *One Eyed Jacks* (1960). Placing *Mutiny on the Bounty* (1962) in this context reveals the ways in which, despite the eighteenth-century location, it represents the period which produced it. The *Bounty*'s crew were Hippies before their time.

A *Bounty* for the Thatcher years

The Bounty (1984) was scripted by Robert Bolt, who had already earned a substantial reputation for epic historical screenplays.[13] It was based on Richard Hough's novel, *Captain Bligh and Mr Christian* (1988), rehearsing the familiar story with new insights and emphasis. It opens with Bligh's summons officially to account for the loss of the *Bounty*. The story is then told in flashback. Once again the tyrannical Bligh is British (Anthony Hopkins) and Christian (Mel Gibson) a colonial. There is affection, even a strange kind of love, between Bligh and Christian. Mel Gibson was by now familiar to audiences, not only for his *Mad Max* (1979) and *Lethal Weapon* (1987) roles, but for *Gallipoli* (1981) in which his youth and idealism were sacrificed as a result of the incompetence of British military authority-figures. This Bligh and Christian knew each other before the voyage, and are on first-name terms. Hopkins is inhibited, but beneath this there is almost fatherly warmth. We see him happily in the midst of his family before the voyage. He gazes lovingly on his wife's portrait when he's at sea. This Bligh is human.

Hopkins looks after his crew in his own way. There are fun and high spirits on this *Bounty* when they cross the Equator. One cannot imagine Laughton or Howard acting in this way. He ensures the crew have their spirits lifted with regular music and dancing, while at the same insisting on good order ('insubordination is no laughing matter'). This is counterbalanced by the considerable ill-feeling amongst the crew themselves. Harmony between Bligh and Christian endures up to the moment when mutiny becomes inevitable. Their friendship is at the base of the fracture, for Bligh is envious of Christian's relationship with native women. There is a clear hint of Bligh's repressed homosexuality. Early signs of the rift are indicated in the return of the formalities of rank. He sympathises with Christian's having to leave his beloved behind on the island, and explains his conduct by saying it was for his own good, 'you needed someone to show you where your duty really lay'. Hopkins's expression as he says this tells all we need to know: he has opened his heart to Christian. There is something big-hearted in this Bligh, who has risen through the ranks to become an officer. He even admits sailing errors. When the ship's doctor, Huggan, dies Bligh shows sympathy, however rough. 'Poor bugger', he says.

Audiences in 1984 would be aware that they were living through the early stages of a new political era.[14] Although the new politics promised success through individual freedom, Thatcherism required the overall control of an almost paternalistic capitalism. Such freedom, paradoxically, required severe limitation on collective action and a greater emphasis on law enforcement. There would be considerable restriction in public expenditure. Discontent showed itself in the worst public riots this century and the Miners' Strike the year *The Bounty* was released.[15] *The Bounty* shows us a man who has risen by his own efforts, desperate to be a high achiever. His accent tells us that he was not born to privilege. He shows his ambition in his determination to circumnavigate the globe by rounding the Cape of Good Hope, but he is brought low by the irresponsible behaviour of his crew. This was a perfect message for the 1980s: individuals must be free to take opportunities to better themselves, and at the same time develop personal responsibility. Groups should not gang up to stifle the enterprise of others. *The Bounty* bodies forth the destruction of deferred gratification by short-term hedonism. Christian loses his judgement because he cannot bear the loss of his native bride. For the crew, life on the Pacific island was the ultimate sexual indulgence, 'all they wear is tattoos in wonderful places . . . Paradise'. Bligh sees that the crew were corrupted 'by the place itself'. The man of enterprise, William Bligh, is exonerated by the court. He weeps to learn the verdict and the mutineers disappear from the scene. This is Bligh's film.

The enduring myth

The historical distortions in the way we continue to apprehend the *Bounty* tell us much about ourselves. The *Bounty* mutiny occurred during the eighteenth-century intellectual fashion for the 'Noble Savage'. Jean-Jacques Rousseau crystallised these themes: that Man was naturally virtuous, free and happy. It was society which corrupted him. The sources of his disharmony were property, inequality and despotism. The closer to nature, the happier Man would be, even though existing institutions might of necessity be retained. Comparisons between degenerate civilised life and unspoiled savagery became a commonplace of European literature between the seventeenth and nineteenth centuries. Notable expressions of the theme are to be found in the novels of François Chateaubriand and James Fenimore Cooper which appeared at the time when the *Bounty* myth was establishing itself. The results of the collision between western progress and apparently pristine societies continue, finding expression in the modern custom for the obligatory student 'gap year' when one sallies forth backpacking through India, Latin America etc., to 'find oneself' before embarking on the undergraduate experience.

The story of the mutiny on the *Bounty* continues to be one of the most beloved stories of sea-going adventure. *Carry on Jack* (1964), in utilising the story further, embedded its position in popular history. Bligh's account has been adapted for use in schools in the UK and USA for some years.[16] The mutineers' trial was the subject of BBC radio and television productions by Stanley Miller, who became so enthralled by the subject that he spent ten years researching the writing of a fictional autobiography of Fletcher Christian, published in 1973, which gives the story from Christian's point of view.[17] The *Bounty* mutiny and its aftermath was serialised on BBC Radio 4's *Storytime* in 1981. In 1983 David Essex released an ambitious concept album 'Mutiny', which led to his hit 'Tahiti'. Two years later he mounted the successful stage show *Mutiny*. In 1981 William Bligh's 'true' account, the Nordhoff and Hall version, was dramatised for BBC Radio 4 and published as an audio tape in 1996.[18] The same year William Kinsolving published a novel about the further adventures of Fletcher Christian, 'the legendary leader of the Bounty Mutiny'.[19] During September 1997 as I began to work on this essay, the History Channel on cable television advertised an upcoming programme in its *History Showcase: Sea Tales* series, 'Where The Past Comes Alive', which purported to tell 'the true story of the mutiny on the "Bounty" '.[20]

In 1997 Dea Birkett published a very disturbing account of Pitcairn Island today which should severely erode the myth of the happy desert island alternative society, but the *Bounty* seems unstoppable.[21] Like Shakespeare's magic island in *The Tempest*, it postulates an alternative world where the past is erased, a fresh start may be made, and perfection is possible. It has the magnetic pull of the American Dream, of a return to innocence. The South Seas as an image of peace and fulfilment away from civilisation dates from long before Gauguin, Robert Louis Stevenson, Rupert Brooke and other professional Bohemians. The discoveries of the pioneering navigators of the sixteenth century were absorbed into cultural discourse and became an image for which the European might long. It is important to note that the paradise-lost version of the *Bounty* story so familiar to us was launched by Nordhoff and Hall in the period immediately following the Great War of

1914–18, in which they served and which was seen as the collapse of hope for modern civilisation.

The *Bounty*'s basic myth is simplicity itself. It bodies forth the New World's right to the pursuit of happiness in the face of the Old World's repression, authoritarianism and decadence. Laughton, Howard, Hopkins represent the old order; Gable, Brando and Gibson the young. The conflict is represented in the most striking way: the Old World is associated with war, slavery, harsh discipline, symbolised in waging war against the elements. The New World involves peace, love and plenty in a perfect climate. It is an aspect of the wide-ranging sentimental yearning for rural simplicity found in Georgianism, the cult of Thomas Hardy, real ale and morris dancing. The 'enduring authority of the myth to promise happiness is enshrined in the Bounty chocolate bar television commercials, 'The Taste of the Exotic', still deployed in promotions in 1998. How effectively the BBC film of Jane Austen's *Persuasion* (1995) signalled the connubial bliss of finally united hero and heroine with a well chosen clip from *The Bounty*.[22]

Notes

1. William Bligh, *The Log of HMS Bounty 1787–1789*, ed. John Bach (London, 1987), p. 20.
2. Robert Hughes, *Culture of Complaint* (Oxford, 1993), p. 8.
3. See William Bligh, *The Bligh Notebook: Rough account – Lieutenant Wm Bligh's voyage in the Bounty's Launch from the ship to Tofua & from thence to Timor: 28 April to 14 June 1789, With a draft list of the BOUNTY mutineers, transcription and Facsimile*, ed. John Bach (London, 1987).
4. See Greg Dening, *Mr Bligh's Bad Language: Passion, Power and Theatre on the Bounty* (Cambridge, 1994), pp. 345–6.
5. *The Hurricane* (1937, remade 1979), *The High Barbaree* (1947) and *Botany Bay* (1952).
6. Nordhoff's early books included *Man-of-War Life* (1855), *The Merchant Vessel* (1855), *Whaling and Fishing* (1856) and *Stories of the Island World* (1857). He was editor of the *New York Evening Post*, and Washington correspondent of the *New York Herald*. He subsequently published books on politics and current affairs.
7. At the time of writing the *Bounty* trilogy, Hall published *The Friends* (1935), a poem about Robinson's poetry.

8. For example, George Mackeness, *The Life of Vice Admiral William Bligh*, first published in two volumes in 1931, reprinted in 1936; Owen Rutter, *Turbulent Journey: A Life of William Bligh, Vice Admiral of the Blue* (1936); H.S. Montgomerie, *William Bligh of the Bounty in Fact and in Fable* (1937); Geoffrey Rawson, *Bligh of the Bounty* (1937).

9. Charles Higham, *Merchant of Dreams: Louis B. Mayer and the Secret Hollywood* (London, 1983), pp. 237–8.

10. Justin Wintle and Richard Kenin, *The Dictionary of Biographical Quotation of British and American Subjects* (London, 1978), p. 311.

11. Leslie Halliwell (ed.), *Halliwell's Filmgoer's Book of Quotes* (London, 1978), p. 162.

12. Ray Connolly, *In the Sixties* (London, 1995), pp. 1–3. See also Peter Furtado (ed.), *The Culture of Youth* (Oxford, 1994), pp. 123–30.

13. These included *Lawrence of Arabia* (1962), *Doctor Zhivago* (1965) and *Ryan's Daughter* (1970).

14. See Robert Hewison, *Culture and Consensus: England, Art and Politics Since 1940* (London, 1995), pp. 209ff.

15. See John MacInnes, *Thatcherism at Work* (Milton Keynes, 1992), Shirley Robin Letwin, *The Anatomy of Thatcherism* (London, 1992), and Edgar Wilson, *A Very British Miracle: The Failure of Thatcherism* (London, 1992).

16. William Bligh, *The Mutiny on Board HMS 'Bounty'*, adapted by Deborah Kestel (New York, 1979). Tim Vicary's novel, *Mutiny on the Bounty*, has been part of a graded reading scheme in the Oxford Bookworms series (Oxford University Press) since 1994.

17. Stanley Miller, *Mr Christian! The Journal of Fletcher Christian, Former Lieutenant of His Majesty's Armed Vessel 'Bounty'* (New York, 1973).

18. The audio tape was produced by Michael Cameron and Stewart Richards, directed by Adrian Bean and released by Mr Punch (Audio) Ltd, 1996.

19. William Kinsolving, *Mister Christian: The Further Adventures of Fletcher Christian, the Legendary Leader of the 'Bounty' Mutiny* (New York, 1996).

20. *Cable Guide*, September 1997, p. 149.

21. Dea Birkett, *Serpent in Paradise* (London, 1997).

22. See Nick Radloe, 'Powers of Persuasion', *Television: The Journal of the Royal Television Society* (November/December 1995), p. 17.

8 *Three* Madame Bovary*s:* Renoir, Minnelli, Chabrol

Alain J.-J. Cohen

'I've seen this movie before . . . every time you see it, it seems to be
different because you're different.'
James Cole, watching *Vertigo* (1958)
in Terry Gilliam's *Twelve Monkeys* (1995)

Prologue

This research proposes a close analysis of three different filmic
versions of the same scene from Flaubert's *Madame Bovary* as directed by Renoir in 1934, Minnelli in 1949 and Chabrol in 1991.
The Ball at Vaubyessard summons a superimposition of readings
and interpretations, highlighted by a combination of methods –
shot-by-shot analysis, narrative construction, recursive images in
competing filmic poetics and various theoretical approaches.[1] Two
versions are by French directors, albeit 50 years apart, and one of
them comes from post-war Hollywood. This focus on the same
scene enables us to compare and control various filmic styles, the
visuality of Flaubert's writing, as well as the spectatorship's cognitive map when comparing the various histories, aesthetics and
methods of interpretation. In the process, the motif of Dance in all
three versions may be explored from within the history of cinema.
This research illustrates also such questions as the models of filmic
composition, the strategies of translation from text to image and
their consequences for interpretation, along with issues of implicit
ideologies and modes of enunciation in the field of film history
and film analysis.

Flaubert's camera, sound-lab and editing-lab

Legions of literary critics have commented upon the painterly or sculptural, the sensuous or plastic aspects of Flaubert's writing and style. Indeed, Flaubert's life (1821–80) overlapped the vast periods of romanticism, realism and early impressionism in painting, as well as the invention of photography (1839). It could just as well be asserted with anachronistic imagination, since the cinématographe was only invented in 1895, that the moves and juxtapositions of the mind's eye, characteristic of the acute visuality of Flaubert's descriptions, correspond to the play of the cinematic image.[2] Witness, for example, this combination of meditation upon the play of light and the minimalist character action in the following typical excerpt of Flaubert:

> Sometimes the sunbeams, coming through the Venetian blind, would stretch what looked like the strings of a lyre from ceiling to floor, and specks of dust would whirl about in these luminous bars. She amused herself by breaking them with her hand; Frédéric would gently seize it and gaze at the tracery of her veins, the grain of her skin, the shape of her fingers.[3]

The seduction scene in *Madame Bovary*, for instance, displays both painterly and filmic qualities. When Emma yields to Rodolphe (with the unforgettable words 'she abandoned herself' which propel the reader–spectator into his/her own sexual imagination), as if in anticipation of early cinema's cut to the sunset after the lovers' kiss, the text then displaces Emma's fluidly shifting passions into a palimpsest of painting styles (romantic, Kaspar Friedrich perhaps, or realistic, Courbet, for example). An emoted landscape is meticulously described: 'Evening shadows were falling', the light filters through the tree-branches in the woods, a skyscape includes the shades of colour of the darkening sky at dusk. Flaubert even includes the diverse harmonics of sounds and birdcries in the forest, in displaced sync with Emma's patent pleasure, overwhelming guilt and foreshadowed death: 'Then she heard a long, lingering, indistinct cry coming from the hills far beyond the forest'. Leaving aside the virtuosity of Flaubert's writing and following this descriptive interweave of Emma's emotions and anthropomorphised nature, the twentieth-century film-spectator may also marvel at the profound anticipation of the soundtrack in cinema in this nineteenth-century text.

Similarly and shortly before this seduction, in the equally legendary scene of the Agricultural Show at Yonville, Flaubert's text portrays a filmic apparatus at work in the virtuoso back and forth crosscut between, on the one hand, the words of the lovers-to-be hidden on the second floor (in his flirting dialogue with Emma, Rodolphe proclaims his contempt for small-town mores in long tirades) and, on the other hand, the speeches by the mayor and other provincial administrators addressing the crowd in the central square of the small town. The controlled editing of the crosscut is so precise that at their paroxysm the two sets of speeches start converging as Rodolphe professes his formulaic love ('A hundred times I was on the point of leaving, and yet I followed you and stayed with you'[4]) whilst the chairman starts auctioning ('For the best of manures'), and the text cuts back to the hackneyed seduction ('As I'd stay with you tonight, tomorrow, every day, all my life'). The effect of the mutual meta-commentary is unmistakable: the literary apparatus juxtaposes in exponential ridicule Rodolphe's words and the chairman's words for the greater laughing pleasure of a constructed reader – whilst the twentieth-century dialogue editor marvels at the craft involved in these punctual match cuts.

Madame Bovary and 'translation'

A work which is so well-known that it becomes indistinguishable from the culture from which it emerges (the same could be said about the *Odyssey, Hamlet,* etc.) poses an irresistible challenge to readers and film-makers alike. Its own aura is inextricably constituted by exegetic and hermeneutic networks woven by generations of commentaries within this universal culture. As a result, every new reading (Borges argued that every reading was in some way a translation) measures itself against all the layers in the history of its interpretations and against the genealogy of its meaning. Thus, either the new reading proposes a salient new way of perceiving a very well known piece of work or it will just be swallowed by the aura of the work to which it refers. A film version of a literary work begins referring to an 'original', but then new versions measure themselves against previous film versions, along with the novel, in a geometric expansion of new effects, inspirations and challenges.

Madame Bovary appears to be a felicitous research example, for several film-makers have tried their hand at conveying their vision of this famous work. The juxtaposition of transposition strategies from the literary to the filmic thus offers object lessons in the field of text-into-film adaptation. It would take a lifetime of punctual work to vet each adaptation or to compare in detail all the versions to one another, and in turn to oppose them to the novel in its totality. It is more productive to focus instead upon the rendition of a single scene by three talented directors, and then to parse the differing results. In so doing, references to other segments of the works are not necessarily to be excluded, and a number of interpretive extrapolations will ensue – inevitably. The fête at Vaubyessard is a unique event in the life of Emma and Charles Bovary. It is central to the discrepancy between Emma's banal everyday existence and her inchoate sense of an inaccessible idealised existence elsewhere (a mental cinema) fed by the reading of too many romanesque books – in this Emma and Don Quixote have a lot in common.

Renoir's *Madame Bovary* (1934)

The Vaubyessard scene (4 minutes, 20 seconds, in a 90-minute film) is made up of eight shots squeezed between a shot of an ecstatic Emma (Valentine Tessier) telling Charles (Pierre Renoir) in their coach: 'This could be the beginning of a new career . . . we could go to Rouen', before a dissolve to the ball, and a shot of Emma in a subsequent sequence on her way to confess her depression and her attraction to Léon to a country priest distracted by schoolchildren. The eight shots are ordered symmetrically: the first one is a high wide-angle deep-focus shot of the Fête, which then tracks forward through the arched-columned and wrought-iron gate where coupled dancers are turning to the sound of a rather fast popular waltz. The eighth shot, the last one, is a reverse track backward shot of the same scene with a similar ongoing waltz on the soundtrack even as the sequence fades to black.

The six shots inserted betwixt the two shots above represent the heart of the matter. Shot 2: the Bovarys in medium shot look startlingly static together in the middle of the agitation of the Fête; Emma keeps looking away offscreen and orders Charles not to dance after he complains about his evening clothes and shoes. They are then separated by an unidentified guest and the marquis (the host) who takes Charles away. Shot 3: the unidentified guest quickly teaches the basic waltz steps to Emma. They waltz along together until the end of the sequence, in medium and long shots, mingled with other dancers, in and out of frame in a track shot that plays with the sometimes wide visual interference of the salon's large columns. The dual movements (camera track and the dancers) isolate even more the static, solitary Charles in a long shot which continues to shot 4 as a mirror reflects the lonely Charles, his back to the mirror, and the festive dancing scene. Shot 5: medium shot of Charles who has moved to another part of the salon as the dancers continue evolving in and out of frame while the camera continues playing with the columns as in the previous shot. Shot 6: axial cut of Charles in a tighter shot looking at a painted portrait of a man whose gaze is looking out at the scene from which Charles is trying to distract himself. The *mise-en-scène* may show Charles's psychological discomfort when trying to strike an attitude as much as when he turns around to observe the dancing, but it also functions as a derivative shot intended to make him even more reified than a portrait. Shot 7 is crucial: (back to shot 5) Charles in long shot in the background, Emma and her partner dancing in midground. When asked by her partner about this bizarre lonely man who seems to follow them wherever they are dancing, Emma disavows Charles: 'I don't know him'; Charles sits down under the portrait, next to a commode upon which rests a small bronze bust surrounded by two flower pots. It is left unclear whether Charles has heard this remark, or whether only Emma's partner and the spectator are its addressees.

The camera move and counter-move (in shots 1 and 8) point to a syntax of inclusion versus exclusion: the invitation to a party at first includes the newly arriving guests along with the spectatorial position; however at the end of the sequence they are excluded, especially with the view of the forebodingly shut wrought-iron gate whilst the sound of the waltz continues – without the Bovarys. In shots 3 to 7, the visual interference of the multiple columns on the dance floor corresponds to the dancers' playfulness, but they exclude Charles from the field of vision: the dancers' moves, just as the camera moves, intensify Charles's static stance. This is similarly highlighted in the mirror shot (shot 4) and in the portrait shot (shot 6). The soundtrack plays equally with the signifiers of inclusion versus exclusion. Except in shot 2 when the music is softened upon the Bovarys' arrival, the repetitive waltz music is ongoing. It endures even as the camera tracks back in high angle, leaving the château and its ongoing fête.

The repetitive (almost grating) sound-image of the waltz, Emma's persistent gaze away from Charles versus Charles's persistent gaze at Emma, the chromatic opposition between men dressed in black versus women dressed in white, the defining opposition of paired dancers versus solitary Charles, the filmic syntax of track forward versus track back at the end, all help constitute the defining concept of inclusion versus exclusion. Albeit with rigorous economy of means and sparse dialogue almost reminiscent of the intertitles of the silent era (after all, in 1934 the sound is still a fresh addition in cinema), Renoir could convey in just eight shots a tragically lonely presentation of Charles and an easily satisfied figure of Emma for whom this fête is the only moment of happiness in the novel and in the film. It is interesting to note that Charles was played by director Renoir's own brother, and to see how the moustache and the costuming remind the spectator of the famous daguerreotype of Flaubert himself.

Minnelli's Madame Bovary (1949)

For Minnelli, the Vaubyessard scene is a lengthy sequence (8 minutes, 45 seconds, in a two-hour film) made up of 38 shots. Its beginning and ending symmetry are framed by a set of close-ups: the dress Emma is wearing at the Vaubyessard party occupies vertically the full frame, and the same dress lies almost horizontally as it is being put away the morning after. Upon their entrance Emma (Jennifer Jones) and Charles (Van Heflin) stand uncomfortably a while until greeted by the marquis, who leads Emma immediately to a quadrille whilst directing Charles to the billiard and card room. Minnelli has Van Heflin cut a gauche and clumsy figure. As opposed to Renoir's distantiated Charles, this Charles is at the same time a rather moving character who tries in vain to bond with the aristocratic men in their billiard or card games, and to join in their drinking and camaraderie.

The husband and wife are positioned into two separate movements and agendas. A few dissolves (as a filmic convention of time elapsing) point to Emma moving from one quadrille to the next – the tempo quickening with every dissolve. At the centre of the men's attention and clearly enjoying herself, Emma becomes frenzied with dance. On the other hand, Charles's frenzy is one of inebriation as he keeps drinking every time the servants' trays come his way. Surrounded by men, Emma looks up obliquely to catch and admire her own image as object of men's desire at the centre of a rounded, ornate garland-framed mirror. She is distracted from her own narcissistic pleasure by the hand of Rodolphe[5] (Louis Jourdan), who leads her despite her resistance into a frenzied waltz.[6] To enhance the ongoing frenzied effect of the dance, the camera pans during the waltz segment in revolving shots from right to left as the partners whirl in the opposite direction, and then the reverse vectors set in when the partners change direction. When Emma complains 'I can't breathe. I am going to faint', windows are broken rhythmically in sync with the heavily punctuating percussion. Minnelli plays here at a double level: first by having it done for Emma, whereas in Flaubert's text Emma simply observes that two window-panes are being broken 'when the air is stuffy'; and second, window-panes are shattered one after the other with mock self-conscious baroque excess, in sync with the rhythm of the music.

Glass and glass-shattering are recursive images throughout this sequence. Twice, high-angled shots of the dancers pan down from the glass chandeliers. Similarly, Charles observes the group of men throwing down their glasses on the marble floor when they finish their drink. In simultaneity with the breaking of the window-panes for Emma, Charles loses his balance and breaks glasses and bottles off a tray in an ongoing shattering rain of glass shards shot both from the inside as well as from the outside of the château. Near the end of the waltz, the blurriness of a rapidly revolving shot signifies the frenzied dizziness overwhelming Emma as well.

In Minnelli's film a scandal occurs: a drunk Charles tries to reach Emma on the dance floor as Emma and Rodolphe keep dancing with even more intensity, but the flux and flow in the movements of the other dancers keep him at bay for a while. When after several tries Charles reaches them with a pathetic 'I want to dance with my wife', Emma leaves the party in a huff. All eyes turn to Charles as the music stops and the floor empties; after a time, he follows her up the short centred staircase with a slightly zigzagging step.

Thus, in Minnelli's *mise-en-scène*, Emma follows a dance motion which she masters whereas Charles is never able to harmonise with the motions of the group of men. High contrast black and white are present, just as much as in the Renoir sequence. Glass and glass-shattering, however, dominate the image-composition of this sequence (chandeliers, drinks, window-panes, mirrors). This sets up a filmic opposition between Emma, for whom glass is broken or who verifies her narcissism in a mirror shot, and Charles, who is fragmented by these images. After they have left the château, where Charles's conduct has provoked scandal, he sleeps in the carriage whilst a pensive Emma holds the horses' reins, the waltz still throbbing in her ears (and on the soundtrack) in sync with the dimmed sound of the horse hoofs. There is no sense of scandal in Flaubert's text nor in Renoir's film. This is part of a larger adaptation and transformation by Minnelli. Moreover, he frames the whole film symmetrically with the legendary trial of Flaubert upon the publication of *Madame Bovary* in 1857. Although the character of Flaubert (James Mason) only utters generalities about the enduring power of art, the representation of Flaubert's trial may also be viewed as an echo of Hollywood's own trials in the late 1940s and early 1950s.[7]

Chabrol's *Madame Bovary* (1991)

In Chabrol's film the Vaubyessard scene is a shorter sequence (4 minutes, 34 seconds, in a two-hour film) made up of 31 fluid shots. Chabrol pursues a different strategy in his version of the scene. No disavowal of her husband by Emma (Isabelle Huppert) nor perpetration of gaffes and scandal by Charles (Jean-François Balmer) prevail in this colour version of *Madame Bovary*. Instead, the *mise-en-scène* follows a rather subdued strategy. The sequence opens with a wide-angle diagonal shot of the musicians in liveried uniforms performing fast pieces softly for dance and entertainment. One of them, following a pizzicato solo violin, is danced minuet-style; the sense of elegance and wealth (again, a high-angle shot of the dancers through glass chandeliers) permeates but does not overwhelm the Bovarys. The class discrepancy is muted (a valet's quizzical expression in reaction to a gauche Charles's introducing himself).

Profile portraiture close-ups of Emma (sometimes with candlelight) alternate with shots of Emma dancing with different partners. An excessively smiling Charles (a visual translation perhaps of his cliché-ridden speech), as proud of his wife as is Van Heflin in Minnelli's film, brings her glasses of champagne in between dances. Emma and her waltzing partner may lock eyes just a while during the time of the waltz, but this is no dancing performance as opposed to the previous film version. Chabrol draws closely from Flaubert's text and from Renoir's film and highlights filmically Emma's subjectivity: she keeps looking away from Charles, walks ahead of him, and her filmic image is spatially distant from Charles – ethereally insulated. Thus Emma by herself overhears directly onscreen, and offscreen as well, the other guests' conversations while Charles doesn't – 'the Colosseum by moonlight . . . you're ravishing tonight, Berthe', 'winning two thousand pounds with my racers in England' – or she overhears the line about the air being 'stuffy' that precedes the matter-of-fact breaking of a single windowpane in Chabrol (two in Flaubert, three in Minnelli, none in Renoir). Chabrol's strategy is to align the spectator with Emma's mental universe as she witnesses these overheard and offscreen voices. The spectator's cognition is thus constituted by Emma's private world which perhaps corresponds to her romanesque readings and fantasies (later she will name her child 'Berthe'). This is a subtle contradistinction to Charles's closed mental universe, solely constituted by looking at his wife 'platitudinously' (to use Flaubert's term) and wanting to be 'platitudinously' reassured that she is happy.

At the end of the party, a muted Strauss waltz playing in the background, the comment repeated twice by Emma, first outside the château at night as they await their carriage, then on board (in profile portraiture again), 'This was the most beautiful day of my life' is surprising; it may be perceived according to Chabrol's subtle strategy. The acting by one of France's most versatile actresses today must have contributed to the construction of a conflicting perception: the event was experienced intensely by the character while played nonchalantly by the actress. Hence, the discrepancy in the comment. Emma felt at one with the world of her dreams at

Vaubyessard, to which she is never to return thereafter except obsessionally in her memories or in her imagination and, by displacement, with Rodolphe.

Ut pictura Madame Bovary

At a minimum, the domain of 'translation' involves philosophy and interpretation, hermeneutics and literary exegesis, art and aesthetics, rhetoric and cultural anthropology. Translation may constitute in and of itself an immense sub-discipline collateral to every single discipline. We are constantly called upon to compare two semiotic systems in order to perceive the rules and logic of their organisation and transformations, whether comparing two cultures, or poetry and painting, or a literary world and its filmic transposition. Whenever we compare a natural language system with a non-linguistically-based system (for which we need what Lotman called a secondary-modelling system), it may behove us to remember at the start that a linguistic lexicon may be finite, whereas a stock of images may seem to be *a priori* non-finite. In translation theory, however, when we compare two systems, whether the analysis moves from text to film, from image to image, or from a film to a new version of the same film, entities are juxtaposed within each other and not within the natural world (where they would indeed be infinite).[8] A finite set of signifiers in a novel is the point of departure for another finite set of possible signifiers and representations from the perspective of the analysis of its translated (or transposed) image variations.

All of the three directors' versions discussed above had to select from the immense (yet finite) material offered by Flaubert's text. For instance, all three versions leave out the fact that in Flaubert's text the Bovarys stay overnight at Vaubyessard and only leave the next day. The elaborate supper and Flaubert's minute description of exotic foods (worthy at least of an extended filmic still shot), the pervasive sense of rich smells so important in all of Flaubert ('Emma felt herself enveloped by a warm atmosphere in which the fragrance of flowers and fine linen mingled with the odour of hot meat and truffles'), are all absent in their filmic counterparts. Similarly, Emma's flashback upon her life at the farm, which occurs during her walk through the party (only presented in Chabrol's version), could have been the occasion for a rich crosscut filmic prowess: 'Thoughts of les Berteaux came to her mind. She saw the farm, the muddy pond, her father in his smock . . . herself as she once had been, skimming the cream with her finger from the jar of milk in the dairy.' Regarding the question of 'faithfulness', we have to accept as axiomatic that 'faithfulness' is not a pertinent factor since the original cannot be replicated, and, moreover, that neither of the three directors was interested in transposing any of the details mentioned above.[9] They confront themselves with other challenges and thus propose other readings and interpretations when shifting this most renowned text into a set of transpositions. What may be noteworthy is that all of them included the dance sequence; and also of interest for the spectator in the history of cinema are the film versions' meta-comments upon one another's interpretations.

An original text offers a point of departure for a possible world with a generally definable cognitive schema to which a new version offers a set of variations and transforms. In addition to the cognitive schema, the text also provides a recognisable affective and aesthetic mapping through which we may applaud or decry an audacious variation, refuse or be pacified by its platitudes. It is because of this aesthetic and cognitive schema that we may wonder about a translator's responsibility. It is this cognitive and affective schema which enables us all at once to highlight in the Vaubyessard Ball sequences a jansenistic or tragically lonely Charles in Renoir's version, a well-meaning but rather gauche and benign Charles for Minnelli, or an imbecilic Charles in Chabrol's film. Similarly, Emma emulates Ginger Rogers in Minnelli's version, dances fairly well albeit not spectacularly for Chabrol, whilst her dancing is clearly of secondary importance in the Renoir version. With reference to the expression of emotions, Emma is ashamed of Charles in Renoir's film, angry at Charles in Minnelli's version and oblivious to Charles for Chabrol. What enables this emotion-schema to be operative is the working-through of something extremely concrete and often recursive in the filmic image: for Renoir the visual interference of the columned dance-space, for Minnelli the lavish shattering of glass during the waltz, for Chabrol the other guests' onscreen/offscreen conversations overheard by Emma in between the dances.

Interlude on Dance in cinema

Dance is a richly polysemic and common occurrence throughout the history of cinema, used for widely different reasons by film-makers and varying from film to film even with the same director. Dance may be a single image in a shot, a motif, a theme, a topos, a recursive figure, a complex configuration, an isotope which integrates itself to a narrative programme, a genre (the musical comedy, where the narrative involving a cast of characters is suspended and subordinated to the dance performance and enjoyment), or a deep structure (as in a choreographic vision of life and play). Every dance sequence presents specific image and narrative integration to a film as a whole: for instance the unforgettably nostalgic dance between Burt Lancaster and Claudia Cardinale at the end of Visconti's *Leopard* (1963) when the old Sicilian aristocrat comes to accept the end of an era, and a new generation's ways of being. The occurrence becomes even more interesting when a deep structure principle connects the figure of a dance with a motivated shot. For instance, several couples execute on cue a superb dance number at the beginning of Scorsese's *Age of Innocence* (1994, based on Edith Wharton's novel); the angle shifts to a bird's eye view of their dance and the overview plays with the notion of rigid social controls from which the lovers do not find respite.

To illustrate versatility, we shall refer very briefly to the transformations and evolution of the use of dance in the work of Bertolucci, a director who includes a dance sequence with different goals and results in most of his films. In *The Conformist* (1971) the fascinating dance number between the two women (Dominique Sanda and Stephania Sandrelli) is a complex configuration, compelling to all the spectators in the restaurant. The latter all become involved in the performance and join the dance themselves – except for the coward (Jean-Louis Trintignant) and the agent who find themselves alone, not dancing. In *Last Tango in Paris* (1973) Bertolucci used the tango with perfection but also in a sequence of parody and derision. In *1900* (1976) the dance number where Sanda pretends to be blind during a peasant dance in a barn is a fleeting motif; however, her affected blindness nullifies temporarily class differences between friends, Robert de Niro (the weak aristocrat) and Gérard Depardieu (the peasant leader), during the early rise of fascism in Italy. In *Stealing Beauty* (1995), a coming-of-age narrative, the young girl dances by herself in her room, just once, to the sound of crashing music.[10] The occurrence remains unexplained and convokes the spectator to construct interpretive strategies.

Clearly *The Conformist* makes the most complex use of Dance by combining the aesthetics of the image with a shrewd twist in the plot. Whatever the case may be, Dance presents a particular challenge for the technical mastery and organisation of disparate elements since it involves a moving character or set of characters, a fixed or moving camera, a static background, the use of sound and music to enhance the fluidity or the awkwardness of the conveyed meaning: all the elements above demand to be articulated in a system's synthesis.

Typologies of translation

Dryden proposed three types of translations in his translation of Ovid's *Epistles*: metaphrasis (*verbatim* translation), paraphrasis (*traductio ad sensum*), and *mimesis* (neither metaphrasis nor paraphrasis).[11] In another research focused on the question of 'intermediality' in translation in three interrelated systems of transpositions (from novel to screenplay, and from screenplay to film), we drew a few conclusions inspired by Dryden regarding the double bind and the paradox of translation, what may be called the structural impossibility of not betraying an original work – the old Italian saying *traduttore–traditore* still holds currency.[12] A heuristic taxonomy of translation flaws and betrayals was thus proposed: 1) a stereotypical translation (the search for corresponding formulaic expressions and images is caricatural); 2) an over-literal translation (the vision of the whole disappears from the target language as faithful translation produces a form of toxic transposition); 3) free translation (when the gap becomes too marked between the object-language and the target language); 4) treacherous translations (those that combine the too literal with the too faithful, and those that have given up on any deontology of translating). Ironically, categories of translation may well be equivalent to types of betrayals.

Going back to the use of dance now apprehended in a quasi-mythological dimension, the three versions by Renoir, Minnelli and Chabrol are clear copies faithful and unfaithful at the same time to the dance scene at Vaubyessard in Flaubert's text. They are translations or transpositions executed in the filmic medium by

directors sensitive and attentive to the implications and potential-
ities of the original, yet who follow other agendas as well. According to the cognitive and aesthetic mapping mentioned earlier, the
reader–spectator readily acknowledges that Emma's disavowal of
Charles is not to be found anywhere in Flaubert's text (although
the narrative voice does remark upon Charles's platitudinous conversation, and Emma does wonder at times why she got married).
In his rather stretching interpretive move, and in his very free
transposition, Renoir heightens a potential meaning in his own
reading of *Madame Bovary*. Minnelli's move is of a different order.
He chooses to push the characters' passions several notches as
Charles repeatedly tries to interrupt the dancers, as Emma leaves in
a huff, as a scandal breaks out. In his version the dance sequence
becomes an end in itself for a virtuoso *mise-en-scène* of glass-
shattering. (If the text presents two shattered window-panes, why
not three? And why not set it to the sound of music?) The translation is so free at this point that Minnelli may have left Flaubertian
paradigms and introduced, as noted earlier, the Fred Astaire and
Ginger Rogers paradigm. The reader–spectator recognises the
genesis of transformations and enjoys the film – but wonders about
code-switching in this hybrid genre.

Chabrol's translation is perhaps of the second type. He may have
studied too well Renoir's film and wanted to avoid his interpretive
move. Emma and Charles are not Renoir's tragic figures, nor are they
possibly Minnelli's passionate figures. Theirs is a far more nefarious
fate. For Flaubert was preoccupied with the weight of commonplace
ideas in the age of the triumph of the imbecilic petite bourgeoisie.
Flaubert's *Bouvard and Pécuchet* and *Dictionary of Commonplaces*
(both unfinished at his death in 1880) are to be read in tandem
with *Madame Bovary*.[13] In Chabrol's version, Charles's reply to
Emma's 'This is the most beautiful day of my life' as they leave
Vaubyessard is to complain about his tight shoes. In this, Chabrol is
strictly faithful to Flaubert: the world of the novel and of this film
is the world dominated by the rigorous description of the banal.

Notes

1. For an illustration of methods, see Alain J.J. Cohen 'Godard/Lang/
   Godard: the Film-within-the-Film', *American Journal of Semiotics*
   vol. 9, no. 4 (1992), pp. 115–30.

2. Sergei Eisenstein (1898–1948), one of the rare directors to be a theoretician of cinema as well, instructed young film-makers to study the inherent filmicity (visuality, montage, sound) within works of literature. He did not mention Flaubert (wasn't it too obvious?) but refers to Maupassant, Pushkin, Zola, and countless others. See his posthumous book S. Eisenstein, *Nonindifferent Nature* (Cambridge, 1987).

3. Gustave Flaubert, *Sentimental Education* (Harmondsworth, 1964 [1869]), p. 271.

4. Gustave Flaubert, *Madame Bovary* (Toronto, New York and London, 1959 [1857]), p. 129.

5. For the sake of narrative economy Minnelli has chosen to conflate the role of the dancing viscount with the later-appearing Rodolphe in Flaubert's text.

6. The prowess of performance may remind the historian of cinema of the musical comedies with Fred Astaire and Ginger Rogers, e.g. *Top Hat* (1935) *et al.*

7. In 1949 the Hays censorship code still prevailed in Hollywood. If there is a hint of the forthcoming McCarthy years by historical association, however, nothing in the film offers much elaboration on the subject.

8. I take here the opposite view to Brian McFarlane in *Novel to Film* (Oxford, 1996), p. 28.

9. Nobody would think that Robert Wilson had an obligation to be faithful to Shakespeare when he proposed a hallucinated reading of *Hamlet*, and Orson Welles's *Othello* (1951) is admirable despite the fact that he rewrites Shakespeare and ellides numerous verses. The stage director and the film director had different agendas.

10. The Italian title *Io ballo da sola* (I dance alone) was more evocative of the centrality of this unexplained dance motif.

11. See John Dryden, 'Preface to Ovid's *Epistles*' (1680) in A. Lefevere (ed.), *Translation/History/Culture* (London, 1992).

12. In an article devoted to the question of translation from one medium to another, see Alain J.J. Cohen, 'The Silence of the Lambs. Trasposizioni: romanzo – script – film', *Carte Semiotiche* no. 2 (September 1995), pp. 74–84. The research focused upon the extreme variants in the ending scene from novel (Lecter just writes a letter to Clarice) to screenplay (Lecter is about to begin his 'work' on a tied Dr Chilton) to finished film (Lecter jokes on the phone 'I'm going to have an old friend for dinner').

13. For my own elaboration, see Alain J.J. Cohen, 'The Passion for Gossip and the Power of Convention. Flaubert and Tarantino', in *Versus*, special issue: *Gossip. Bavardage. Pettegolezzo* (forthcoming 1998).

9 *The fiction is already there: writing and film in Blair's Britain*

Stuart Laing

A well-established means of considering the relationship between writing and cinema is through direct comparison of written texts and their filmed adaptations. A study of, for example, a novel and a film version would have value in its identification of the specific properties of each text, in being a case study of an adaptation task and in its illumination of the intrinsic technical possibilities and limitations of novel and film as specific art forms. Such a study would typically conclude either by specifying how the film adaptation had narrowed, sharpened or altered the core meanings of the novel or by stressing the importance of seeing the novel and film as separate works, each with its own integrity and to be judged without necessary reference to the other.

This essay takes much from this approach, but also differs from it in some substantial respects. For while academic criticism may wish to emphasise the specificity and separateness of individual filmic or literary texts, the way in which such narratives and stories circulate in our contemporary culture is often much less pure and is unaffected by concern for textual integrity. As with fairy-tale, myth or romance, the existence of different forms of the same story (novel, film, play, radio adaptation, etc.) creates a more generalised, somewhat imprecise, cultural object, the meaning and significance of which derives from the interaction and overlapping of meanings of the multiple versions, as well as from its place among more general cultural themes and symbolic forms. In particular, five adjacent areas of meaning construction will be of relevance here: those of novel (or autobiographical) text; film; published film-script;

press, publicity and media representation; and general cultural resonance.

The discussion here considers three films, *The English Patient*, *Fever Pitch* and *Crash* (each based on successful, or controversial, books), on general release in Britain in the spring and summer of 1997, just prior to or following the historic New Labour election landslide on 1 May. Each set of narratives is considered in turn, followed by some concluding comments on how these narratives contributed to, and gained meaning from, some broader cultural themes circulating within Britain in 1997 and 1998.

The English Patient

Michael Ondaatje's novel *The English Patient* won the Booker Prize, the pre-eminent British fiction award, in 1992, followed by paperback publication in 1993. It is written through the voice of an omniscient author, who has full access to the actions, thoughts and feelings of all the characters. From this perspective the central narrative (events in the spring and summer of 1945 in the Villa San Girolamo, a semi-derelict former nunnery turned temporary military hospital) is interleaved with the past lives of Almásy, the 'English patient', of Kip, a Sikh sapper, and (more fragmentarily) of Hana and Caravaggio, Canadian war exiles in Europe. Both the events narrated and the linguistic choices of the writing (through the language of the narrator and the characters, especially Almásy) are designed to allow a fluid interplay between four levels of significance: those of the eternal or elemental; the historical; the political and military present; and the personal. The power of the novel resides in the skill with which these four levels become mutually reinforcing and are all plausibly present within the realistic depiction of characters and events in situations of historical and personal extremity.

A sense of the elemental and eternal is sustained through the specific environments of the novel's events: the desert (and its metaphorical other – the sea), the winds (of the Sahara and of India), the thunder and lightning of Tuscany, the moon, the fires (of Almásy's crash, of the bombs and mines which Kip struggles to disarm, of Hiroshima), the carefully marked passage of spring and summer surrounding the villa. A long historical perspective is linked to this, especially through the device of Almásy's edition of Herodotus and his additional jottings and annotations: 'there were traditions he had discovered in Herodotus in which old warriors celebrated their loved ones by locating and holding them in whatever world makes them eternal – a colourful fluid, a song, a rock drawing'.[1] Almásy is driven by the search for ancient desert civilisations and their geographical topography, while the presence of medieval and Renaissance Italian religious, and military, icons and traditions underpins particularly Kip's experience of Italy. The cultural frameworks offered by the characters themselves also cross historical periods (Milton, Tolstoy, Pliny, Fenimore Cooper, Herodotus).

The present of the novel is one of extreme social dislocation and stasis – the moment between peace and war. All the characters have found the set trajectory of their lives disrupted in a time in which all national identities and norms are called into question. The 'English Patient' is not English and is an enemy spy; Kip's loyalty to the English values and cause is destroyed by the realisation of what the atomic bomb has done to Asian civilians. Hana loses her lover and her father; Caravaggio's identity as a thief is destroyed by the mutilation of his hands. Within these shifting perspectives personal identities are constructed and re-formed through a language and set of perspectives which might be seen as simplistically romantic and individualistic if they were not shown to be caused and validated by the environments, histories and the present experience of the villa's inhabitants. As Caravaggio, for example, remarks on the loss of their past lives, 'now there is hardly a world around them and they are forced back on themselves' (Ondaatje, p. 41).

It is the context of this kind of language and its demonstrated roots in the specific experience of the characters which gives substance to what would otherwise be the rhetorical hyperbole of extreme romantic and sexual desire between Almásy and Katherine:

All that is alive is the knowledge of future desire and want. What he would say he cannot say to this woman whose openness is like a wound, whose youth is not mortal yet. He cannot alter what he loves most in her, her lack of compromise, where the romance of the poems she loves still sits with ease in the real world. Outside these qualities he knows there is no order in the world.

(Ondaatje, p. 257)

The novel does not, however, simply offer this intensity of feeling (nor even the mutual seeking of human comfort of the parallel relationship of Hana and Kip) as some kind of intrinsic human good defeated by external forces. Both the origins of the relationships and their temporary nature are parts of the same pattern of experience, brought to a swift and shattering conclusion as the inhabitants of Hiroshima suffer the same fate as the English patient himself. Within the structure of the novel the task of the reader is to take the various blocks of information and sections of narrative and make comparisons and connections between present and past, between the different characters and between the levels of significance (with their various forms of language) and compose a pattern of meaning which will transcend that of any character and of the authorial voice itself.

The film, *The English Patient*, written and directed by Anthony Minghella, won nine Oscars in March 1997. While it keeps at the core of the narrative the key comparisons between the two settings of the North African desert and the Italian villa/monastery, and the two relationships of Almásy/Katherine and Hana/Kip, the film excludes some key elements of the novel's setting of context and also radically reshapes the plot. As Ondaatje himself has noted, 'the long roots of Hana's and Caravaggio's psyches, Kip's training in England, his reaction to the atomic bomb, and his eventual fate, will always remain in the country of the novel'.[2]

The film replaces these elements with new explanations for key events of the narrative – in such a way as to heighten the contrast between the demands of the contemporary political and military conflicts and the imperatives of individual relationships and desires. The plane in which Almásy crashes and is burned is now shot down by Germans (his own allies) rather than simply misfiring through disuse; Caravaggio's mutilation is directly caused by the success of Almásy's espionage rather than by his being caught as a thief; Madox's suicide is reported as being directly caused by his learning that his greatest friend, Almásy, has become a German spy, rather than by a more generalised depression about the advent of war. Almásy's personal dilemmas of loyalties and betrayals become sharper and more significant, as does the representation of the progress and demise of the relationship between Almásy and Katherine. Several key scenes in the film are not directly derived from the novel at all; these include the crash of the jeep in the desert which leads to Almásy and Katherine being together through the sandstorm, Clifton waiting all night in the taxi while his wife is with Almásy, and the episode in which British troops go through ordered Christmas festivities in the outdoor heat of the courtyard of the British ambassador's residence, while Almásy and Katherine make love with rough and hasty passion in the storeroom alongside.

This particular scene also illustrates how the film makes use of the capacity of the medium for simultaneous contrastive meaning, since the scenes are shot from inside the shade of the building so as to contain both the foreground of the darker interior settings of the lovers and the bright ordered formal proceedings of the military party. In the published film-script (which, unlike a published play-script, is not so much an instruction manual to be turned into a performance, as an attempt to provide a written equivalent of one definitive performance) Minghella's 'stage-directions' for this scene read: 'It's as if the world has stopped and there's only their passion, overwhelming reason and logic and rules' (Minghella, p. 85). This comment indicates how the film concentrates the four levels of interacting meaning of the novel into a powerful binary opposition between the individual/eternal and the constraints of the social order; it also indicates how, in the overall construction of *The English Patient* as, in Ondaatje's words, 'a communal story made by many hands' (Minghella, p. ix), the printed screenplay has its own distinctive part to play in specifying particular meanings in a way which neither the film itself nor the novel can do.

Equally Minghella's film contains elements which the screenplay cannot capture. The film, unlike the novel, uses a circular narrative with identical opening and closing scenes of the plane with Almásy and the dead Katherine high over the desert. The image of Katherine all in white – the white silk of the parachute with which Almásy covers her to carry her into the Cave of Swimmers to meet her death and which is still clothing her as he keeps his promise to carry her out years later – was selected, on British release, by many reviewers as the defining image of the film. The whiteness is both that of the bridal gown (being carried over the threshold) and of the shroud, which together underlie the dominant message in press advertising and on the cover of the subsequent British video release: 'In memory, love lives forever'.

Fever Pitch

Nick Hornby's autobiographical *Fever Pitch* was published in 1992 when it won the William Hill Sports Book of the Year Award. *Fever Pitch* is presented by Hornby as the anatomy of an obsession, 'obsessives are denied any kind of perspective on their own passion. This, in a sense, is what defines an obsessive (and serves to explain why so few of them recognise themselves as such). . . . *Fever Pitch* is an attempt to gain some kind of an angle on my obsession.'[3] The author then promises to disprove the rule that an obsessive cannot understand his own obsession by offering a new form of revelation. The form is that of an autobiographical journal (each two- or three-page section being generated by memories of a particular soccer match which Hornby saw between 1968 and 1992), but one structured through reflection and re-interpretation of the past as much as by the wish to recapture it on its own terms. Therefore while there are developing, if weak, narratives – of the author's progress through school, university and adulthood, of the changes in British football, of the cyclical progress, decline and triumphs of Arsenal – the core is the thoughts, feelings, self-analysis and emotional development (or retardation) of the author. The book essentially ends where it began, describing 'a nil-nil draw, against a nothing team, in a meaningless game, in front of a restive, occasionally angry but for the most part wearily tolerant crowd, in the freezing January cold . . .' (Hornby, p. 247).

Around this core of personal confession are the cultural worlds within which this psycho-drama is played out. The general social, political and cultural history of the UK from 1968 to 1990 serves as a backdrop, with particular changes in the world of football as a microcosm. Hornby comments on changes in styles of play, costs of attendance, the effects of the Heysel and Hillsborough tragedies, the consequent debates on ID cards and the creation of all-seater stadia. Foregrounded here is the experience of supporting one club, but particularly of the significance of regular attendance as part of the crowd:

> What do I imagine would happen to me if I didn't go to Highbury for just one evening. . . . I am frightened that in the next game, the one after the one I have missed, I won't understand something that's going on, a chant or a crowd's antipathy to one of the

players; and so the place I know best in the world, the one spot
outside my own home where I feel I belong absolutely and unques-
tionably, will have become alien to me.

(Hornby, pp. 214–15)

The result is a text with access to the inner life of only one character, but nevertheless peopled by a densely referenced cultural
context: the author's family (especially his father) and the suburban
milieu of Maidenhead (contrasted with the partly mythicised setting
of North London), the Arsenal players through different eras, who
stand as metaphors for various aspects of success, failure, persist-
ence or ambition, and an eclectic list of popular and high cultural
references – film (Woody Allen, Jane Fonda, Schwarzenegger, James
Bond, *Kes*), literature (*King Lear*, Martin Amis, Rushdie, Germaine
Greer), music (Led Zeppelin, Dire Straits, Jagger, ballet). *Fever Pitch*
is consciously a commentary on how such people as the author
might position themselves culturally in terms of the past and present.
There is first the culture rejected: 'And what is suburban middle-
class culture anyway? Jeffrey Archer and *Evita*, Flanders and Swann
and the Goons, Adrian Mole and Merchant-Ivory, *Francis Durbridge
Presents* . . . and John Cleese's silly walk . . .' (Hornby, p. 49).

The particular claim of *Fever Pitch* to offer itself and its values
as a replacement for such culture is closely linked to its role as a
definer of masculinity and the New Man in a consciously post-
feminist world:

It's easy to forget that we can pick and choose. Theoretically it is
possible to like football, soul music and beer, for example, but to
abhor breast-grabbing and bottom pinching (or, one has to concede,
vice versa); one can admire Muriel Spark and Brian Robson. Inter-
estingly it is men who seem to be more aware than women of the
opportunities for mix n'match.

(Hornby, p. 80)

This use of cultural reference points, particularly the mixing of
different cultural worlds and levels, is a central feature of how the
writing seeks to uncover and present the distinctive experience of
the obsessive, and then to explain it – 'my coolness towards all
things Arsenal had nothing to do with rites of passage, or girls, or
Jean-Paul Sartre, or Van Morrison, and quite a lot to do with the
ineptitude of the Kidd–Stapleton strikeforce' (Hornby, p. 97). A

more extended example is the taking of the popular journalistic cliché of an intense moment of sporting success being better than sex and endorsing it on the basis of a detailed argument: 'Maybe if I hadn't made love for eighteen years, and had given up hope of doing so for another eighteen, and then suddenly out of the blue, an opportunity presented itself . . . maybe then it would be possible to recreate an approximation of that Anfield moment' (Hornby, p. 230). It is with these modern metaphysical conceits (yoking together supposedly disparate areas of experience) and metaphors of extremity that Hornby seeks to persuade the reader of the significance of his experience. In doing so he begins to reflect and create a new cultural landscape of 1990s Britain.

Both the appearance and success of *Fever Pitch* as a new kind of writing in a new genre were dependent on ground laid by the soccer fanzine in the late 1980s. The language, audience and approach of the fanzines (over 600 had come in to existence by 1992), especially the national *When Saturday Comes*, together with the resurgence of soccer in Britain following the 1990 World Cup, almost certainly helped persuade publishers that a book such as *Fever Pitch* would find a readership. The book in fact speaks to two sets of readers. In part it is designed for a certain type of male readers to recognise themselves, but also to allow others (especially women) to gain an understanding. *Fever Pitch* was published in paperback in 1993 and by 1997 had sold half a million copies.

As Hornby says in introducing the published screenplay of the 1997 film, 'Because it is in effect an autobiography, the book has a narrative of sorts, but it is just as much a book of essays as it is a rites-of-passage memoir, and the timescale, the football, the cast of thousands and the structure all suggested that the book would not make for a straightforward adaptation'.[4] The first two tasks for Hornby (who wrote the screenplay himself) were then to re-construct the core of meaning of *Fever Pitch* as fiction and to create a plot. The result is a film structured around a strong and explicit series of oppositions with two massive variations from the shape of the book – the focus of the story on one season in 1988–89 and the introduction of a female lead character (Sarah) to balance the male lead (now named Paul). This latter point significantly shifts the film away from the dominance of the single perspective and voice of the book since, even though there is a considerable presence of Paul's voice-over (which allows him to retain the dominant perspective), the existence of many scenes between Sarah and her friend Jo allows an alternative perspective on Paul's obsession to develop. In effect some of Hornby's ability, in the book, to pre-empt any criticism by intense self-awareness and irony is split off into the female characters' amazement at Paul's obsession with Arsenal, with Paul becoming more unremittingly myopic in his denial of the needs of others (particularly Sarah), thus setting up a sharp conflict needing resolution through the narrative.

The two parallel plots (of Arsenal's progress to their eventual League championship and of Paul and Sarah's romance) illustrate this first opposition around which the film is structured. Secondly the chronology of the book and the story of Hornby's childhood apprenticeship as an Arsenal supporter and its roots in his family history is told through flashbacks, frequently with voice-overs which contrast past and present in Paul's life. Thirdly the film uses very clear male/female oppositions – Paul's obsession with football and untidy flat, and apparent valuing of soccer over romance and even family responsibility, against Sarah's tidiness, concern for personal relationships and plea for Paul to behave as a mature adult. A fourth opposition is made possible by the decision to make both the main characters English teachers, thus setting up an opposition between the school as the site of official cultural values (whether English literature or general school discipline) and popular culture as the site of authenticity and spontaneity. Paul's support for Arsenal is presented, through his relationship with Robert (a pupil whose father has left home), as a means of providing genuine personal help going beyond the obligations of duty. Finally Paul's (at times) extreme selfish behaviour towards Sarah is presented as (and almost justified by) a depth and intensity of feeling which is to be set against the dull conformity of those who have no impossible dreams – 'maybe there's a bit of you that's gone missing somewhere. Maybe everyone should want something they've always wanted' (Hornby, screenplay, p. 124).

The film uses the concluding match of Arsenal's 1988–89 season (the achievement in the last minute of an unlikely win at Liverpool) to resolve all these oppositions in a single event. All the characters of the film are shown watching and sharing in the victory. As Sarah becomes completely involved in the victory celebrations outside the ground, Paul's voice-over which closes the film reveals that the end of this eighteen-year wait for Arsenal success has moderated the scale of his obsession. The unifying of the private and the public through the communal street celebrations suggests a legitimation of popular culture (soccer and the kind of popular music which is central to the film), especially when presented through the knowing self-awareness which the film itself embodies. *Fever Pitch* provides, then, both through its messages and its form (which, through the dominance of interiors, dialogue and close-up shots, is more like good British television drama than the expansive feature-film settings and style of *The English Patient*), a celebration of a new kind of cultural synthesis within England.

Crash

J.G. Ballard's novel *Crash* was first published in 1973 and is recognisably a product of its period. Like most of Ballard's novels, *Crash* is not formally complex. The whole novel is narrated through a single first-person voice who offers an easily comprehensible series of events in a simple chronology – the novel begins in a present (after the death of Vaughan, the main character) to which all the events of the novel return. There is a gradual psychological and physical deterioration in the main male characters, culminating in the last meeting of Vaughan and the narrator during an acid trip (the only point at which the consciousness of the narrator, as opposed to the events narrated, enters the surreal).

Crash depicts an urban world, recognisable and very precisely located on the western edges of London, but on the edge of a new future. It is a world of airports, TV commercials, film and photography, endemic traffic-jams on a landscape of urban highways, and of sexual obsessions and encounters divorced from any traditional familial constraints, romantic associations or even simple lust. Centring all this is the reality and symbol of the car crash with its interaction of machine and human body – the body becoming refigured as a machine as the narrator and Vaughan propel themselves into an obsession with observing, rehearsing, recording and repeating crashes and the remakings of the human body (through damage or sexual activity) which accompany them. For the narrator ('Ballard') the crash (specifically his own crash) is a key to the 'remaking of the commonplace'[5] which reveals the nature of the modern world – 'a unique vision of this machine landscape' (Ballard, p. 54).

The novel's impact depends certainly on the number and variety of car crashes and sexual encounters, but perhaps more on the particular forms of language and cultural references used. Perhaps the most common adjective is 'stylized' – a word used repeatedly to distance the descriptions of the sexual encounters and the obsession with cars from being seen as the expression of some natural spontaneous emotion. The arrangement of bodies within cars (whether for sexual acts or in the aftermath of crashes) is described in a language which combines formal medical terminology with the vocabulary of technical drawing (another favourite word is 'angular'). The narrator reflects on his crash as 'the failure of the technical relationship between my own body, the assumptions of the skin and the engineering structure which supported it' (Ballard, p. 58).

While the narrator's feelings may be stated, there is no extensive metaphorical language to describe or embody emotion. As the narrator remarks, it is a matter of 'conceptualized acts abstracted from all feeling' (Ballard, p. 129) presented through 'an exact language of pain and sensation' (Ballard, p. 90). Equally the society presented is one without traditional cultural reference points; these are replaced by the icons of modern American popular culture, especially those of Hollywood, stardom and sudden death – James Dean, Jayne Mansfield, President Kennedy, Marilyn Monroe and, above all, Elizabeth Taylor, the central figure of Vaughan's fantasy of amalgamating the worlds of the photographic image, the famous, sexual orgasm and the fatal car crash. While the language itself is not designed to replicate or evoke the sensation and depth of visual experience, the world described is one almost overrun by mechanical reproduction – it is the obsession with the recording and repetition (for the camera) of crashes, as much as the crash itself, which dominates the minds of both Vaughan and the narrator.

Introducing the republication of the book in 1995 Ballard saw the social tendencies identified by *Crash* in the early 1970s as having only intensified: 'We live in a world ruled by fictions of every kind – mass-merchandizing, advertising, politics conducted as a branch of advertising, the pre-empting of any original response to experience by the television screen' (Ballard, p. 4). This comment suggests some of the aspects of the novel which made adaptation rather more complex and problematic than the simplicity of its narrative form might have suggested. In fact Cronenberg's screenplay is much closer to the original novel than is the case with the other two films already discussed. The core of the narrative remains intact, and all the main characters retain their structural positions in the plot and patterns of character involvement. Much of the dialogue is directly copied from the novel and even the extensive 'stage directions' in the published screenplay are typically close approximations to the descriptive language of the novel, which is particularly concerned with precise depictions of the physical relations between body and machine in sexual encounters and car crashes. Perhaps the only major shifts from the novel's structure are the complete omission of references to Elizabeth Taylor and the introduction of an ending in which 'Ballard' and Catherine are seen as consciously attempting to cause each other's death as part of a final consummation.

It was, however, precisely because the novel was significantly concerned with the nature of visual representation in mass society (television, film, photography) that close reproduction of its arguments and scenes on film itself generates an extra set of meanings and a further level of impact. Cronenberg writes of his intention in 'replicating the tone of the book, which was absolutely unrelenting and confrontational'[6] and notes that Ballard (the author) 'says that I go even further than the book, that delights me. I don't know how accurate it is though. I think it might just be a difference in the media. The immediacy of movie reality might do that on its own' (Cronenberg, p. xi). The implication of this comment for *Crash* may not be so much the obvious contrast between the different denotative features of a visual and a written medium as the shift from Ballard's deliberately abstract and de-personalised language of description of sexual encounters to the necessarily greater sensuousness and physical presence of the rough, uncomfortable and obsessive sexual encounters of the film. In particular the film's opening caused a good deal of comment, as Cronenberg noted in an interview in March 1997:

> I also think that there is a formal problem here. The film opens with three sex scenes in a row, and there are other moments in the film where there are sequential sex scenes. I think the only place

where people have seen this before is in pornography, and therefore they can't make the leap that, while this is a film that might use a structure that is familiar from pornography, it's still not a pornographic film. They confuse the structure with the intent.[7]

The way in which the film *Crash* came to acquire cultural meanings in the UK during 1997 had in fact much more to do with debates about its fitness for public viewing than with any direct consideration of its aesthetic or entertainment qualities. Having won the Special Jury Prize at the 1996 Cannes Film Festival (and generated some notoriety among the British popular press), it took five months to gain a certificate for general release from the British Board of Film Classification (BBFC), but remained under a ban from some local authorities (including Westminster where the major West End cinemas are situated). A certificate for video release was not granted until spring 1998. The nature of the concerns generated and the range of attributed meanings for the film can be summarised briefly by considering divergent views taken from just one *Observer* feature article by Andrew Anthony, on James Ferman, the director of the BBFC in March 1997. For Anthony the film is 'the story of two lovers whose sexual experimentation leads them to seek their gratification among the carnage of car crashes'; for a Dr Britton, a forensic psychologist commissioned by the BBFC, it is 'wall-to-wall pornography. It should never be released. No one should see it'; for Ferman, 'the message of the film . . . is not to have promiscuous sex'; and finally unnamed MPs are reported as saying '*Crash* might lead some viewers to cause car accidents for sexual kicks'.[8]

The range of views here as to the film's supposed content and likely effect indicates a significant difference from *The English Patient* and *Fever Pitch* in how cultural impact took place. In the case of the latter two films there was general critical consensus as to their intentions and likely effects; any disagreement revolved around the degree of aesthetic success and the level of seriousness of the messages. With *Crash* the occasion of the film generated both entirely opposing views as to its messages on sexual behaviour and car culture, and a sharp resurgence of a recurrent debate on artistic freedom, censorship and the boundaries of acceptability within English culture. As for the film itself, it may be that the observations of Holly Hunter, who plays one of the female leads in the film, provide as clear-sighted a view as any: 'It's describing a bleak, destructive, non-committed life those people are living. But they are struggling to connect – although they don't know how to do it any more. It's as if their humanity is missing. . . . I felt the movie was in some way a tragedy.'[9]

Conclusion: Britain 1997–98

The speech in *Crash* which caused most offence embodies the philosophy of Vaughan: 'the car crash is a fertilizing rather than a destructive event – a liberation of sexual energy that mediates the sexuality of those who have died with an intensity impossible in any other form' (Cronenberg, p. 42). In the aftermath of the extraordinary intensity of emotion accompanying the traumatic and tragic death in a car crash of Diana, Princess of Wales on 31 August 1997, such language, while remaining no less disturbing, has now further resonances beyond those of the deaths of the public figures (such as James Dean, Jayne Mansfield and John Kennedy) on which the novel and film make repeated play. Certainly it is clear that the scenario of the death of lovers (one an internationally famous beauty and media personality and both with varied sexual histories) in a car crash at speed, with photographers in chase and among the first to arrive at the scene – and the unanticipated level of personal grief felt by many, as well as the collective media hysteria – suggests not so much any uncanny predictive power of Ballard or Cronenberg, but rather the accuracy of Ballard's perception of key symbolic features of our modern consciousness.

The death of a beautiful English woman (a woman who is the very symbol of romantic passion) in a crash abroad also resonated with *The English Patient*. Katherine's last words – as Almásy leaves her in the cave – are a plea to be returned home,

> I don't want to die in the desert. I've always had a rather elaborate funeral in mind, with particular hymns. Very English. And I know exactly where I want to be buried. In our garden where I grew up. With a view of the sea. So promise me you'll come back for me.
>
> (Minghella, p. 144)

Katherine's words are almost a series of instructions for the Princess of Wales's elaborate and formal public funeral, with Elton

John's 'Goodbye England's rose' being as 'Very English' as anyone could have wished; this followed by burial on the island covered by flowers and in the park where Diana walked as a child, surrounded by water. Again this comparison is made not to suggest either some predictive power or any conscious copying, but rather to refer to the common reference points both the film and the public response to the Princess's death touched on in their compositions of the narratives of high romantic tragedy.

There are no such direct connections between these events and the more mundane world of *Fever Pitch*; yet Hornby's synthesis of the new masculinity, the acknowledgement of strong emotion and the endorsement of popular culture have perhaps most in common with the general style and self-image of Blair's new Britain. Certainly the televised scenes in May 1998 of Arsenal fans celebrating their club's achievement of their first 'double' since 1971 bore a very strong resemblance to the closing scenes of *Fever Pitch* recreating the 1989 celebrations of the first championship since 1971. A comparison of the two sequences of footage as televisual events calls to mind again Ballard's comments that,

> we live in a world ruled by fictions of every kind . . . the pre-empting of any original response to experience by the television screen. We live inside an enormous novel. It is now less and less necessary for the writer to invent the fictional content of his novel. The fiction is already there. . . .
>
> (Ballard, p. 4)

It is with this awareness of how meanings circulate within our culture that we should understand the relations between imaginative writing and cinema and the realities which they both seek to represent.

Notes

1. Michael Ondaatje, *The English Patient* (London, 1993), p. 248. Further page references are cited in the text.
2. Michael Ondaatje, 'Foreword' in Anthony Minghella, *The English Patient* (London, 1997), p. viii. Further page references are cited in the text.
3. Nick Hornby, *Fever Pitch* (London, 1994), pp. 10–11. Further page references are cited in the text.

4. Nick Hornby, *Fever Pitch the Screenplay* (London, 1997), p. 7. Further page references are cited in the text.

5. J.G. Ballard, *Crash* (London, 1995), p. 52. Further page references are cited in the text.

6. David Cronenberg, *Crash* (London, 1996), p. xvi. Further page references are cited in the text.

7. David Cronenberg, in the *Guardian*, 31 March 1997.

8. Andrew Anthony, feature article on *Crash* in the *Observer*, 30 March 1997.

9. Holly Hunter, quoted in the *Guardian*, 6 June 1997.

10 Public spaces and private narratives – the plays and films of David Hare

Stephen Lacey

For some time, all useful ideas in art have been extremely sophisticated. Like the idea that everything is what it is, and not another
thing. A painting is a painting. Sculpture is sculpture. A poem is a
poem, not prose. Etcetera. And the complementary idea: a painting
can be 'literary' or sculptural, a poem can be prose, theatre can
emulate and incorporate cinema, cinema can be theatrical.

Susan Sontag, *Film and Theatre* (1966)

David Hare is a particularly good test-case for anyone wishing to
assess the validity of Sontag's second 'useful idea'. A prolific writer
for, and director in, the theatre, with a career that has spanned
over 27 years and shows no sign of faltering, Hare has also directed films and written screenplays, some of which are adaptations
of his stage plays, and has also written for television. His theatre
work has been seen as 'filmic' (although his film work has not been
seen, by and large, as 'theatrical', which in the language of film
criticism would be a more damning epithet). It is certainly true
that the lines of demarcation between the two media frequently
blur in Hare's work. On the one hand, ideas, motifs and arguments
are often carried across plays and films written/produced close to
each other: *Plenty* (1978) is linked thematically to *Licking Hitler*
(1978) in its pessimistic view of the legacy of the Second World
War, for example; and *Strapless* (1989), *Paris by Night* (1988)
and *The Secret Rapture* (in both play and film form) are linked in
their depiction of the consequences of Thatcherism. On the other
hand, there is a similarity of technique, with certain approaches to
narrative construction, that, whichever medium they are associated

with, can be traced in both films and plays. If Hare's plays are considered filmic, it is often because they seem to employ forms of montage in their narrative construction as well as in the composition of images. And there are distinctive generic patterns and characteristics, particularly those that owe a debt to film noir, that infuse his work in both film and theatre.

Part of the reason why Hare should be so at home in different media is that he did not come to the theatre along the same path as many of his contemporaries, but was much more indebted to film than to either mainstream or alternative theatre. In an interview, Hare explained his rejection of much contemporary theatre as a rejection of a particular kind of naturalism, 'when I grew up, the stage was the prisoner of the closed set, the one-room play, the psychological drama etc.'.[1] It was the cinema that excited him, especially the European cinema of the French New Wave and British popular genres. What he got from his exposure to film was a sense of engagement with the contemporary world that lay beyond the narrow, class-bound observances of much West End theatre – European rather than British in its sensibilities. Hare commented: 'It was from the cinema that I got all the richness, the sense of life's passage, history on the hoof, you know, that you went to Truffaut or Louis [Malle] or Godard for' (Zeifman, p. 19).

The cinema also offered a more open and fluid approach to story-telling that he was anxious to exploit in the theatre: 'why shouldn't it [the theatre] have the same freedom as the cinema to move where it wants to, to show the passage of time boldly? . . . Why shouldn't you tell stories that are just as melodramatic as the stories the movies tell? Why shouldn't the fun of the cinema be on the stage?' (Zeifman, p. 19). This was linked to Hare's sense that, as a writer acutely aware of his own historical context, the stories he wished to tell required a different kind of narrative: his attraction to the formal possibilities opened up by film 'coincided with a way of looking at things which was not suited to box sets' (Zeifman, p. 19).

Hare is, in general terms, of the Left, and his radicalism is no less a force in his work for being often idiosyncratic and against the grain of much orthodox Left politics in post-war Britain. As the examples quoted above suggest, both his plays and his films can be seen as responses to two defining historical moments, that of 1945 (the Labour government of Clement Atlee and the creation of what is often referred to as the post-war settlement) and of 1979 (the election of a Conservative government under Margaret Thatcher, which led to a progressive unravelling of that settlement). Hare saw the journey from 1945 as a remorseless process of loss and disillusion with the post-war world, and these can be traced through nearly of all his work in this period. They are etched into the plays that cut a swathe through post-war history, like *Plenty* (1978) and *Brassneck*, as well as those that cut deep into a particular historical moment, like *Knuckle* (1974), *Teeth 'N' Smiles* (1975), *Licking Hitler* and *A Map of the World* (1982) (which pursues similar concerns in an international context).

In the 1980s and early 1990s, his work was created in the shadow of Thatcher's victory and explores the fall-out from that cataclysmic event. He has been particularly attracted to the distinctive characters of the Thatcher era; writing about *Paris by Night* (1988), Hare noted that 'there has been a considerable body of plays about the economic results of Thatcherism [but] almost nothing about the characteristics and personalities of those who have ruled over us'.[2] Clara, the powerful and attractive MEP in *Paris by Night*, and Marion in *The Secret Rapture*, who is a government minister, are good examples. Hare has also been concerned with the way that British institutions have adapted to the Thatcherite onslaught on their legitimacy. This project, which has been pursued primarily in the theatre, embraces Hare's and Howard Brenton's attack on the supine liberal response to the destruction of press freedom heralded by the Murdoch revolution, *Pravda* (1984); his 1990s trilogy of plays for the Royal National Theatre, *Racing Demon* (1989), which examined the Church of England; *Murmuring Judges* (1991), on the institutions and processes of justice and the law; and *Absence of War* (1993), which followed the Labour Party through a failed election campaign.

We noted earlier that, as well as making films, Hare is often said to be writing plays that are 'filmic'. Notions of the 'theatrical' and the 'filmic' are notoriously slippery, their meanings often owing much more to the context in which they are used than to innate properties of the media themselves. There are two particular senses in which Hare's plays should be considered filmic. The first is to do with the way that Hare has chosen to confront the problem of the spatial restrictions associated with the stage. Film, it is sometimes claimed, has a freedom that is denied theatre; as

Raymond Williams has argued, the film camera is not constrained by the four walls of the naturalist box set, but can move out into the world that lies beyond and represent it directly.[3] 'Opening out' the narrative is still the dominant strategy adopted when a play is transferred onto the screen. Film can 'show' a society rather than simply refer to it metonymically, and this is clearly a gain for documentary realism of the sort that, say, underpinned northern, working-class cinema in the late 1950s and 1960s (much of it adapted from successful stage drama). ·

However, it was in the theatre, rather than film, that Hare, like many of his contemporaries, confronted the inherited problems of the 'box set' play. Set against the act/scene structure of the intensive, tightly focused naturalist play, with its single playing space, condensed time-span and limited range of action, Hare has adopted an approach that is more episodic, representing a wider field of action and setting, and often covering an extended time-span. Hare's plays move between the public and private, the domestic and the institutional, only rarely accepting the restrictions of the single-set space, as in *Skylight* (1995), and often disrupting a conventional chronology in the process. The opening three scenes of *Plenty*, for example, move from a Knightsbridge flat in 1962, to a field in France in 1947, to the British Embassy in Brussels; in *Racing Demon*, which concerns the crisis of conscience of a Church of England minister, Lionel Espy, Hare contrasts the domestic interior of Lionel's home with the public spaces of church, Synod and the lobby of the Savoy Hotel; and in *Murmuring Judges*, about the operation of the criminal justice system, the action moves between settings including a courtroom, the Hall at Lincoln's Inn, a prison cell and the Crush Bar at the Royal Opera House. Such an approach may be termed filmic (and has certainly been termed Brechtian) and is based on the primacy of action and situation, which is often common to both the theatre and cinema. As Hare has noted, 'the movement of a play is like the principle of film-cutting – you must not cut until something has happened'.[4]

The second way in which the filmic is important to Hare's plays is associated with the concept of montage.[5] That this is purely 'filmic' is open to question (Sergei Eisenstein, with whom the idea of montage is normally associated, actually developed the concept in the theatre before applying it to film). Hare's use of montage is complex, and it produces effects that are sometimes to be read as cinematic, and at other times are essentially, or simultaneously, theatrical. This has been particularly true since the production of *Plenty* at the National Theatre in 1978, after which Hare has worked predominantly in large, well-resourced theatres, with the capacity to deploy formidable new lighting and stage technologies. This has led to a fluid process of staging (indicated in the published texts, and not simply imposed by the production) that has aimed at combining the representation of a variety of different settings with complex and fully realised (though not always 'realistic') designs. The technique employed in *The Secret Rapture*, for example, is to overlap scenes, allowing each one to bleed into its predecessor, often by bringing on characters who are heard by the audience before they are seen. The stage directions at the end of Act 2 Scene 5, which is set in Isobel and Irwin's new offices, read as follows:

> Before they [Isobel and Irwin] can leave, we hear the sound of Marion's voice as she approaches from the back. The scenery changes as the others leave, and we are in Tom's office. . . . Tom is already at his desk to greet his wife. . . .[6]

The effect is one that is reminiscent of the cinema, where a common technique is to allow the soundtrack from one scene to play over that which precedes it.

However, montage of this sort is theatrical as well. One of the most striking examples of the way that Hare montages scenes and images can be found at the end of Act 1 Scene 7 of *Murmuring Judges*, where there is a complex cross-cutting between three separate scenes, the first set in a police station, the second in a prison cell and the third on the staircase outside the Crush Bar at the Royal Opera House. The scene has a particular importance as it comes at the end of the first act, and brings a temporary resolution to three separate narrative threads, focusing on three characters who are at the centre of each location: DC Barry (in the police station), Gerard, the prisoner (in the cell), and Irina, his lawyer (at the Opera). The effect of this sequence is to encourage the audience to place each of the three characters in relation to each other, to judge the nature of the dilemmas they face in the context provided by the other two, and in this way, to connect up the separate parts of the system of justice in a single image.

Hare has argued that: 'What theatre can do are those extra-ordinary collisions of the kind that you get in *Murmuring Judges*, which *only* theatre can deliver' and the scene described above is clearly theatrical rather than filmic, even if the technique initially connotes 'cinema' (Zeifman, p. 7). Theatrical in this sense refers to the way that space is used; each scene is occurring simultaneously, and visibly, on different parts of the stage, with the power of control over what the audience may focus on relinquished in a way that does not normally happen in the cinema. Although the dialogue moves between locations, directing attention at any given moment, the audience has a choice of viewpoint normally only available in the theatre; it has, for example, the freedom to choose to look at one scene whilst listening to another, and to take in two different spheres of action at the same time.

So far we have been mainly concerned with some of the inter-connections between the theatrical and the cinematic in Hare's plays: but what of his films? Given Hare's success as a playwright and the obvious theatricality of his plays, it is relevant to ask why he should have turned to film-making in the 1980s. That he should do so is due to several reasons, not the least of which was the existence of the new opportunities for film-making created by the establishment of Channel 4, the independent television company with a policy of supporting new British film-making. It was also to do with the particular way that Hare views film, and how this relates to his project as a writer.

We noted earlier that the narrative fluidity that film permits is often used to show society in its operations – that it is social, often realist (and at one extreme documentary) in its effect. However, Hare sees the potential of film differently; film is interesting to him not because it captures the external, public world better than theatre but because it can capture the workings of memory and the sub-jective consciousness, the interior life and the a-logical patterning of dreams. 'In any narrative in which dream plays a large part', Hare has written, 'film wins hands down.'[7] In Hare's films, as in his plays, memory is often of a past that is irrevocably lost, and is the subjective parallel to the sense of historical loss that we have already noted. There is a very telling moment in the film version of *The Secret Rapture*, in which the central character, Isobel, is look-ing at a home movie of her family taken by her father, whose death she is mourning. Isobel reaches out and touches the screen, as if to reclaim a past that eludes her. It is a gesture that turns the movie into a metaphor for the dual nature of film; it is 'present' at the moment it is screened, yet, in preserving the past, it is also 'burdened with memory' in Sontag's memorable phrase.[8]

Hare's characters are often similarly burdened with memory, and he uses the narrative fluidity of film to connect a subjective, interior landscape to the determinants of social context. *Wetherby* is a particularly good example. At the centre of the film is a suicide, committed by John Morgan, at the home of Jean Travers, a woman he had only just met. The suicide occurs early in the film, and much of the rest of the main narrative is concerned with unravelling the motivation for, and the significance of, the event for everyone touched by it, especially Jean. The main narrative line concerns the investigation, but this is intercut with flashbacks, which re-construct Morgan's arrival at the town and the circumstances by which he, and the girl he is following, arrive at Jean's door. This narrative is also intercut with the story, which is partly a memory, of Jean's passionate relationship with a young soldier, who is eventually killed in Malaya in the early 1950s. To lay out the narrative in this way does not capture the complexity with which it actually unfolds, since the film constantly moves between these different narrative strands. Cutting is often related to the inner lives of the characters, especially Jean, rather than being motivated by the demands of narrative clarity; it is the deep emotions stirred by Morgan's suicide, which threatens to overwhelm her, that trigger her memories. It is a film that attempts to give shape to what Hare has termed the contrast between 'the ordinariness of people's lives [and] the operatic passions of their unspoken feelings' (Hare, p. 130).

The view of his films that Hare offers above is one that connects to what he sees as a new emphasis in his work, one which relates to the 'secular spirituality', which animates both *The Secret Rapture* (in play form at least) and *Racing Demon*, but which is particularly to be found in his films. This points towards a source of motivation for his characters that is independent of social and political determinants. 'I've found myself in *Wetherby*, in *The Secret Rapture* and in *Strapless* drawn more to feeling that there's something which isn't just what we're conditioned by', he confessed to an interviewer; 'If a writer doesn't have a sense of the other, by which I mean spirit or soul, I don't want to know'.[9]

This suggests a radical departure from the forms and politics of Hare's drama; it is, however, not so much a departure as a refocusing of elements that had always been present. Threaded through the political, moral and ideological actions and arguments of all his work has always been a parallel concern with interiority and the subjective, with the determining power of emotion and the irrational, which is often placed 'outside' history and in tension with it. This tension is not always reconciled; one of the difficulties with *Plenty* (and a source of its emotional power), which the film version does not resolve, is that it is not always possible to 'explain' Susan's choices and the despair that they bring, in terms of the socio-economic context against which her personal drama is played out. It is not so much that there is a dialectic between the personal and the social, but rather that the personal is played out in a political/historical context that delimits the possibilities for action; it is a liberal rather than a Marxist view of the relationship between human beings and the world they inhabit.

Much of the interior world of Hare's plays is conceived in sexual terms. Hare has drawn attention to his fascination with the transformation of everyday reality produced by sexual desire and love: 'the view of the world it [romantic love] provides, the dislocation it offers, is the most intense experience that many people know on earth'.[10] It is the compressed, inexplicable and disorientating power of love that makes Anna, the heroine of *Licking Hitler*, remain steadfastly committed to Archie, the man who violently deflowered her. Love is equally important as a source of transformative power in his later work, especially *Strapless*, in which the central character, Lillian, is liberated through her love for a man, Raymond, who lives in a permanent romance. In a much more optimistic film than *Licking Hitler*, Lillian's transformation is both personal and political; she becomes both accepting of her need to be herself, and of her sister Amy, who becomes pregnant, and takes an active role in the campaign to resist budget cuts in the hospital in which she works.

Hare's search to find a narrative form in which to explore the subjective and the interior world and relate it to the public, social one has extended to his use of genre. Hare has never been an easy writer to identify in generic terms, but several of the films he has made – notably *Paris by Night* and *The Secret Rapture* – owe a debt to one of the more enduring of Hollywood genres, film noir.

Also, *Knuckle*, an early stage play, is a self-conscious re-working of the noir thriller format, and gains much of its energy from the transposition of noir characters and situations to the English Home Counties.

Film noir is the name given retrospectively to a group of films made, roughly, between the end of the Second World War and the late 1950s (although there have more recent attempts to fashion noir to a new age), many of which were adapted from 'hard-boiled' detective fiction written before the war. The world of film noir is dark, nihilistic – often misogynistic – and set in an urban landscape, in which violence, crime and corruption are foregrounded. Noir films do not constitute a genre in any strict sense, nor is the term confined entirely to thrillers. As Michael Walker has argued, 'film noir is not simply a certain type of crime movie, but also a generic field; a set of elements and features which may be found in a range of different sorts of film'.[11] These elements are: a distinctive visual style (the city, shot at night and often in the rain, the lighting dominated by neon, car head-lamps and fractured by shadows); recurrent narrative patterns (normally crime and the pursuit of its perpetrators, an activity that is by no means guaranteed of success, and in which the investigator may be as culpable as the criminal); and character types (the 'seeker-hero' – often a detective, the 'victim hero' or the 'femme fatale'). The world of film noir is an erotic one, in which sexuality, violence and death are intertwined; as Borde and Chaumeton have noted, 'a Noir film is a film of death'.[12]

Like most recent noir writer/directors, Hare does not simply reproduce the specific world of film noir but rather works within, and extends, the generic field it maps. Hare is clearly drawn to the expressive potential of noir landscapes, and, indeed, of noir generally, to reveal the subjective experiences of his characters. As Paul Schrader has written, some of the best film noir 'is an uneasy, exhilarating combination of realism and expressionism'.[13] Hare wrote of *Knuckle* that 'to go for a thriller style . . . was one way of putting the character's inner feelings into the outer form of the play'.[14]

Both *The Secret Rapture* and *Paris by Night* dramatise city environments drawing on noir visual iconography. The action of *The Secret Rapture* moves out of the largely domestic and office interiors of the original play into the streets of London, invariably at night, and almost always in the rain (noir has an almost Freudian attachment to water). A key scene is re-located from an office, in the play, into the shell of a building, dimly lit and with smashed windows, a transposition that emphasises the sense of threat and danger that is bearing down on the central character, Isobel. The title of *Paris by Night* is illustrative of the setting of most of that film, which is mainly in cities – London as well as Paris – shot in a way that draws on the nightmarish and expressive urban landscapes of noir. The interiors are framed in a way that emphasises their expressive meanings in this film. As the central character, the Tory MEP Clara Paige, attempts to keep at bay the chaos she has unleashed as a result of the impulsive murder of an ex-business partner, the interiors – chiefly hotel rooms – are shot in ways that often de-centre the characters, placing them in semi-shadow, and giving a direct expression to the feeling of terror and violence that eventually engulfs her. It is best to pursue these arguments further by looking at two texts in detail, one play (*Knuckle*) and one film (*Paris by Night*).

Knuckle, as a stage play, has a different relationship to noir than Hare's film. It cannot draw on the specifically cinematic visual iconography of film noir, although its characters and narrative are unmistakably of that world. The play concerns the attempt by a gun-runner from Guildford, Curly Delafield, to unravel the mystery of the disappearance of his sister, Sarah, last seen on a beach in Eastbourne. His investigations uncover a world of shady property dealings, sexual deviance and betrayed idealism, that centre on his father, a City broker. In fact, the play also refers to the popular fiction from which noir sprung, in particular the device of the first-person narrative, translated into monologues delivered by Curly. Curly is in the tradition of the noir 'seeker-hero', the active protagonist who seeks to uncover the 'truth'. Unlike many noir heroes, he does discover a truth of sorts. However, the truth he uncovers is not what he anticipated, and what is thrown up on the way unsettles his view of himself and his family. He discovers what he thinks has happened – that his father is involved in the disappearance of his sister, who has committed suicide – and decides to suppress it, only to discover that Sarah has faked her own disappearance in order to implicate her father.

Hare also re-defines one of the other main character types of film noir, the femme fatale. This role is given to Jenny, a night-club hostess and childhood friend of both Curly and Sarah. Constructed in this way, Jenny is signalled as having the characteristics of the femme fatale, representing both sexual possibility and danger to the protagonist, Curly. The femme fatale is a male construct, an attempt to demonise active female sexuality as untrustworthy and a threat, and is a direct expression of the misogyny that runs through many noir films. However, it rapidly becomes clear that Jenny is not a femme fatale, but a rather different, and more familiar type of Hare heroine. Jenny has as much knowledge of the situation as Curly – more, as it transpires, as she is the recipient of Sarah's last letter, which reveals that the suicide/murder is fake. She also carries more of the moral and political conscience of the play, a role that Hare often ascribes to women. She has an awareness of the way that women are subject to a lifelong harassment at the hands of men. 'Young women in Guildford must expect to be threatened', she says in a speech that shows both a consciousness of the world in which she moves and a self-awareness of her role in that world: 'Men here lead ugly lives and girls are the only touchstones left . . . the only point of loveliness in men's ever-darkening lives'.[15]

The noir world is typically one where social reference points are less important than psychological ones. The world of *Knuckle*, however, is an explicitly political one, in which the self-interest that motivates nearly all the characters is placed in the context of a society predicated on, and organised around, money and greed. The cynicism of this world is such that nobody pretends that it is otherwise, and Sarah's indignation and determination to ensure that everybody should be told the truth is dangerous. As in so much of Hare's work, personal deceptions are of a piece with, and made possible by, the lies that govern society as a whole – a theme to which he returns in both plays and films (see especially *Plenty* and *Licking Hitler*). The thriller is a mechanism for exposing both.

Paris by Night concerns a ruthless and ambitious Thatcherite MEP, whose impulsive murder of a previous business partner whom she thinks (wrongly) wishes to blackmail her, eventually leads to her own death. The film, which is classically noir in its narrative trajectory as well as its visual style, inhabits a world of shadows and confusions. Clara is plagued by phone calls, in which a man announces 'I know who you are'; she leaves her handbag at the scene of the murder, and desperately attempts to find it. The anxiety that she – and we – experience attests to the quality of dream and nightmare that infuses both this film and noir films generally, and which is linked to specific plot mechanisms and the air of unpredictability and violence; as Borde and Chaumeton observed, 'there is something of the dream in this incoherent and brutal atmosphere, the atmosphere common to most noir films' (Borde and Chaumeton, p. 24). What is important about the oneirism of *Paris by Night* is the disorientation it produces, and the way that it connects private nightmare to political logic in a world that is both recognisable and social (the public meetings and the political cabals, in which Clara moves) and private and unfamiliar.

Clara is a development of the 'seeker-hero' noir figure, mainly because she is a woman, and there is a strong ideological resistance in film noir to the idea of a seeker-heroine. Like Curly, Clara knows less than she thinks she does, and her lack of knowledge of her specific dilemmas is related to a wider misunderstanding of the political world in which she moves (she is in this sense also another kind of noir figure, the victim-hero/heroine). She is wrong about the intentions of her former business partner, and wrong about the identity of her mysterious caller. The world that she seeks to dominate is almost exclusively male, and, as the narrative progresses, it is made clear to her that she can only enter it on their terms. The meeting with which the film opens is saturated with male unctuousness, and her erstwhile benefactor, Adam Gillvray, a Tory historian, is revealed to be the man on the other end of the telephone.

The values of this world are ostensibly to do with personal freedom, which Gillvray defines at a dinner party, at which Clara is present. As a socialist, he was troubled by guilt: 'Then I saw the light. I do remember this weight being lifted. No more having to think. Not wasting your life in uncertainty and guilt. Do what you want to. . . . That's the basis of freedom.'[16] 'Do what you want' resonates at both the political and personal levels. When Clara asks her husband for a divorce, he notes, in a phrase that rings in the clear tones of Thatcherite ideology, that she is being true to form: 'I've seen you do it to everyone, since you were a girl. If they don't shape up, kick 'em out' (Hare, *Paris by Night*, p. 65). It is a philosophy that leads to Clara's own destruction.

The balance of sympathy in the film, however, is less easy to establish than this account of Clara as arch-Thatcherite might suggest, for one effect of the disorientation produced by the oneiric quality of the narrative is that it makes easy judgement of Clara's actions more problematic. *Paris by Night* shares with noir generally the aim to create a 'state of tension instilled in the spectator when the psychological reference points are removed' (Borde and Chaumeton, p. 25). Clara is both murderer and victim, the instigator of action over which she has no control. The violence with which she is killed is that reserved for the noir villain – spattered against the wall by bullets – yet her murder seems like the last stage in a nightmare which controls her. Hare clearly wanted an audience to be unsure how they should respond to Clara. Writing about the film, he described the experience of filming the scene in which Clara has just made love to the young Englishman, Wallace, she has met in Paris, and is laying out her philosophy of life:

> Clara is talking from her own experience, mixed up with a certain amount of confused political prejudice, yet a combination of things – the context in which she speaks, the tenderness with her lover, the play of light, Charlotte's [Rampling] exquisite conviction in the role – combined to produce in those of us watching a feeling of total disorientation. We simply did not know what our response to Clara was. . . . We were all robbed of our usual reactions. This is something I have so long wanted to do as a writer. . . .
>
> (Hare, p. ix)

The world of film noir, then, allows Hare to pursue concerns that animate all his writing, for the stage as much for the screen, whilst giving them a particular inflection.

Through much of the 1990s, Hare has returned to working exclusively in the theatre, and the kind of formal experiment, often drawing on film, that we have been discussing is less in evidence in recent work. However, Hare remains a good example of what is generally true in post-war culture: that despite periodic calls for a 'pure' theatre and a cinema that is freed from the tyranny of the 'theatrical', it is not longer possible to write – or, indeed, direct, design or act – as if other media did not exist.

Notes

1. Hersh Zeifman, 'An Interview with David Hare' in H. Zeifman (ed.), *David Hare: A Casebook* (New York, 1994), p. 18. Further page references are cited in the text.
2. David Hare, 'Introduction' in D. Hare, *Paris by Night* (London, 1988), p. vii. Further page references are cited in the text.

3. Raymond Williams, 'A Defence of Realism' in N. Belton, F. Mulhern and J. Taylor (eds), *What I Came to Say* (London, 1989).

4. David Hare, quoted in Janelle Reinelt, *After Brecht: British Epic Theatre* (Ann Arbor, MI, 1994), p. 123.

5. See John Russell Brown, 'Playing with Place: Some Filmic Techniques in the Plays of David Hare' in Zeifman (ed.), *David Hare: A Casebook*.

6. David Hare, *The Secret Rapture* (London, 1988), p. 59.

7. David Hare, 'On *Wetherby*' in D. Hare, *Writing Left-Handed* (London, 1991), p. 130. Further page references are cited in the text.

8. Susan Sontag, 'Film and Theatre' in G. Mast, M. Cohen and L. Braudy (eds), *Film, Theory and Criticism: Introductory Readings* (4th edn, Oxford, 1992), p. 370.

9. David Hare, quoted in Vera Lustig, 'Soul Searching', *Drama* no. 170 (1988), p. 18.

10. David Hare, 'A Lecture Given at King's College, Cambridge: March 5 1978' in D. Hare, *Licking Hitler* (London, 1978), p. 69.

11. Michael Walker, 'Film Noir: Introduction' in I. Cameron (ed.), *The Book of Film Noir* (New York, 1992), p. 8.

12. Raymond Borde and Etienne Chaumeton, 'Towards a Definition of Film Noir' in A. Silver and J. Ursini (eds), *Film Noir Reader* (New York, 1996), p. 19. Further page references are cited in the text.

13. Paul Schrader, 'Notes on Film Noir' in Silver and Ursini (eds), *Film Noir Reader*, p. 56.

14. George Gaston, 'Interview: David Hare', *Theatre Journal* no. 45 (1993), p. 219.

15. David Hare, *Knuckle* in D. Hare, *David Hare: Plays 1* (London, 1996), p. 219.

16. David Hare, *Paris by Night*, pp.15–16.

11 *Preserving machines: recentering the decentered subject in* Blade Runner *and* Johnny Mnemonic

Mark Bould

How science fiction (SF) came to be accepted as a legitimate object of academic enquiry is a long and twisty tale. I have no intention of exploring its byways here other than to note that, to the extent that this acceptance does exist, it is in no small part due to the challenge presented to traditional literary studies by cultural studies and newer textual disciplines more amenable to critical theory. Arguably, SF has an exaggerated affinity with one of the basic precepts of twentieth-century critical theory: by naming and describing things which do not exist, are as yet unknown, and cannot (yet?) be known, it repeatedly emphasises a Saussurean conception of language as arbitrary and unmotivated, as a framework placed over the valueless, meaningless flux of existence. Such a framework enables us to make sense of the world by dividing it up into categories (e.g. big/small, red/blue, trousers/hat) which we internalise and normalise, failing to recognise that our experience of the world is always already mediated by language. Whereas fantasy and horror tend to name and describe the occasional non-existent or unknown, SF regularly elaborates such things in the most verisimilitudinous manner, underpinned by a scientific and logical rigour. The sports produced by fantasy and horror might trouble pre-Saussurean notions of language, but the tendency within SF to generate total worlds of non-existents and unknowns is rather more traumatic, demonstrating the lack of any necessary connection between signifying practices and 'reality'.[1] Such foregrounded textuality makes SF and post-Saussurean theory natural bedfellows, and in this whistle-stop essay I intend to outline some elements of their congress, particularly the ways in which SF and theory can illustrate and illuminate each other's problematisation of the subject. In order to do this, I shall draw upon examples from the following text-clusters:

Blade Runner cluster, henceforth BLADE RUNNER:
Philip K. Dick, *Do Androids Dream of Electric Sheep?* ([1968] London, 1982), henceforth *Androids*.
Blade Runner (film: Ridley Scott, 1982 – the international cut), henceforth *BR*.
Blade Runner: The Director's Cut (film: Ridley Scott, 1991), henceforth *BR: TDC*.
K.W. Jeter, *Blade Runner 2: The Edge of Human* (London, 1995), henceforth *BR2*.
K.W. Jeter, *Blade Runner 3: Replicant Night* (London, 1996), henceforth *BR3*.

Johnny Mnemonic cluster, henceforth JOHNNY MNEMONIC.
William Gibson, 'Johnny Mnemonic' ([1981] in William Gibson, *Johnny Mnemonic: The Story and the Screenplay*, New York, 1995), henceforth 'JM'.
William Gibson, *Johnny Mnemonic: The Screenplay* (in William Gibson, *Johnny Mnemonic: The Story and the Screenplay*, New York, 1995), henceforth *JM: TS*.
Johnny Mnemonic (film: Robert Longo, 1995), henceforth *JM*.
Terry Bisson, *Johnny Mnemonic* (novelisation of the film; New York, 1995), henceforth *JM: nov*.

Individual texts will be referred to by their abbreviation; *Blade Runner* will refer to *BR* and *BR: TDC* considered together.

These clusters, whose boundaries are as arbitrary as the boundaries of the individual texts they contain, have been selected for three reasons. First, they are familiar. It seems to have become impossible when discussing post-1980 SF not to talk about *Blade Runner* and/or the cyberpunk fiction of William Gibson. Second, there is a serendipity to the way in which these clusters take us from the precursors of cyberpunk through to 'the day cyberpunk died'.[2] Third, and most importantly, the nature of the production of these texts raises as many issues concerning notions of authenticity and originality as do the texts themselves.

The decision to examine clusters rather than privileging individual texts derives from an unwillingness to become the critical equivalent of a blade runner. Just as Rick Deckard (Harrison Ford) must track down replicants, deciding en route who is human and who is not, so the traditional textual critic finding himself faced with 'essentially [six versions of the movie] which have been seen by the general public', must decide which is authentic (whatever that might mean).[3] However, there is no critical value in championing *BR: TDC* over *BR*, as the majority of popular and academic criticism has done, merely because it bears the director's imprimatur. Such complicity in promoting the re-mix too easily slides back into declaring the director to be the source and guarantee of the movie's meaning. Indeed, the complex history of *Blade Runner* suggests that *BR: TDC* is best considered as an unsuccessful attempt to reconstruct an earlier, non-existent version of the movie.

Jeter, too, rejects the role of blade runner. Although *BR2*'s jacket blurb asserts that it is intended to function as a sequel to both *Androids* and *Blade Runner*, and to resolve many of the discrepancies between them, Jeter refuses the opportunity offered by the authorised nature of his work to give precedence to any prior text or to establish a definitive reading. Filled with the characters and terminology of the movies, its plot is generated from the famous continuity error about the number of replicants. Such key elements of *Androids* as Mercerism, Buster Friendly and the widespread ownership of artificial animals are omitted. Absent from the movies, *Androids*' J.R. Isidore reappears and meets Deckard for the first time, even though they have already met for the first time in the novel.

Clearly no sequel to *Androids*, neither is it a sequel to any version of the movie. Instead, it hesitates between being a sequel to *BR* and a sequel to *BR: TDC*. For example, *BR* ends with Deckard and Rachael (Sean Young) flying into the wilderness, Deckard's voice-over informing us that she does not have the built-in four-year replicant lifespan; *BR: TDC* ends with nothing to suggest an escape into the mountain country, and the implication of Rachael's second visit to Deckard's apartment is that she does have the standard replicant lifespan; *BR2* opens in the Oregon wilderness, but Rachael's lifespan is nearly used up. This compromise utilises elements of both movies but gives precedence to neither, and Jeter further muddies the water by referring to police surveillance booths (pp. 121–6), which only appear in the Workprint of the movie. This refusal to eradicate the ambiguities and contradictions of the movies is typified by Jeter's Dick-ian response to that most vexed of *Blade Runner* questions: is Deckard a replicant? *BR* raises the possibility that he might be; *BR: TDC* suggests that he is; *BR2* argues that he is not, but that even if he is, it is an irrelevant technical distinction. Jeter's novels might, then, be best understood as sequels to a non-existent version of a movie called '*Blade Runner*' which glide away from the milieu of the existing movies into one more typically Dick-ian in its characters, settings and preoccupations.

Similar issues of precedence and authenticity are raised for the reader of *Androids* – a novel Dick refused to suppress in favour of a ghosted novelisation – by this unusual note which appears on the unnumbered copyright page of the reprinted tie-in:

> In 1968, Philip K. Dick wrote *Do Androids Dream of Electric Sheep?*, a brilliant science-fiction novel that became the source of the motion picture *Blade Runner*. Though the novel's characters and backgrounds differ in some respects from those of the film, readers who enjoy the movie will discover an added dimension on encountering the original work. Granada Publishing is pleased to return this classic novel to print.

Although ascribing to it classic status and recognising its chronological precedence, the publishers are rather apologetic for its digressions from the movie. There is something contradictory in this. Since canonicity and chronology are recognised then surely it is the movie that should be seen to diverge from the book, but in begging pardon for the 'original work' the publishers suggest that the movie is more significant. Similar irresolvables attach to JOHNNY MNEMONIC. Is *JM: TS* of greater significance than *JM* because it is by Gibson and has chronological precedence? How are we to consider it in relation to his earlier 'JM'? And what of *JM: nov*, based on 'JM' and *JM: TS* but not on *JM*?

'The Preserving Machine': the radical indeterminacy of texts

In Dick's 1953 short story 'The Preserving Machine', Doctor Labyrinth, inspired by an apocalyptic vision of global destruction, manufactures a device to transform musical scores into creatures who will survive the war and flourish in its aftermath. In this manner, the music he loves will outlive the suicidal folly of the race which created it. But the machine does not work in quite the way he intended. Instead of the hardy, fierce burrowing creatures he had envisaged, the machine produces an exotic array of mozart birds, beethoven beetles, schubert animals, brahms insects, bach bugs, and so on. Released into the wild they continue to adapt to their new environment, and when Labyrinth attempts to undo a bug's transformation the resultant score is a hideous, barely recognisable distortion of the original fugue.

The unhappy Labyrinth has learned 'the lesson of the Garden of Eden: that once a thing had been fashioned it begins to exist on its own, and thus ceases to be the property of its creator to mold and direct as he wishes'.[4] It is easy to interpret this story as a Barthesian allegory about the death of the author. A text is fed into a wonderful contraption (the reader) and Labyrinth (the author) cannot determine what strange creature (story) it will create. Dick's story concludes with a beethoven beetle, suddenly aware of the narrator's scrutiny, 'turn[ing] abruptly and enter[ing] its building, snapping the door firmly shut behind it' (p. 207). In our allegorical interpretation, this exclusion from the new ecosystem signifies the expulsion of the author from the text. Just as the new creatures exist in relation to other creatures rather than in relation to their creator, so texts exist in relation to other texts. Post-Saussurean criticism argues that a text becomes intelligible when, in the process of consuming it, the reader or viewer recognises the similarities and differences between that particular text and all the other texts he or she has encountered. Because the reader can only make sense of a text through its participation in a sign-system, the text is at least generated, if not determined, by the sign-system rather than by the author.

Mosaics

In Kristeva's words, Bakhtin perceived the text as 'an *intersection of textual surfaces* rather than a *point* (a fixed meaning), as a dialogue among several writings'.[5] Whereas earlier models considered the text a unit of meaning transmitted from author to reader, this dynamic model not only challenges the unitary nature of the text, but also recognises that the addressee is a conceptual construct which only exists within the text's discourse. Therefore, an understanding of text as a communication between subjects must be replaced with an understanding of the text as intertextual. The 'text is constructed as a mosaic of quotations' (Kristeva, p. 66), and meaning is not the product of the text but of its intertextual relationships. For example, the visual style of *Blade Runner* is that of the film noir but its milieu is science-fictional. It tells a hard-boiled detective story about a burnt-out cop chasing robots: the mosaic nature of the film exhibits a quintessentially postmodern 'complacent eclecticism'.[6] This is echoed within the film by both Gaff's (Edward James Olmos) cityspeak – a language which draws attention to its own hybridity – and the production design which makes Los Angeles look more like Manhattan, with retrofitted architecture quoting Egyptian and Mayan design alongside Frank Lloyd Wright, and streets teeming with Chinese, Arabs, Hispanics, Hare Krishnas and punks.

Androids' opening also demonstrates this intersection of textual surfaces. It 'is recognizable that the universe Dick presents in his work corresponds very closely to his situation as a writer, facing a blank white sheet, the story unformed and awaiting his god-like direction'.[7] Startled awake, it is as if Deckard has suddenly sprung into existence. Beside him, his wife Iran stirs. As a result of having set his Penfield Mood Organ to 'D', he is in a buoyant mood whereas Iran is irritable from having only set hers to 'C'. So they argue, and he hesitates between dialling for a 'thalamic suppressant (which would abolish his mood of rage) or a thalamic stimulant (which would make him irked enough to win the argument)' (p. 8); she threatens to dial whatever it would take for her to win. He backs down, and they discuss which moods they should dial for the day ahead, including (pp. 8–10): 3: the desire to dial a mood; 481: 'awareness of the manifold possibilities open to me in the future'; 594: 'pleased acknowledgement of husband's superior wisdom in all matters'; 888: the 'desire to watch TV, no matter what's on it'; 'ecstatic sexual bliss'; and 'self-accusatory depression'. This reduction of emotion to generic moods, randomly numbered and labelled on the Penfield's dial, demonstrates an understanding of language as arbitrary and conventional. Flat characters round themselves out with textual fragments we recognise from medicine, popular psychology, self-help literature, and so on. But it is the author, not the characters, who makes these choices, selections from the intertext, that 'corpus of texts, textual fragments, or textlike segments of the sociolect that shares a lexicon and . . . a syntax with the text'.[8]

Forming and decentering the subject

The constraints placed upon Dick's characters by their accommodation to the emotional economy of the Penfield is suggestive of Benveniste's contention that subjectivity itself is a possibility only provided for by language.[9] The word 'I' – that which identifies the subject – is, like all other words, just another marker of difference within the system of difference that is language. In order to produce meaning, the individual must identify himself with 'I', must accept being positioned by language as the subject. When the visored and datagloved Johnny Mnemonic (Keanu Reeves) enters cyberspace – which we can regard as being, like language, a symbolic realm – a division occurs between Johnny, sitting in Crazy Bob's computer store, and virtual Johnny, his avatar roaming cyberspace. In order to function in the Matrix, Johnny must identify himself with his avatar and accept being represented by it, even though it is merely a sign.

The replicants' prosthetic memories – encoded personal histories implanted in them so that they can function within the social formation – exemplify the linguistic construction of the subject, and this is emphasised by Deckard's recitation of Rachael's memories and Gaff's awareness of his unicorn dream. McCaffery's discussion of domestic mnemonic technologies signals the indistinguishability of replicants from humans in this respect:

> our memories of many of the key events of our past are now recollections not of 'actual' past events, but of the photographs or videos we have taken of them. . . . [P]eople now often use the 'real experience' . . . as a 'pretext' for the more 'substantial' later experience of 'reliving' these experiences through reproduced sounds and images that magically conjure up for us our past, a conjuration that seems more 'substantial' precisely because it can be endlessly reproduced.[10]

This substantiality is represented in *Blade Runner* when, for a moment, Rachael's photograph seems to come alive in Deckard's hand, and explains the replicants' – and Deckard's – obsession with photographs.

The first generation of *BR* viewers received a rare insight into this technological inscription of memory. For us, Harrison Ford was always already Han Solo and Indiana Jones. This was the preview audience's memory of him and because of this identification of Ford with specific roles – a phenomenon significantly different from Cary Grant always being Cary Grant and James Garner always being James Garner – they found Deckard unrecognisable. Hence *BR*'s voice-over, effectively an extra-textual attempt to shape Ford's affectless performance with a recognisable voice, a voice doubly familiar in that it belonged to both Ford and to the hard-boiled tradition. This voice wrote in a past which diverged significantly from our memory of him, taking him from cynical hero resisting Evil Empires to world-weary, sanctioned killer, working for a corporate tyranny. As we watched, our memories were re-written for us.

Lacan's discussion of the mirror stage of infant development further emphasises the ascendancy of language over the subject.[11] He argues that the new-born infant has no sense of identity, experiencing existence as a series of fluxes, drives and desires with no core of self and no clearly defined borders. On confronting his reflection, however, he becomes aware for the first time of differentiation, of the division of the universe into subject (self) and object (not-self), into signifier (self) and signified (mirror image). This first division of the world into categories marks the infant's entry into the symbolic and the origin of identity. In *JM: nov*, Jones, the dolphin, dreams of his prelinguistic past in which 'the sea and not the swimmer was the subject'. Cyborged, trained and heroin-addicted by the US Navy, he was torn 'away from his world and imprison[ed] . . . in a smaller one, of individual personality'; disconnected from the 'Mother Waters', he has entered into the Symbolic, and now has 'two monkeys on his back, heroin and self' (p. 224).

Having learned to distinguish between 'I' and 'not-I', the infant learns to identify himself with a subject position created by language so that he can express his needs and desires. In order to interact with others who also identify themselves as 'I' he will go on to identify with a variety of subject positions, and constantly shift between 'I', 'you', 'him', and so on. This ability to occupy a variety of subject positions ensures that discourse is mutually intelligible, but it problematises subjectivity, fragmenting and distributing it over a cluster of frequently inconsistent and contradictory subject-positions around an absent centre.

Lacan further argues that the mirror stage does not produce a unitary subject but instead opens up a gap between the perceiving 'I' (the infant) and the perceived 'I' (the mirror image). This is reinforced on the infant's entry into language by a secondary split between the 'I' posited by language and the 'I' who does the speaking. The spoken 'I' is inevitably only an arbitrary and conventional representation of the speaking 'I'. The speaker exists in excess of the word 'I', just as Johnny exists in excess of his avatar, and it is in this gap between one 'I' and another that the unconscious comes into being as a storehouse of that which cannot be expressed. Entry into the symbolic enables the infant to express his desires and simultaneously renders him incapable of articulating those desires which remain unconscious. The net-surfing 'Johnny''s identification with the 'Johnny' he becomes in cyberspace isolates him, minimising his interactions with non-virtual people, and his 'room-service' flip-out registers this inarticulacy. It is therefore possible to consider the subject as being formed by a contradiction, and as an unending process of construction without direction or centre.

JM opens with a headlong rush through the Internet, the text of Johnny's wake-up call forming ahead of us, racing toward the screen in his hotel room. As we are behind the screen, the text appears reversed. Static, then the alarm wakes Johnny, and the message is reflected on his eye. For a moment it appears as if it is actually being displayed there, as if the dataspace we hurtled through is inside him. This ambiguity is maintained throughout the movie. With the exception of the Crazy Bob sequence, it is unclear whether the dataspaces we see represent the information he is smuggling, the architecture of his wetware implant, or that of his brain. This suggests that no clear demarcations can be made between these dataspaces, and the location of 'Johnny' becomes unclear. The subject as a centre disappears, or rather becomes defined not as 'a fixed locus but [as] a function, a sort of nonlocus in which an infinite number of sign-substitutions come into play'.[12]

The preserving machine: ideology

And so we return to preserving machines. Not Dick's Barthesian contraption this time, but ideology. Marx contended that 'the mode of production of material life conditions the social, political and intellectual life processes in general. It is not the consciousness of men that determines their being, but . . . their social being that determines their consciousness.'[13] Social being is determined by signification and discourse which function in the interest of the dominant class so as to reproduce social relations of inequality. The term 'ideology' describes 'knowledge' whose social origins are suppressed or deemed irrelevant in order to make it seem natural and universal; in a class society, 'ideology is the relay whereby, and the element in which, the relation between men and their conditions of existence is settled to the profit of the ruling class'.[14]

In *Androids*, Deckard dials for 'a creative and fresh attitude toward his job, although this he hardly needed: such was his habitual, innate approach without recourse to Penfield artificial brain stimulation' (p. 11). This suggests that he experiences, interprets and understands his emotions by comparing and contrasting them with the artificially generated moods, and adopts the Penfield's categorisations to describe them. Deckard's recognition of this requirement of labour under capitalism as something habitual and innate indicates the extent to which this 'knowledge' has become naturalised. The characters' willingness both to use the Penfield and to restrict their understanding of emotional experience to its preconstructed settings demonstrate its efficacy in managing the consent of the masses to the interests of the dominant classes. When *Androids'* Deckard is arrested, he is booked for a '304. . . . And 612.4 and let's see. Representing himself to be a peace officer . . . 406' (p. 87). The parallels between criminal activities and the Penfield settings are clear. Crimes, like emotions, have numbers and tags. The arbitrariness and inadequacy of such systems to describe a wide range of human activities are obvious. Although the legal and law enforcement apparatuses function in the public sphere by violence or the threat of violence, and the mood organs operate in the private sphere by consent, they are both regulatory forces working to reproduce subordination to the relations of production.

The subject, formed by language and discourse, is also an ideological construction. Common sense tells us that we are autonomous, unique individuals with a discrete consciousness which is the source of our beliefs and actions. This appears to be natural, obvious and true, and denies the linguistic, discursive, ideological formation of the subject. Like Jones, we are all selfhood junkies and, therefore, when we are addressed as autonomous subjects we respond by misrecognising ourselves in this address and freely assuming the subject positions (wage-slave/consumer) required of us as participants in the social formation. BLADE RUNNER and JOHNNY MNEMONIC are fundamentally concerned with the ideological and repressive apparatuses involved in generating and maintaining this misrecognition, and managing consent to it. In *BR* language mediates our first encounter with Deckard. Sat in blank silence between the lights in the shop window and of the advertising blimp, between the drone of its spiel and of his voice-over, he lists the various professional and familial subject-positions (cop, blade runner, killer, husband) he no longer occupies. This 'cold fish' is in a similar position to the renegade replicants: emotionless, he has rejected his role within the social formation. His reluctant return to headquarters reverts him to that role.

Throughout BLADE RUNNER massive institutional power is brought to bear on those considered to be artificial, and the method of determining their artificiality – the Voigt-Kampff Empathy Test – depends upon a complex interrogation procedure in which scenarios involving cruelty towards animals are described. The respondent attempts to give the 'correct' answers, and thus to adopt the position of a legitimate subject. Verbal responses are ignored, however, in favour of measuring involuntary physiological reactions which indicate whether or not the respondent experiences instinctive empathic responses. Despite insisting these reactions are natural, the V-K test obviously measures learned responses. *Androids* explains that in the immediate post-World War Terminus period 'not taking care of an animal' (p. 15) was deemed criminal; although subsequently decriminalised, it is still considered 'immoral and anti-empathic' (p. 68). This ethic is clearly a result of widespread consent to (repressive) legislation. That the legal framework was necessary to enforce this ethic, and that such a framework could be later removed without weakening the social sanction it had both developed from and enshrined, is suggestive of the internalisation of an ethical code that does not 'instinctively' arise in those who are human. The human who felt indifference or antipathy towards animals but chose to make an ethical decision in accordance with dominant ideology would fail the V-K test. He would make the correct verbal responses, but not the correct physiological ones, and thus be executed as if he were an android. It is clear from this that the test is about policing conformity to the requirements of dominant ideology. The suspicions voiced by Rachael and *Androids'* Luba Luft about the nature of the questions – they seem to be more concerned with policing sexuality and domestic power relations than with empathy towards animals – underscore this.

Androids suggests that anyone – androids, schizoid or schizophrenic humans – who experiences a 'flattening of affect' (p. 33) would fail the test. However, the widespread dependence on Penfields for the generation of emotion suggests that humans everywhere are suffering such a flattening. The role of the android/ replicant in BLADE RUNNER is akin to that Baudrillard famously ascribed to Disneyland: they are presented as false 'in order to make us believe that the rest [are] real'.[15] The V-K test is, then, part of the repressive state apparatus for locating and exterminating those improperly constituted individuals who are incapable of playing the required roles of production and consumption. Such inauthentic subjects must be destroyed because as simulations they threaten the 'very principle of reality' (p. 38) by revealing that that principle is itself an ideological construction. The Penfields perform the necessary adjunct role of concealing a possibly universal flattening of affect, and enabling people to perform the functions required of them by the hegemonic order.

Recentering the subject

In order to make room for his wetware implant, Johnny had to 'dump a chunk of [his] long-term memory': his childhood. A rootless yuppie, he has no surname. In order to get ahead, he sacrificed his past and conventional markers of social identity; like *BR*'s Deckard, he has abandoned familial and corporate subject-positions. His marginal, problematic position within the social formation is indicated not so much by his criminal activities but by their freelance nature. During the final hack on his own brain, Johnny recovers, downloads and broadcasts the Pharmakom data and regains his childhood memories which have somehow been encoded and stored in an area of either his brain or the Internet he could not previously access. The hitherto tantalising glimpses of his home, his mother, and his birthday party cohere. He rejects the frightening corporate ethic which sought to suppress the cure for the fatal Nerve Attenuation Syndrome in favour of the more profitable treatment of its symptoms, and is saved by a dolphin and an African-American – those quintessentially 1980s/1990s bearers of liberal conscience – and the love of two good women, with one of whom he has become romantically involved. *JM: nov* gives this even greater emphasis, and 'JM' concludes with Johnny, Molly and Jones in business together, financially successful and heading, perhaps, towards legitimacy. Individuals are thus incorporated back into family units, ones which might prove more conducive to the hegemonic order.

However, rewritten Johnny, whilst undeniably human, is effectively a replicant. This emphasises once more that subjectivity is a linguistic construction, but ideology works to obscure this insight. We are bombarded instead with spectacular images of the brainhack, the sentimental 'authenticity' of home movie footage, the constitution and reconstitution of families, and the destruction of the 'bad' capitalists. Similarly, Deckard grows from 'sushi' to an ethical being, and is rewarded with a romantic partner. *BR* promises their escape and survival, *BR: TDC* concludes on a less optimistic note but at least the hero gets the girl, and *BR2* and *BR3* play variations on this theme. *Androids* takes a rather more mournful tone, indicating the traumatic nature of conforming to the requirements of the dominant order. In both BLADE RUNNER and JOHNNY MNEMONIC the audience recognises the terrible nature of the corporate global order yet celebrates the protagonists' new-found eligibility as members of it. We pay to see movies which indict capitalist excess whilst practising it, and to identify with loners whose success is figured in terms of their incorporation into the social formation. Thus are we interpellated as wage-slaves and consumers, and we love it.

Notes

1. Vivian Sobchack in *Screening Space: The American Science Fiction Film* (New York, 1991) argues that although this 'tension between "invention" and "convention" informs any symbolic activity that is

not merely replicative, it is most consciously privileged and doubly articulated in SF – heightened and stressed as constituting both the genre's mode of discourse and its discursive object' (p. 303). No matter how unfamiliar SF requires its materials to be, its non-existents and unknowns must be representable. This is as true of the most smugly reassured and reassuring SF text as it is of that proposed in my highly idealised model of the genre. SF's own crisis of representation, this is most easily recognised in the neologism – robot, android, cyborg, replicant, terraform, flivver, conapt, urbstak, cyberspace – which must conjure an unknown in knowable terms. Such coinages when first encountered threaten to dislocate the signifying chain, but the signifying chain works to counter this effect, to contain and fix meaning among its links.

2. Arthur and Marilouise Kroker, 'Johnny Mnemonic: The Day Cyberpunk Died' in Hacking the Future: Stories for the Flesh-Eating 90s (Montreal, 1996), p. 50.

3. Paul M. Sammon, Future Noir: The Making of Blade Runner (New York, 1996), p. 395. Sammon lists The Workprint, The San Diego Sneak Preview, The Domestic Cut, The International Cut, The Director's Cut and the 1986 US network television cut. In addition to these, it is not unreasonable to suggest that any dubbed, subtitled, domestically censored and panned-and-scanned versions be considered 'essentially' different versions.

4. Philip K. Dick, 'The Preserving Machine' in P. Dick, Beyond Lies the Wub: Volume 1, The Collected Stories of Philip K. Dick (London, 1990), p. 203.

5. Julia Kristeva, 'Word, Dialogue, and Novel' in J. Kristeva, Desire in Language: A Semiotic Approach to Literature and Art, ed. Leon S. Roudiez, trans. Thomas Gora, Alice Jardine and Leon S. Roudiez (Oxford, 1981), p. 65.

6. Fredric Jameson, Postmodernism or, the Cultural Logic of Late Capitalism (London, 1991), p. 18.

7. David Wingrove, 'Understanding the Grasshopper: Leitmotifs and the Moral Dilemma in the Novels of Philip K. Dick', Foundation: The Review of Science Fiction no. 26 (October 1982), p. 28.

8. Michael Riffaterre, 'Intertextual Representation: On Mimesis as Interpretive Discourse', Critical Inquiry, 11 September 1984, p. 142. He defines the sociolect as 'language viewed not just as grammar and lexicon but as the repository of society's myths ... represented by themes, commonplace phrases, and descriptive systems' (p. 160n).

9. Emile Benveniste, Problems in General Linguistics (Miami, FL, 1971).

10. See Larry McCaffery, 'Introduction: The Desert of the Real' in L. McCaffery (ed.), Storming the Reality Studio: A Casebook of Cyberpunk and Postmodern Science Fiction (London, 1991), pp. 1–16.

11. Jacques Lacan, *Ecrits: A Selection*, trans. Alan Sheridan (London, 1989).

12. Jacques Derrida, 'Structure Sign and Play in the Discourse of the Human Sciences' in J. Derrida, *Writing and Difference*, trans. Alan Bass (London, 1981), p. 280.

13. Karl Marx, *Karl Marx: Selected Writings*, ed. David McLellan (Oxford, 1977), p. 176.

14. Louis Althusser, 'Marxism and Humanism' in L. Althusser, *For Marx*, trans. B.R. Brewster (London, 1969), pp. 235–6.

15. Jean Baudrillard, 'The Precession of Simulacra' in J. Baudrillard, *Simulations* (New York, 1983), p. 25.

12 *From SF to sci-fi: Paul Verhoeven's* Starship Troopers

I.Q. Hunter

With its giant Bugs, ultraviolent special effects and a script that even admirers might regard as cheesy, *Starship Troopers* (1997) is undeniably a state of the art 'sci-fi' action movie.[1] Directed by Paul Verhoeven, it belongs to the period of science-fiction cinema's greatest commercial success. Whereas the majority of recent sci-fi films, from *Independence Day* (1996) to *Men in Black* (1997), drew on either mainstream novels, comic books or old movies, *Starship Troopers* was adapted from the classic SF novel written in 1959 by Robert Heinlein,[2] one of the genre's most distinguished practitioners. The film has a tone of irony that, while not unique among contemporary blockbusters, is unusually complex and ambiguous. As a case study it allows comments not only on the relation between science fiction film and literature, but also on the specific thrills of that most disdained and, to many critics, ideologically transparent genre, the big-budget action movie.

Since moving from Holland to the USA in 1983, Verhoeven had made *RoboCop* (1987) and *Total Recall* (1990), two of the period's most profitable and, in the latter's case, most expensive sci-fi movies. After the erotic thriller *Basic Instinct* (1992) confirmed him as one of Hollywood's more provocative 'bad boys', Verhoeven achieved less welcome notoriety with *Showgirls* (1995), which was a critical and box-office disaster. *Starship Troopers* was therefore a return – or retreat – to a proven commercial formula. Verhoeven depicts a war between mankind and giant alien insects with all of his trademark comic-book imagery, extreme violence and stylishly tongue-in-cheek approach to the blockbuster. Despite a budget of $100 million and major publicity and marketing campaigns, the film achieved only modest success at the box-office and was critically received as an entertaining 'no brainer'. But, as aficionados of written SF might well insist, its merit as exemplifying the current state of sci-fi can also be seen as its greatest failing. In catering to the global mass audience for action movies, Verhoeven distances his film from both Heinlein's novel and SF's 'serious' literary tradition, which remains to a large extent the taste of a specialised genre readership.

Starship Troopers, moreover, from a certain point of view, is symptomatic of contemporary Hollywood at its most spectacularly meretricious and shallow. Seemingly a big dumb entertainment like *The Lost World* (1997) or *Titanic* (1998), it sacrifices characterisation and narrative depth to technical gimmickry and fast-paced shocks. The film's heroes are as one-dimensional as the stars of teen comedies, and the early scenes play like a pastiche of the television series *Beverley Hills 90210* or *Saved by the Bell*. Instead of the atmospheric tech-noir of *Alien* (1979) or *Event Horizon* (1997), its design has the cartoonish gloss and busy flatness of TV soap opera, with scenes brightly lit to display the dazzling CGI (computer-generated imagery) realism of Bugs and vast starships manoeuvring in outer space. The tone throughout is slickly ironic and referential, with nods variously to 1950s creature features like *Them!* (1954), flag-waving combat movies, and even the Nazi propaganda documentary, *Triumph of the Will* (1936). To its detractors, this is popcorn postmodernism at its most violent and seductive, a cinema of allusions, jolts and surfaces, with the movie itself merely a pretext for spin-off toys, theme park rides and computer games.[3]

How different from literary SF, in which, as Kingsley Amis suggested, ideas are the real hero.[4] Critics with an investment in legitimating the genre have long regarded SF novels as more subtle and imaginative than sci-fi movies, which till recently were chiefly valued for their ideological subtexts. Hostility to sci-fi movies typically rests on the assumption that film, being a mass art, is incompetent to deal with abstractions and intellectual complexity. From this perspective, SF literature is what Edward James calls 'a form of elite fiction, the elite being of a technocratic, rather than a literary, intelligentsia', while the sci-fi film is its populist bastardisation.[5]

It is revealing that science-fiction cinema – like the action movie – has attracted relatively little serious critical attention. While written SF is the subject of a considerable body of academic work, the few books on sci-fi movies have gravitated towards the same canonical films, with a narrow ideological focus cruelly insensitive to art direction and special effects. Although I'm not persuaded that cinema is any less able than theatre or television drama to communicate 'ideas', sci-fi's critics are right in one important respect. The peculiar exhilaration of a film like *Starship Troopers* lies in its specifically visual qualities. From the antiseptic modernism of *Things to Come* (1936) to the smoke and neon Gothic of *Blade Runner* (1982), sci-fi cinema has been 'about' its look – the aesthetic thrill of sensuous design, the delicious estrangement of novel and incomprehensible sights.[6]

Science-fiction literature and film differ in their attitudes towards the genre's basic themes. Since the 1950s the films have consistently depicted outer space as threatening rather than expanding human possibility, a theme lately revived with *Independence Day* (1996) and *Mars Attacks!* (1997). James notes that film and written SF have come to stand for very different perspectives on science and space:

> written sf liked to believe that humanity, through science and rationality and by abandoning old social conventions (or re-establishing an imagined golden age), could build a better world; the films preached that there were things humanity should not dabble in, that the status quo should be defended against all attempts to change it, that emotion is more important than reason, and that the cold and essentially unwise scientist cannot be trusted.
>
> (James, p. 82)

Generically, the films are closer than written SF to horror and fantasy. Owing more to comic books and juvenile 'pulps' than to SF's 'serious' tradition, they prefer bug-eyed monsters to meticulously detailed alien civilisations, and disguised fairy-tales, like *Star Wars* (1977), to technological speculation and prophecy. Generally speaking, as John Baxter remarks, 'Science fiction supports logic and order, sf film illogic and chaos'.[7] Above all, sci-fi cinema is bracingly dystopian, and echoes the horror film's injunction to leave nature and the universe well alone. Even when celebrating in every frame the technological achievements of special effects, the films remain suspicious of the future and scientific advance.

Sci-fi cinema has of course offered benevolent visions of both the future (*Things to Come, Bill & Ted's Excellent Adventure* (1986)) and encounters with aliens (*E.T.: The Extraterrestrial* (1982) and *Contact* (1997)). There is even a strain of humanistic optimism and progressive satire in apocalyptic classics such as *The Day Earth Caught Fire* (1961) and *Planet of the Apes* (1968). But on the whole dystopianism – or at least anti-utopianism – has become obligatory in sci-fi films, reflecting both a 'postmodern' loss of faith in narratives of progress and a well-founded suspicion that utopianism implies totalitarian fantasies of regimentation and homogeneity.[8] Achieved utopias, as in *Logan's Run* (1976) and *Gattaca* (1998), invariably turn out to be fascist states in disguise.

Starship Troopers is therefore unusual because it depicts a mature utopia. What looks like a totalitarian nightmare is presented as an ideal social and political system.[9] This utopianism derives from Heinlein's novel, which was immediately controversial. For the most part it is a novel not of action, but of intensely argued political ideas, projecting Heinlein's American conservatism into the world of the twenty-fourth century. In this approvingly described utopia, to become a citizen one must first volunteer to spend a period in military service and learn the values of honour, sacrifice and obedience. In a first-person narrative the novel follows the career of Juan Rico, a recruit from Buenos Aires, as he endures boot camp training and a war with the 'Bugs', giant Arachnids from the planet Klendathu. The war itself, though vividly described, is often incidental to long passages of futuristic political philosophy that detail the failures of twentieth-century democracy. Heinlein's politics are put across by the teachers (all veterans) of History and Moral Philosophy (H&MP) classes, which Rico attends at High School and as part of officer training. Major Reid explains:

> Superficially, our system is only slightly different; we have democracy unlimited by race, colour, creed, birth, wealth, sex, or conviction, and anyone may win sovereign power by a usually short and not too arduous term of service. . . . But that slight difference is one between a system that works, since it is constructed to match the facts, and one that is inherently unstable. Since sovereign franchise is the ultimate in human authority, we insure that all who wield it accept the ultimate in social responsibility – we require each person who wishes to exert control over the state to wager his own life – and lose it, if need be – to save the life of the state.
>
> (Heinlein, pp. 145–6)

This has much in common with the 'Cold War paranoia' associated with 1950s sci-fi films like *Invasion of the Body Snatchers*

(1955) and *Red Planet Mars* (1952). Alasdair Spark suggests that 'Heinlein's opinions really belong to the "native and proud of it" school epitomized by sceptical pundits such as H.L. Mencken, or the vulgar Nietzsche of Ayn Rand; he is perhaps best considered as a social Darwinist, whose ideal society is one in which the individual is free to rise to his "natural" level of power, wealth and authority'.[10] Heinlein offers his crypto-fascist utopia only as one possible functioning world, from the tendentious point of view of an enthusiastic future citizen. The considerable pleasure of his novel lies in the extremism of its liberal-baiting ideas, which are deliciously outrageous and estranging.

Ed Neumeier, the co-author of *RoboCop*, had written an original scenario (*Outpost 7*) about bugs in space before the decision was taken to buy the rights to Heinlein's novel.[11] In adapting it, he was faced with much more than another potential 'creature feature'. His source was a canonical, albeit very controversial SF novel, whose reputation depended on political attitudes very much of its period. Considered as material for an action movie, however, the novel was an ideal 'hyphenate' of the combat and SF genres: a Second World War story in outer space.

The film focuses on a group of high-school friends from Buenos Aires: Johnny Rico (Casper Van Dien), his girlfriend Carmen Ibanez (Denise Richards), Zander Barcalow (Patrick Muldoon), Dizzy Flores (Dina Meyer) and Carl Jenkins (Neil Patrick Howard). The actors were virtually unknown, having mostly graduated from television. They volunteer for Federal Service, and after harsh-but-fair basic training, the friends graduate to their respective military roles. Rico stays in the infantry, keen for revenge against the Bugs after they nuke his home city; Carmen becomes a pilot; and Carl Jenkins's psychic abilities are put to use by Military Intelligence. In a series of brilliantly orchestrated battle sequences, the last hour of the film stages the gruesome war against the Bugs, played out on their bleak and featureless planets. Of these scenes, which are astonishingly brutal and exciting, it is relevant to cite Yvonne Tasker's comments on the action film: '[T]he cinema as sensuous experience is too often neglected. Features such as the breathtaking nature of visual spectacle, or the feelings of exhilaration at the expansive landscape in which the hero operates, are fundamental to the action cinema.'[12] Eventually the troopers capture a Brain Bug, one of the aliens' high command. A FedNet broadcast – a fusion of television and the internet – informs us that victory against the Bugs is assured.

While the visuals are sophisticated, and the battle scenes numbingly realistic, the film's dialogue is unnervingly camp and clichéd. Neumeier's solution to updating the novel was to rework it, saying 'one of the main goals of *Starship Troopers* the movie is to suggest the feel of those boys-turns-into-warrior stories of the 1940s and '50s'.[13] Although he parodies Heinlein's novel, he does not obscure its underlying ideas. Indeed the new context lends them fresh meaning and relevance. Through a loving pastiche of the discourses of the Second World War and the Cold War, Neumeier wryly acknowledges the historical context of both Heinlein's novel and the 1950s sci-fi movies that inspire the film's xenophobic imagery. Appropriating Heinlein's ideas allows, too, for deadpan satire of authoritarian trends in contemporary America. Verhoeven, who came to the project after the script was written, agreed to retain the novel's ideas because 'When I started, I thought this country's starting to flirt with those ideas and so we could make a little bit of a joke out of that'.[14] He also saw the chance to return to the themes of *Soldaat van Oranje* (*Soldier of Orange*), his 1977 film about the Dutch resistance to Nazism.

Heinlein's philosophy is condensed in a speech by the philosophy instructor Rasczak (Michael Ironside), a character invented for the film, who sternly espouses the merits of military authoritarianism. The seriousness of his lecture is drolly undermined by shots of bored pupils sending cartoon love messages to each other on touch-screens:

RASCZAK: Why are only citizens allowed to vote? . . . When you vote, you're exercising political authority. You're using force. And force, my friends, is violence, the supreme authority from which all other authority derives. . . . Whether it's exerted by ten or ten billion, political authority is violence by degree. The people we call citizens have earned the right to wield it.

DIZZY: My mother always says that violence never solves anything.

RASCZAK: Really? I wonder what the city fathers of Hiroshima would have to say about that. You.

CARMEN: They probably wouldn't say anything. Hiroshima was destroyed.

RASCZAK: Correct. Naked force has settled more issues in history than any other factor. The contrary opinion, 'violence never solves anything', is wishful thinking at its worst.

In keeping with the film's parodic intention, the Bugs' subspecies echo the 'the faceless World War II Axis troops and exaggerated weaponry seen in old Hollywood propaganda film. . . . The Warriors are the ground-based troops, the Plasma Bugs are the heavy artillery, the Hoppers are the air force, and the Tankers are like flame-throwing tanks' (Magid, p. 73). Despite the troopers' futuristic technology, they mostly engage in hand-to-mandible warfare with the Warrior Bugs. In fact, the film, like the novel, is a traditional 'grunt's eye-view' of war.

FedNet broadcasts interrupt the narrative, hectoring us in pompous tones to volunteer for Federal Service. Asking 'Would you like to know more?', they fill in details about the world of the future. Criminals are executed live on the Net; children are encouraged to handle guns and to further the war effort by crushing insects underfoot. The FedNet works in the satirical manner of the TV broadcasts that punctuate *RoboCop*, in which beaming idiots jokingly relate news of social breakdown and nuclear accidents. Elsewhere, however, there are no obvious cues to ironic distance. The political address throughout seems to be that of a derangedly over-the-top recruitment film. As tends to happen with postmodern films, you either 'get' the joke or you don't. The style of the film is impeccably fascist, *Triumph of the Will* with a cast of bubbleheaded jocks and co-eds. The Federal government meets against a background of regimental eagles; echoes of Nazi iconography abound, from the chiselled Aryanism of (some, not all) the troopers to the SS leather coats of the intelligence officers. The twist is that these signifiers of Nazism are associated with the 'Allies' in what is otherwise a familiar American war film. On the one hand, Heinlein is confirmed retrospectively as an embarrassing fascist; on the other, the ideological function of the war film is made inescapably clear. The audience is manipulated into identifying with and cheering on 'Nazis'.

Verhoeven takes the clichés of the American war movie and exaggerates them to bloodthirsty excess. The standard scene in which a Drill Sergeant challenges recruits to fight ends here with his breaking one recruit's arm; to emphasise the usefulness of knives in combat, he impales another recruit's hand to a wall. Similarly, the characters are treated with hyperbolic – and hilarious – ruthlessness. Carmen vomits as she dissects a Bug; Rico grins triumphantly while covered in ridiculous green alien goo. Women are ripped apart; brains are slurped from their skulls; the ground is littered with dismembered torsos and headless trunks. Despite this carnage, the troopers are gung-ho to the point of mindlessness, with their 'Death from Above' tattoos and cries of 'Rasczak's Roughnecks!'.

Crucially, none of them questions the basis of their society. This obedience is of course essential to a utopia, whose citizens must universally recognise its perfection. In contrast to *RoboCop* and *Total Recall*, there are no signs of the conventional postmodern dystopia: no megalopolis, anarchic underclass, or evil corporate leadership. Equally, no one resists utopia, as in *Zardoz* (1973) or *Demolition Man* (1993). The Federation is presented as integrated, non-sexist, universally accepted and even pleasurable. The platoons are impeccably multi-racial. Women fight wars and play American football alongside men; the sexes even shower together. As Andrew O'Hehir remarks, in a brilliantly insightful review, 'Heinlein's "utopia" may have been a deadly earnest prescription, but for Verhoeven it becomes an aesthetic and ideological field of play'.[15] Heinlein's 'fascism' of the consensual 1950s is hijacked to satirise the intolerant conformisms of both Right and Left. As Verhoeven said:

> In my opinion, the world of *Starship Troopers* and recent America are not so far apart. I recently heard someone on the news say that the free speech we are experiencing here would not be possible in Japan – but how can you say that after Watergate, Irangate, Whitewatergate and all the other gates? The belief in spiritual freedom is the most powerful myth in this country.[16]

Most important, *Starship Troopers* carefully makes its utopia politically correct, in the most reductive and dimwitted sense that each of the characters is an inoffensive 'strong' stereotype. Emotional uplift is offered to all – and especially to women, whose 'musculinisation' has increasingly been in a feature of action films (see Tasker, pp. 14–34). The disabled have their honoured place: a biology teacher is blind, while paraplegic veterans are held in the highest respect. Racism meanwhile is reserved for the inhuman Bugs. The heroes might look Aryan, but they are South, not North Americans; and when the Federal Marshall resigns, he is replaced by a middle-aged black woman. Everyone – except one cowardly general – is a perfect role model.

This oppressive utopianism relates the film closely to the despised lap-dancing satire *Showgirls*, which also depicts a system (Las Vegas) that runs by clearly understood and generally obeyed rules: in *Showgirls* the desire for money and power; in *Starship Troopers*, for career and conformity. In the first, it is others who are sacrificed; in the second, it is potentially oneself. What disturbs in either case is that no alternative is offered. Escape and resistance seem equally unthinkable. Although Nomi flounces out of Las Vegas at the end of *Showgirls*, it is only so that she can pursue her dreams in Holly-wood. Whereas *RoboCop* and *Total Recall* depict individuals rebel-ling against corrupt corporatism, *Showgirls* and *Starship Troopers* are darker visions of societies in which ideological complicity is inescapable and absolute.

As well as being perversely utopian for a sci-fi film, *Starship Troopers* slyly subverts the conventions of the action movie by dwelling on the collectivist ethos of the war genre. Action heroes tend to be macho individualists who, though ultimately working on society's behalf, are hostile to authority and the strict letter of the law. At the same time action films tend to articulate the popu-list assumption that governments are conspiracies against the elec-torate. *Starship Troopers* reverts to the pattern of *The Sands of Iwo Jima* (1949), in which individual heroism matters less than the forging of collective identities, and when there were causes still worth dying for. The result masquerades as the first pro-war film since *The Green Berets* (1968). In few films are the heroes so at ease with the society that sends them to their deaths.[17]

To some extent, as in *Independence Day*, the film's sardonic political correctness reflects the difficulty of attaching any negative connotation to an identifiable group of humans. Bug-like aliens are perfect because no one will take offence or picket cinemas on their behalf.[18] Verhoeven noted, 'The US is desperate to find a new enemy. . . . Alien sci-fi gives us a terrifying enemy that's politically correct. They're bad. They're evil. And they are not even human' (Van Scheers, p. xiii). Of course the revived motif of the hostile alien is not entirely without political interest. From film to film, it seems to mean something very different: fear of 'wetback' illegal aliens (*Men in Black*); an excuse to replay Desert Storm (*Stargate* (1994)); or simply, as in *Independence Day*, a paradigm of 'structuring otherness', something to define Americans against.

Up to the end of the Cold War, the Bugs would have been understood to 'represent' Communists of some description. Or, since the imagery of emotionless inhumanity is more or less reversible, they might have stood for Germans, as in the television series *V* or *Dr Who*. At any rate there was the pressure of some insistent subtext, some identifiable signified. This is not the case in *Starship Troopers*. Insofar as the film appropriates the combat genre, the Bugs do indeed stand-in for the 'Nazis' or Second World War Japanese, though, to confuse matters, it is the troopers who sport quasi-Nazi regalia. And while the film echoes the anti-Communism of both the novel and 1950s sci-fi movies, the Bugs are neither Russians nor the Asian Communists that Heinlein seemed to have in mind:

> Heinlein's description of the Bugs fulfils the familiar 'yellow peril' stereotype of an Asian enemy, updated with Communist overtones during the Cold War. . . . The Bugs are caste-stratified (divided into Workers, Soldiers, Brains, and Royalty), inscrutable, and 'inhuman', chiefly in their willingness to spend lives. . . . The comparison of alien and Asian Communist is interesting, not least for the term 'Bugs'. . . . This evokes the pejorative applied to other Asian enemies such as Japanese, Koreans, and subsequently Vietnamese – people who, as GI memoirs repeatedly mention, were not considered human, but as mere 'gooks'.
>
> (Spark, pp. 156–7)

This signified now refers nostalgically to a time when otherness seemed absolute and enemies were more readily identified. Alternatively, as Spark implies, the Bugs might be read in the light of the representation of 'Charlie' in Vietnam war films. We are reminded too of the Western, with the Bugs as Indians fighting off genocidal colonists. The film is a compendium of knowingly reworked and culmulatively devastating allusions to the ways in which war films dehumanise the enemy. This promiscuity of reference baffles the usual reductive interpretations. At one point, when the Bugs besiege an outpost, the film irresistibly recalls *Beau Geste* (1939) and *Zulu* (1964). At another, celebrating a victory by breaking out the beer and fiddling 'Dixie', the troopers weirdly turn into Confederate Rebels, which presumably makes the Bugs Yankees. At another level of representation, the Bugs are simply very big insects, phobia-inducing monsters to be exterminated. But here again the film unsettles. The Bugs surprise the Federation with their intelligence and military cunning, and win the first skirmish of the war. The captured Brain Bug is not quite the gross, squashy termite queen that it appears. Carl reads its mind and announces that 'It is afraid!'; a cheer goes up from the massed troops and the music swells to mark their triumph. But it makes for an unsettling recognition that the Bugs are not really like the insects of earth, that most disposable of life-forms. This insect can think, and feel emotions. By the end of the film, parallels between the Bugs and the humans have become inescapable. Both species are colonialist, hierarchical, and made for war. (Carl himself is a kind of human Brain Bug; he enters Johnny's head to direct him to Carmen, as the Bug literally penetrates Zander's.) Evolution has done to the Bugs what social engineering is doing to the humans. As the blind biology teacher implies in an early scene, while her students dissect Arachnids, the ideal citizen of utopia would be an insect.[19]

The representation of the Bugs is a free-wheeling parody of how the enemy other is demonised in films and its genocide made palatable. Goading us to think like fascists (in other words, like the ideal audience of any militaristic movie), the film rouses us against the absurdly overdetermined otherness of the Bugs. Even as it does so, the film insinuates that, biology aside, there is little to choose between the troopers and their foe. The movie illustrates the untrustworthy nature of narrative and comments on the power of popular forms to mask ideologies.

So far my reading of *Starship Troopers* has taken its 'irony' for granted, largely by seeing it through the lens of authorial intention (Neumeier's as well as Verhoeven's). I have presented it as, first, a parody of Heinlein's novel; second, a wicked deconstruction of the xenophobic militarism of both 1950s sci-fi and the war film; and third, a deliberately camp and overblown pastiche of the contemporary blockbuster. Even so, the 'ironic' reading is not necessarily the obvious or dominant one. It is true that Verhoeven stressed the film's satire in interviews, and that most reviewers picked up on it. But the irony of this kind of 'modest proposal' is much less conspicuous than the exultant parody of *RoboCop* or the slapstick farce of *Mars Attacks!*. Critics were bemused by rather than hostile to the film and audiences respond to it with extremes of rapture and loathing. Certainly the film is exceptionally ambiguous and divisive, perhaps too clever and contradictory for its own good. As with *Showgirls*, a certain (elitist?) cultural capital is required to turn out the kind of ironic interpretation that recognises 'eye-candy' as an auteurist masterwork. It requires, for instance, not only a liking for what might be called 'heterosexual camp', but also an awareness of Verhoeven's ambivalent fascination with American low culture. His American films are models of postmodern double-coding, from *RoboCop*, with its action scenes for 'the masses' and anti-capitalist satire for the critics; through the equivocal narratives of *Total Recall* and *Basic Instinct*; to *Showgirls*, which was so deeply sunk in self-parody that no one understood it.[20] *Showgirls'* satire of America is more intelligent than its innumerable critics allowed, but the near universal hatred the film inspired is proof that Verhoeven badly miscalculated his audience's tolerance for camp 'subversions from within'. The disappointing revenues for *Starship Troopers* imply that his quirky brand of postmodern irony is starting to alienate the multiplex audience.

Starship Troopers is postmodern, then, in the crude sense that it can be read straight or ironically. While one part of the audience laughs with the film, the other laughs at it, or cheers on the troopers. Others still might point out that irony is not necessarily 'progressive'. An attitude of 'not really meaning it' can smuggle through much that is ideologically pernicious. Like parody, irony tends to amoral nihilism, raising style above content: aestheticising politics by disavowing the meaning of what it says.[21] A game with the signifiers of fascism might still produce a fascist film.

Contemporary Hollywood films are ideologically complex partly because they have to reach out to multiple demographics and provide something for everyone. As a result they are highly self-conscious, parodic and reflexive, all of which unsettles any confident diagnosis of their 'real' latent content. *Starship Troopers* is a extreme manifestation of this tendency and openly embraces the suspect ideological baggage of popular genres. The subtexts are on the surface, all spelt out and suspiciously readable. Faced with an ironic and self-aware film like *Starship Troopers*, the critic is like one of the troopers confronted with an apparently dumb, homogenous Bug – only to find that it is not quite as stupid as it looks. Finally, the film's overwhelming visuals remind us that the success of a work of science fiction is not reducible to its portable 'ideas', any more than its meaning is exhausted by 'deep' ideological analysis. Verhoeven's complex and sardonic treatment of the novel ensures that the film, though mere 'sci-fi' rather than 'SF', is altogether more rich, complex, beautiful and troubling.

Notes

1. 'SF' or 'sf' are the preferred terms among the science fiction community; 'sci-fi' is used by journalists and the ignorant public, most usually for TV series and films. I've never seen the harm in referring to 'sci-fi', and so I'll stick to popular usage and refer throughout to 'sci-fi' films, reserving SF as useful shorthand for the written stuff.
2. Robert Heinlein, *Starship Troopers* ([1959], New York, 1987). Further page references are cited in the text.
3. Galoob released a range of *Starship Troopers* action figures. See Richard Holliss, '*Starship Troopers*', *Area 51: Sci-Fi Collecting* no. 4 (March 1998), pp. 59–62.
4. Kingsley Amis, *New Maps of Hell* (London, 1969).
5. Edward James, *Science Fiction in the Twentieth Century* (Oxford, 1994), p. 31. Further page references are cited in the text.
6. See Scott Bukatman, *Blade Runner* (London: British Film Institute, 1997), p. 9.
7. John Baxter, *Science Fiction in the Cinema, 1985–1970* (London, 1970), p. 10.
8. On utopianism in recent sci-fi films, see I.Q. Hunter, 'Capitalism Most Triumphant: Bill & Ted's Excellent History Lesson' in Deborah Cartmell, I.Q. Hunter, Heidi Kaye and Imelda Whelehan (eds), *Pulping Fictions* (London, 1996), pp. 111–24.
9. The film's ironic reversal of sci-fi's dystopian imagery 'attracted predictable liberal outrage in the US'. See 'Starship Stormtroopers', *Sight and Sound* vol. 8, no. 1 (January 1998), p. 7.
10. Alasdair Spark, 'The Art of Future War: *Starship Troopers, The Forever War* and Vietnam' in Tom Shippey (ed.), *Essays and Studies 1990: Fictional Space: Essays on Contemporary Science Fiction* (Oxford, 1991), p. 136. Further page references are cited in the text.
11. Paul M. Sammon, 'Bug Bytes', *Cinefax* no.75 (March 1998), p. 68. For a detailed account of the film's production, see also Paul M. Sammon, *The Making of Starship Troopers* (London, 1997).
12. Yvonne Tasker, *Spectacular Bodies: Gender, Genre and the Action Cinema* (London: Routledge, 1993), p. 6. See also David Bordwell, *Making Meaning: Inference and Rhetoric in the Interpretation of Cinema* (Cambridge, MA, 1989), pp. 263–74, for a discussion of

'sensuous criticism'. A technical description of the movie's Oscar-nominated special effects can be found in Sammon, 'BugBytes', and in three articles in *American Cinematographer* vol. 78, no. 11 (November 1997): Les Paul Robley, 'Interstellar Exterminators' (pp. 56–66); Ron Magid, 'Starship Maneuvers' (pp. 67–72); and Ron Magid, 'Pest Control' (pp.73–78). Further page references are cited in the text.

13. Bill Warren, 'Writing *Starship Troopers*: Ed Neumeier', *Starship Troopers Souvenir Magazine* (London, 1997), p. 19.

14. Verhoeven in Jeff Dawson, 'Basic Insect', *Empire* no. 104 (February 1998), p. 81.

15. Andrew O'Hehir, review of *Starship Troopers*, *Sight and Sound* vol. 8, no. 1 (January 1998), p. 54.

16. Verhoeven, in Rob van Scheers, *Paul Verhoeven*, trans. Aletta Stevens (London, 1997), p. xii. Further page references are cited in the text.

17. Even here Verhoeven's intention is ambiguous and thought-provoking. Since the Second World War was a 'good war', its purpose impossible to satirise, the film cannot help but come across as 'pro-war'. Although politically distasteful, the film's fascist utopia enables the soldiers eventually to gain the upper hand. The troopers' willingness to obey authority and die for their race might contradict standard anti-war sentiments, but a similar willingness was pretty useful in defeating the Nazis. As Verhoeven put it, in *Starship Troopers* 'the society which is so successful in fighting these aliens is a society you might, perhaps, disapprove of', quoted in Anonymous, 'Space: A Bug and Beyond', *SFX* no. 34 (January 1998), p. 48.

18. *Basic Instinct* was picketed by gay rights activists for depicting bisexual and lesbian women as serial killers.

19. The scientist's 'rational' assumption that creatures unclouded by ego and morality will not only be 'perfect' organisms but will ultimately succeed humanity is a familiar one in sci-fi films. It echoes fears of how democracy would cope with a truly ruthless foe, whether Nazi or Communist. Mark Jancovich argues, against the critical orthodoxy, that 1950s sci-fi was not simply anti-Communist, but that it used the imagery of depersonalised aliens to criticise the period's faith in science and conformism. This implies that *Starship Troopers*' ambiguity and social criticism are more in keeping with 1950s sci-fi than conventional interpretations of it would lead us to expect. See Mark Jancovich, *Rational Fears: American Horror in the 1950s* (Manchester, 1996).

20. On Verhoeven's use of ambiguity and indecipherable narratives, see Paul Verhoeven, *Showgirls: Portrait of a Film* (London, 1995), p. 21.

21. See Chuck Kleinhans, 'Taking Out the Trash: Camp and the Politics of Parody' in Moe Meyer (ed.), *The Politics and Poetics of Camp*, (London, 1994), p. 198.

Part Four
Writing about Cinema

13 *Writing and reputation: The Searchers 1956–1976*

Douglas Pye

During the 1970s *The Searchers* achieved a very unusual status among Hollywood movies – celebrated both by critics and by young American film-makers who quoted it, re-worked scenes, or re-cycled its narrative.[1] Once a work achieves such widespread acclaim the judgement implied can seem both natural and permanent, even when we are attuned to the ways in which styles and reputations are commodified and consumed. The implications of a film's or a film-maker's status, the cultural meanings of reputation, the history of debate and polemic that produce shifts in the canon, are often rendered invisible in the assumption of common assent. *The Searchers* is just a single case in a process by which the cultural status of Hollywood cinema has been transformed, but it is also a striking example of how the past is constantly mined and re-forged to reflect the concerns of the present.

Ford and authorship I

The first considered accounts of Ford as a director of films on specifically American themes were developed by the journal *Sequence* after the Second World War. *Sequence* writers (notably Lindsay Anderson) celebrated aspects of Ford's career – especially his genre movies – which had received little critical attention. Anderson stressed the distinctiveness of Ford's direction in films like *They Were Expendable* (1945), *My Darling Clementine* (1946), *She Wore a Yellow Ribbon* (1949) and *Wagonmaster* (1950) as the work of a 'poet' of the American past: 'there is a sense ... of regret for ways of living at once simpler and more colourful than those of today ... [and an] ... implied lack of concern with contemporary issues'.[2] His vision seemed to Anderson 'inspired by an optimistic faith in man's nature, a reverence for the human creature . . . combined with a firm emphasis on discipline . . . on moral and social duties . . .' (Anderson, p. 31). *Sequence* was important in bringing Ford's genre films into critical focus, judging them not by the apparent 'seriousness' of their subject matter but by the individuality and resonance of their direction. In these terms, Ford's most personal films were often the least 'showy'. This argument, and *Sequence*'s view of Ford as a traditional artist, rooted in the American past, established crucial frameworks for later criticism.

The Searchers: 1956

The film was extensively reviewed, and on the whole positively received as a major new Western. But significant reservations were also expressed and these are interesting for the evaluative criteria they imply and for the ways in which they show reviewers grappling with unusual aspects of the film. Several of the issues which became central to later accounts of the film are in fact present from the outset, and two of these – characterisation and narrative structure – posed particular problems.

In one of the most positive reviews, in the *Daily Worker*, the film's characterisation is related to recent developments in the Western: 'The characters have stopped being black-and-white. . . . They now quite often take on the colour and depth of real people . . . with feelings and motives and ideas which go a long way past the simple old Western philosophy of just being against bad men.'[3] More generally though, questions were raised about unexplained motivation. For *Variety*, '[Ethan's] motivations . . . are unclear'[4] and the *Daily Sketch* reviewer was similarly puzzled: 'so little of the motivation is explained on the screen. Why has the surly Mr Wayne such a chip on his shoulder about all Indians? Why, at the end, is he ready to shoot his own niece – in the supposition that she is now a squaw . . . ?'[5] Expectations that motivation will be explained are paralleled by criteria for the coherence of narrative structure. *Motion Picture Herald*'s view that 'The story is straight and strong'[6] was very much a minority. More characteristic were views like those of the *Monthly Film Bulletin* that 'the narrative . . . becomes a little aimless in the middle passages'; the *Daily*

Worker that 'Ford tells a slow, sometimes disjointed, story'; and *Tribune* that the 'final effect is rambling and discoursive'.[7] *Tribune* was particularly critical: 'The search progresses in fits and starts, lingers ... over particular incidents, switches back too often to the Texas starting point, and finally a love affair of Marty's holds everything up just at the moment when the child is finally found. ... the tension is snapped, and the rescue comes more in the nature of an epilogue than a climax.'

The representation of racism in the film, a major preoccupation of more recent critics, was touched on by few reviews. The *Evening Standard* identified the racist attitudes expressed in the film and took them to be shared by the film: 'There is an unpleasant undertone of race hatred in Wayne's continually stressed nausea at the very thought of a white woman living with a red man'.[8] The *Daily Worker*, on the other hand, saw the film's handling of racism as a significant strength: 'Ford's way with the primitive race hatred is not to pretend that it didn't exist or to introduce a high-minded character to argue it away. His method is to show it for what it was, an irrational reaction which no warm-hearted person could sustain when it became a matter of individual people instead of abstractions.'

Because of his earlier championing of Ford, Lindsay Anderson's review is particularly interesting.[9] He found the film unsatisfactory in ways similar to those identified by other reviewers: there was 'too much' story for a director whose best films 'have relied less and less on narrative and more on mood' (Caughie, p. 76); the acting and the moods of the film were 'uneven', with Wayne's performance in particular lacking 'either complexity or consistency' (Caughie, p. 77). The character of Ethan, in fact, was central to what Anderson felt was wrong with the film: 'its hero, Ethan Edwards, is an unmistakable neurotic, devoured by an irrational hatred of Indians. ... His search for his little niece ... abducted by Comanches seems ... inspired less by love and honour than by an obsessive desire to do her to death as a contaminated creature' (Caughie, p. 76). However, unlike other reviewers, Anderson's critical response was driven by what he saw as the strengths of Ford's earlier work and by what he interpreted as a failure of 'inner conviction' on Ford's part in *The Searchers* (Caughie, p. 76). For a Ford movie it seemed to have the wrong character at its centre: 'The only way, one would have thought, that Ford could give such a story significance was to make its hero not Edwards but Martin Pawley. . . . At least here is a character who stands for something. [But] It is . . . Edwards who stands at the heart . . . what is Ford, of all directors, to do with a hero like this?' (Caughie, p. 76).

The assumptions at work in the reviews are striking. While only Anderson's sprang from a considered view of Ford's artistic identity, most reviewers attributed the film essentially to Ford and commented positively on his reputation as a director of Westerns. But the dominant frameworks are those of entertainment and of genre. Although the *Daily Worker* saw Ford as having 'done as much as any man to elevate the Western into a work of art', the word 'elevate' eloquently implies the cultural position the Western was generally seen to hold and this in turn circumscribed the claims reviewers made for the film. While they identified aspects of the film which distinguish it from many other Westerns – especially the unusual narrative structure and Ethan's confusing motivation – criteria of well-crafted narrative led them to identify these as weaknesses. The reviews strongly suggest that while the dramatic power of *The Searchers* was clear, the film didn't fit the available frameworks, even though one or two acknowledged that the Western itself was in the process of change. Anderson's review was extraordinary for the clarity with which he identified (on the basis of his view of Ford as the optimistic poet of the American past) a good deal of what was problematic about *The Searchers*, but like other reviewers he found the film unsatisfactory because it didn't fit the framework he brought to it.

When the film was 'discovered' fifteen years later, frameworks and cultural context had changed substantially and some of the issues puzzled over or criticised by reviewers became central to new ways in which the film came to be viewed.

Ford and authorship II

One index of changes in critical taste and cultural status is provided by lists of film critics' 'all-time greats', the most high-profile of which has been conducted in *Sight and Sound* every decade since 1952.[10] In the first three polls Hollywood sound cinema was represented only by Chaplin and Welles. 1982 therefore represented a major break with *Citizen Kane* (1941) joined by Kelly and

Donen's *Singin' in the Rain* (1952) at joint third, Hitchcock's *Vertigo* (1958) at joint seventh and *The Searchers* at joint tenth. In 1992 *Singin' in the Rain* had vanished but *Vertigo* was fourth and *The Searchers* fifth. The presence of two Hollywood sound movies in addition to the apparently permanent *Citizen Kane* hardly constitutes a revolution but it marks a significant inflection of cultural standing in the wake of the critical battles over Hollywood cinema in the previous decades.

The approaches to Hollywood cinema pioneered in France in the 1950s and developed in Britain and the US in the early 1960s with the appearance of *Movie* and Andrew Sarris's work in *Film Culture*, laid the basis for a remarkable transformation of attitudes to Hollywood cinema. They focused on the work of the director as the controlling figure in the realisation of a film and identified directors who had created distinctive bodies of work within the studio system. Although Ford and Hitchcock already had well-established reputations, both became central to the development of 'authorship' approaches to Hollywood.

Unlike Hitchcock, however, Ford was marginal to the initial debates about Hollywood cinema that centred first on *Cahiers du Cinéma* in France and then on *Movie* in Great Britain.[11] Andrew Sarris wrote on Ford in *Film Culture*, particularly on Ford's concern with American history, but few extended accounts appeared in the early 1960s.[12] But Ford was a pivotal figure in the second wave of authorship approaches, in the late 1960s and early 1970s, with the result that by 1975, in the flood of film books that signalled the increasing cultural significance of cinema in Britain and America and the gradual institutionalisation of film studies, Ford had become one of the most written about of Hollywood directors. His significance was such that in 1981 John Caughie chose him as the sole director case study in his reader, *Theories of Authorship*.

New versions of Ford's authorship emerged slowly during the early 1960s. In a *Cahiers du Cinéma* review of *Cheyenne Autumn* (1964) in 1965, Jean-Louis Comolli commented that 'for a good twenty years he [Ford] has been painstakingly dismantling the myths that he himself more or less created. . . . Ford hasn't waited for Sam Peckinpah or Robert Aldrich in order to make "anti-Westerns"' (Caughie, pp. 109–16), one of the earliest claims for Ford's modernity and a perception that anticipates later accounts of *The Searchers*. A month or two before, Peter Wollen's first discussion of Ford appeared in *New Left Review*.[13] Wollen probably played the major role in redefining Ford's authorship during the 1960s, beginning with this article and continuing in a more overtly theoretical context in *Signs and Meaning in the Cinema* (1969).[14] Like Anderson, Wollen associated Ford with specifically American themes but he outlined a very different Ford: someone whose work was 'full of contradictions' (Caughie, p. 103) which he traced in his politics, his representations of the military, Indians, his ideas of 'home' and 'community'. *The Man Who Shot Liberty Valance* (1962), for instance, was 'ambiguous in its attitudes towards legend and truth, towards the necessity of progress and the values of the past . . . ambiguities not of confusion or deception, but of a contradiction which Ford cannot resolve. . . .' (Caughie, pp. 107–8).

These ideas of 'ambiguity' and 'contradiction' were developed in *Signs and Meaning in the Cinema* within a more theorised approach to authorship, based on the structuralist analysis which informed a number of other publications of the time.[15] Wollen identified recurrent structural oppositions in Ford's films: 'garden versus wilderness, plough-share versus sabre, settler versus nomad, European versus Indian, civilised versus savage, book versus gun, married versus unmarried, East versus West' (Wollen, p. 94). The 'contradictions' he identified in the earlier article are analytically focused as thematic and ideological 'antinomies' – inflections of polarised images which 'have dominated American thought and literature' – through which the ambiguities of Ford's films could be identified and their development across his career charted (Wollen, p. 96).

Between the publication of Wollen's two accounts of Ford, Andrew Sarris's *The American Cinema* and Peter Bogdanovich's Ford interview book appeared.[16] Bogdanovich's introduction was significant for its overview of Ford's career and for the consolidation of ideas touched on by Sarris and Wollen, that defeat and failure were Ford's recurring themes (Bogdanovich, p. 23). *The American Cinema* codified Sarris's approach to Hollywood by ranking directors in a series of categories. His purpose was explicitly evaluative; authorship was for Sarris a principle for identifying individuality within what was perceived as the largely undifferentiated 'forest' of Hollywood and at the top he identified fourteen

'Pantheon Directors', one of whom was Ford. He saw Ford's career as 'a rising parabola from *Steamboat Round the Bend* to *Seven Women*' (Sarris, p. 47), implicitly placing greatest emphasis on the later work, but in overall emphasis Sarris at this point had more in common with Anderson than with Wollen's growing emphasis on contradiction. He identified values of 'the agrarian order of family and community', saw 'Ford's visual treatment of the past as a luminous memory more real than the present' and suggested that Ford's vision of the world remained 'unified' (Sarris, p. 48).

The flood of writing on Ford began in the 1970s. 1971 saw Ford issues of *Film Comment* and *Focus on Film*, the first book on Ford in English (John Baxter's *The Cinema of John Ford*, 1971) and, in the first three extended accounts of *The Searchers*, the claim that the film was a masterpiece.[17] One other important article on Ford was also published in 1971: Robin Wood's excellent ' "Shall we Gather at the River": the late films of John Ford'.[18] Although Wood criticises aspects of Wollen's analysis of Ford and his approach to the films is very different, some of Wood's analytical terms are not dissimilar to Wollen's. For instance, he writes: 'diverse pulls and impulses have always existed in Ford. At times they can give rise to a rich complexity ... or carefully defined ambivalence ... at others to confusion and self-contradiction' (Caughie, p. 88); and 'The ambivalence of Ford's attitude to civilization that reaches full explicitness in *Liberty Valance* is implicit in all his work' (Caughie, p. 92).

Although in some of this new writing references to cultural perspectives beyond cinema (notably to Henry Nash Smith's *Virgin Land*[19]) were beginning to suggest more complex ways of placing Ford, the discussions were dominated by authorship. But the image of Ford was changing from the optimistic, unselfconscious poet of the American past to someone whose films were seen as characterised by 'contradiction', 'ambiguity', 'oppositions', 'antinomies', 'ambivalence'. These emphases created an intellectual framework within which *The Searchers* could emerge as a crucial film. It already has a significant place in both Wollen's and Sarris's accounts of Ford. Wood hardly mentions it, although in discussing Ford's relationship with contemporary America he poses a question which almost defines ways in which *The Searchers* came to be understood: 'What can Ford possibly be expected to make of contemporary American society – whether one calls it disintegrating or permissive

– where no values are certain or constant, all traditions questioned
and most rejected, all continuity disrupted, and where the army is
a dirty word?' (Caughie, p. 95).

The Searchers: 1969–1976

Film criticism, like any discourse, is marked by its historical moment.
When the first extended accounts appeared, a variety of contextual factors may well have influenced the identification of *The
Searchers* as a key film. America was embroiled in the Vietnam
war and experiencing a period of almost unprecedented challenge
to traditional values, associated with the anti-war movement, civil
rights and feminism. Major changes had taken place in Hollywood
following the break-up of the studio system, including changes in
audience and challenges, linked to contemporary ideological crises,
to genre conventions. This affected all genres of male action but
notably the Western, which was entering its final great phase in
Hollywood production, dominated by Peckinpah and the 'Vietnam
Western'.[20] In many of these films both the protagonist's moral
identity and his range of power are questioned and traditional
narrative functions are removed from the hero, so that the symmetry
of moral rightness and control over significant action is broken.
The view of white American society is correspondingly bleak.

   One of the central emphases in accounts of *The Searchers* was
on its hero, now described in terms very different to the 1956
reviews. For Peter Wollen 'Edwards is ambiguous; the antinomies
invade the personality of the protagonist himself. The oppositions
tear Edwards in two: he is a tragic hero' (Wollen, p. 96). Wollen's
terms are strikingly value-laden: greater complexity becomes a
criterion of value and the idea of psychic division leads to Ethan
receiving the culturally loaded designation of 'tragic hero'. But
Wollen also stresses Ethan's links with the villain, Scar, and therefore his moral ambivalence – a hero who is also 'savage'. This is a
significant inflection of the familiar description of the Western
hero as someone who straddles civilisation and wilderness but
whose moral identity is rarely in doubt and it is striking that in the
same year Jim Kitses described Anthony Mann's heroes in similar
terms.[21] In these revaluations of Western tradition, versions of the
traditional Western hero were being discarded and a hero for the
Vietnam period was being defined.[22]

None of the accounts of *The Searchers* that appeared in 1971 refer to Wollen, although each refers back to earlier writing on Ford and all offer revisionist accounts. Baxter begins his chapter: 'Is there any more American film than *The Searchers*, any work that more concisely sums up the dichotomy in American consciousness between the pioneer and the businessman, the soldier and the farmer? In its extraordinary economy, its efficiency of technique, the memorable playing of its principals and supporting cast it is perhaps Ford's most perfect philosophical statement' (Baxter, p. 144). 'Dichotomy' continues the growing insistence on thematic conflict. The idea that the film might be seen as a 'philosophical statement' strikes a new note, as does Baxter's suggestion that 'The deep thinking of *The Searchers* is subliminal, carried on in the Ford language of gesture, visual metaphor and action which he uses for his most personal statements' (Baxter, p. 145).

For Sarris *The Searchers* 'manages to sum up stylistically all the best of what Ford had been with all the best of what he was to be' (Caughie, p. 78) and he also evokes a duality of meaning in which the drama is immediate and specific yet at the same time resonant with wider significance. These rather vague evocations represent shared ground among the 1971 writers and an important strand in the growing consensus that in its realisation, its style and imagery, *The Searchers* achieves its potency through implication and suggestion rather than by overtly addressing its themes. More tangibly, Sarris, like Wollen, identifies the divisions within Ethan as a major source of the film's power, but he values what the reviewers criticised, the aspects of motivation which are not made explicit: 'The dramatic struggle ... is ... within the protagonist himself. ... The mystery of the film is what actually happened to Wayne in that fearful moment when he discovers the mutilated bodies of his [family]. Surly, cryptic, almost menacing even before the slaughter, he is invested afterward with obsessiveness and implacability' (Caughie, pp. 80–1). The 'neurotic' nature of the hero, which Lindsay Anderson found inimical to his conception of Ford, and the apparently opaque motivation which reviewers disliked are becoming the keys to the film's emerging stature in the 1970s – an emphasis rather different from Wollen's idea that Ethan's divisions make him a tragic hero but again one that celebrates the unconventional nature of the hero and the film's critical interrogation of specifically American themes.

The most developed of the 1971 articles was McBride and Wilmington's 'Prisoner of the Desert', which probably more than any other established the terms within which the film came to be critically discussed. It shares major emphases with the other writers but in some respects goes much further. They begin and end by stressing that the film is *about* America: Ford's use of Monument Valley is his major metaphor of America itself – the promised land as barren desert. And they end: 'It is the story of America' (McBride and Wilmington, p. 214). This is the most extreme of the various claims that were beginning to be made for *The Searchers* as a specifically American work and the intention is to appropriate a discourse applied to American literature and apply it to a *movie* – an important polemical strategy and an implicit demand that the cultural blinkers that consigned movies to the margins of serious culture should be removed. But in arguing that the film is 'the story of America' they are claiming an even more privileged status for *The Searchers* as a text which illuminates concerns fundamental to America as a nation and which belongs to the great tradition of symbolic fiction which begins with Cooper. They argue that the film is about the settlement of America, the establishment of 'civilisation' and the relationship between community and the Western hero, but suggest that it fundamentally questions traditional generic assumptions and carries in its realisation an insistent metaphorical or even mythic resonance.

Thus, like Baxter and Sarris, they associate some of the power of *The Searchers* with qualities that are difficult to describe: '[It] has that clear yet intangible quality which characterises an artist's masterpiece'; but introduce other, archetypal, frameworks to define the film's resonances, linking Ethan's journey to Homeric models and to a version of the knightly quest; and they introduce the term 'Myth' ('The first images of *The Searchers* are the invocation of a myth') as a further way of reaching towards the unusual status which they attribute to the film (McBride and Wilmington, pp. 210–12).

Their sense of the film's critical relationship to its material centres on Ethan, 'a nomad tortured by his desire for a home', driven mad by the events which bedevil him, 'who turns his violence *against* the family', and whose heroism is increasingly difficult to distinguish from Scar's villainy (McBride and Wilmington, pp. 210–12). Their terms therefore overlap with Wollen's and Sarris's, but in a more developed way than other writers they place *The Searchers* within the traditions of the post-war Western, as one of a number of films which 'criticise the basic assumption of the genre – that the solitude of the hero, because it is an instinctive revulsion against the hypocrisy of civilised society, is *a priori* a good thing' (McBride and Wilmington, p. 212). Indeed, they suggest that in transferring the heroic deeds (finding Debbie, killing Scar) to other characters, 'Ford is destroying the myth of the heroic loner' (McBride and Wilmington, p. 213), an idea that implies not only that the film has the power of myth but that it subjects American myth to critical scrutiny.[23] They also develop an argument that the events of the film are 'bizarre', Ethan's quest is 'absurd', the role of Mose in relation to Ethan produces a 'grotesquerie' accompanied by 'anarchic humour' in which the comic elements provide 'a continuous commentary on the meaning of the drama' (McBride and Wilmington, p. 213). In these ways, the film achieves a dual vision, 'that what is most terrifying in life is frequently a hair's breadth from howling absurdity' (McBride and Wilmington, p. 211). They were also the first writers to take up again the issues of racism that had been touched on in reviews. They argue not only that miscegenation is a central concern of the film but that Ford's grip on the material is critical and essentially coherent, and also (a perception developed in their book) that these racist attitudes and actions are seen by the film as deeply embedded in white society. As part of this they perceive the huge shift in Ford's representations of the cavalry: 'eulogised in his 1940s Westerns, [they] have ... become vindictive white supremacists' (McBride and Wilmington, p. 213).

McBride and Wilmington's juxtaposition of authorial, generic and mythic perspectives was important for the developing reputation of *The Searchers*. Nevertheless, for them Ford's authorship gives the film coherent artistic form. If from later perspectives this can seem a limitation, the desire to make the film cohere and their establishment of elaborate patterns within their overall schema of symbolic meaning gave their account great interpretative power. Strikingly too, the emphasis on the film's implicit critique of American myth and its view of life as 'absurd' cast their discussion into distinctly modernist terms, while its representation of deep-rooted racism gave it a clear contemporary relevance. The 'story of America' which they claim the film tells feels very much like the story of the time in which McBride and Wilmington were writing:

to use Robin Wood's words, a 'disintegrating' America, 'where no values are certain or constant, all traditions questioned . . . all continuity disrupted . . . where the army is a dirty word' (Caughie, p. 95).

But these accounts of *The Searchers* remained firmly within the discourses of criticism, making no reference to contemporary events or wider debates. The appropriation of the film by young American directors, on the other hand, linked it firmly, if indirectly, to the cultural concerns of the 1970s. In an unprecedented way the film became a rich source of reference, particularly for Martin Scorsese and Paul Schrader, but also for directors as diverse as George Lucas and Michael Cimino.[24] For Scorsese and Schrader, making films about contemporary America, their early careers involve almost obsessive re-workings of Ford's film.[25] This generation of American film-makers was the first to have attended film school and their interest in Ford was fed by the developments in criticism referred to above. For Scorsese and Schrader *The Searchers* was both a model and a source for ways of dramatising the present. Not surprisingly, given their film school background and reading in film criticism, they expressed what they found valuable in *The Searchers* in terms similar to those used by the critics. Asked why *The Searchers* was important to him and other directors of his generation, Schrader replied: 'the frailty of the great American hero, the psychological instability of the pioneer. . . . taking the great iconographic hero and breaking the icon down.'[26] 'Breaking the icon down' is close to McBride and Wilmington's sense that 'Ford is destroying the myth of the heroic loner' and Schrader also implies a self-conscious play with established images: 'Wayne is playing with his persona . . .' (Schrader, p. 155).

Both the instability of the hero and the critical distance from his traditional identity fed directly into Schrader's and Scorsese's writing and directing. *Taxi Driver, Rolling Thunder* and *Hard Core* all draw on the narrative of the search, the ambivalence of the hero's (and the film's) relationship with 'home' and his links with the villain. Each film's 'dialogue' with *The Searchers* became a regular topic in critical commentary. *The Searchers*, then, offered ways of thinking about and dramatising problems of pressing concern to contemporary American cinema in the Vietnam period and beyond, and ways of addressing the problem of how to create narratives in which, as Andrew Britton wrote of Vietnam movies, a 'hero-function' was still pivotal but his 'agency appears as compulsive and psychotic'.[27] More recent film theory and criticism have addressed some of these issues from within the discourses of gender studies, and ideas about the divided hero have been articulated in sexual and psychoanalytical terms in work on masculinity in American cinema. But in the period with which this article is concerned both the movies and criticism were less articulate about sexuality and gender. As the discourses of film theory and criticism developed, aspects of *The Searchers* initially seen as confused or unsatisfactory were increasingly appropriated into a view of the film as embodying a radical challenge to the traditions and values that had sustained the Western. Its contradictions, critique of the iconic hero, ambivalence about family and community, overt analysis of racism in white society, made it a crucial modern, almost modern*ist*, movie, which anticipated many of the preoccupations of the late 1960s and 1970s. In its apparent reflection of contemporary American culture, it became in effect an honorary Vietnam Western.

There is inevitably something arbitrary about choosing a date at which to end this account, particularly as *The Searchers* has continued to be the subject of critical debate. But the focus of this article on the establishment of the film's reputation perhaps makes 1976 less arbitrary than most. Of all the films which drew on *The Searchers*, *Taxi Driver* (1976) is probably the most significant, partly because its great success highlighted *The Searchers'* key role for Scorsese, Schrader and their generation and partly because it makes the most complex and problematic use of *The Searchers'* inheritance. 1976 was also the year in which *Screen Education*, the pedagogical journal of the Society for Education in Film and Television (SEFT), produced a special issue on *The Searchers*.[28] This was significant both as an assertion of the centrality of Ford and *The Searchers* to the debates and practices of the growing film education movement, and because it examined the film from several perspectives, only one of which was authorship. Indeed, in his stress on ideological analysis in the article which addresses the principle of authorship, John Caughie challenged views of the film's artistic coherence, particularly in its tangled handling of relationships between the races, by placing Ford within the traditions of genre and wider social determinations, emphases which became increasingly marked in subsequent debate.[29]

Notes

1. *The Searchers* (CV Whitney Pictures, Warner Brothers, 1956), directed by John Ford.
2. Lindsay Anderson, '*They Were Expendable* and John Ford', *Sequence* no. 11 (Summer 1950), p. 26. Further page references are cited in the text.
3. Thomas Spencer, untitled review of *The Searchers*, *Daily Worker*, 27 July 1956.
4. Unattributed review of *The Searchers*, *Variety*, 14 March 1956.
5. Harold Conway, review of *The Searchers*, *Daily Sketch*, 27 July 1956. See also Isobel Quigley, review of *The Searchers*, *The Spectator*, 5 August 1956.
6. Unattributed review of *The Searchers*, *Motion Picture Herald*, 17 March 1956.
7. 'J.W.', review of *The Searchers*, *Monthly Film Bulletin*, August 1956; Eleanor Wintour, review of *The Searchers*, *Tribune*, 5 August 1956.
8. Alan Brien, review of *The Searchers*, *Evening Standard*, 26 July 1956.
9. Lindsay Anderson, '*The Searchers*', *Sight and Sound* vol. 26, no. 2 (Autumn 1956), reprinted in John Caughie (ed.), *Theories of Authorship* (London, 1981), pp. 75–7. Further page references to Anderson's review are to the reprint in Caughie's book.
10. *Sight and Sound* vol. 2, no. 8 (December 1992) contains the most recent poll and summaries of the others.
11. *Cahiers du Cinéma* published a few articles on Ford (see Caughie (ed.), *Theories of Authorship* for articles by Louis Marcorelles and Jean-Louis Commolli, from 1958 and 1965). *Movie* published only one article on Ford in issues 1–19.
12. See *Film Culture* nos. 25 and 28 (Summer 1962 and Spring 1963).
13. 'Lee Russell' (Peter Wollen), 'John Ford', *New Left Review* no. 29 (January–February 1965), reprinted in Caughie (ed.), *Theories of Authorship*, pp. 102–8.
14. Peter Wollen, *Signs and Meaning in the Cinema* (London, 1969). Page references are cited in the text.
15. See, for instance, Geoffrey Nowell-Smith, *Visconti* and Jim Kitses, *Horizons West*, both London, 1969, published in the same series as *Signs and Meaning in the Cinema*.
16. Andrew Sarris, *The American Cinema* (New York, 1968); Peter Bogdanovich, *John Ford* (London, 1968). Page references are cited in the text.
17. John Baxter, *The Cinema of John Ford* (London, 1971). Page references are cited in the text. Andrew Sarris, '*The Searchers*', *Film Comment* vol. 7, no. 1 (Spring 1971), reprinted in Caughie (ed.), *Theories of*

Authorship, pp. 78–82; Joseph McBride and Michael Wilmington, 'Prisoner of the Desert', *Sight and Sound* vol. 40, no. 4 (Autumn 1971). This latter article was later adapted for their book, J. McBride and M. Wilmington, *John Ford* (London, 1974). Page references cited are to their original article.

18. Robin Wood, ' "Shall we Gather at the River": The Late Films of John Ford', *Film Comment* vol. 7, no. 3 (Fall 1971), reprinted in Caughie (ed.), *Theories of Authorship*, pp. 83–101.

19. Henry Nash Smith, *Virgin Land* (Harvard, 1950).

20. See Douglas Pye, '*Ulzana's Raid*', *Movie* no. 27–28 (1981), reprinted in Ian Cameron and Douglas Pye (eds), *The Movie Book of the Western* (London, 1996), pp. 262–8.

21. Kitses, *Horizons West*. Kitses describes the Mann hero as 'at the mercy of an irrational drive . . . morally ambiguous, his actions carrying a nihilistic undertone' (p. 35), and as 'neurotic' (p. 43).

22. See, for instance, Robert Warshow, 'Movie Chronicle: The Westerner', *Partisan Review* (March–April 1954), reprinted in R. Warshow, *The Immediate Experience* (New York, 1962), pp. 89–106.

23. The uses of 'myth' in the article are relatively undefined but one can identify two main inflections: 'myth' as a fictional mode in which events carry archetypal resonance; and 'myth' as inherited belief or as image or story which embodies inherited belief, as in 'myth of the heroic loner'.

24. Films involved include *Who's That Knocking on My Door* (Scorsese 1968), *Mean Streets* (Scorsese 1973), *Taxi Driver* (Scorsese 1976, scripted by Schrader), *Rolling Thunder* (John Flynn 1977, story by Schrader), *Star Wars* (George Lucas 1977), *The Deerhunter* (Michael Cimino 1978), and *Hard Core* (Schrader 1979).

25. Lesley Stern has reflected at length on Scorsese's use of *The Searchers* in L. Stern, *The Scorsese Connection* (London, 1995).

26. Paul Schrader, *Schrader on Schrader and Other Writings*, ed. K. Jackson (London, 1990), p. 155. Further page references are cited in the text.

27. Andrew Britton, 'Sideshows: Hollywood in Vietnam', *Movie* no. 27–28 (1981), pp. 2–23.

28. *Screen Education* no. 17 (Winter 1975–76).

29. John Caughie, 'Teaching through Authorship', *Screen Education* no. 17, pp. 3–13.

14 *Writing on film: practical propositions*

Reynold Humphries

1960, 1972: two dates which have marked the annals of writing on film and which correspond to the first public showing of Michael Powell's *Peeping Tom* and of Sam Peckinpah's *Straw Dogs*. The violent critical reaction to these two films, which, I would suggest, can be seen as a form of collective pathology, still has lessons for us today: Charles Barr's trenchant article is as relevant now as it was in 1972.[1] It is with this study, one of the most incisive and intelligent I have read on some of the most urgent and fundamental questions that this volume is addressing, that I shall start the ball rolling.

In his analysis of the critical discourses that accompanied *Straw Dogs* and *A Clockwork Orange* (1971), Barr evokes 'certain shared beliefs and criteria' to be found in the reviews of the numerous critics he quotes and adds, 'passion swamps control, and they succumb to that loss of control which they diagnose in Peckinpah, victims of a process which is a leading subject of the film' (Barr, pp. 18, 20). I shall offer presently an interpretation of the ideological reasons underpinning this situation, but first I wish to draw attention to what is, for the purposes of this essay, the most striking aspect of Barr's intervention and Ian Christie's presentation of the circumstances surrounding the reception of *Peeping Tom*: the little matter of 'details'.

With justifiable cruelty Charles Barr points out that *Sight and Sound* systematically reproduced stills of *A Clockwork Orange* 'wrongly printed, reversed left-to-right', a 'comical lack of precision' that also characterised the summaries of the plot of *Straw Dogs* (Barr, p. 17). Ian Christie quotes one reviewer of *Peeping Tom* who accused Powell of using 'phoney cinema artifice and heavy orchestral music to whip up a debased atmosphere'.[2] Christie has stressed the fact that the only music in the film is a solo piano, but perhaps even more to the point is the formula 'phoney cinema artifice'. For if ever there existed a film which insists on the reality of film-making and film-going, implacably stripped of anything remotely phoney or artificial, then it is *Peeping Tom*.

Arguably the most important shot in Powell's film is that where the prostitute turns, looks into the camera and says: 'It'll be two quid'. Two details are paramount here: the presence of a hairline cross (as if we are looking through the viewfinder of a film camera); and the fact that she looks the spectators directly in the eye. Now we have already seen the man who approaches her hiding a movie camera *at waist level*, which means that it cannot be his camera she looks into. So, even before the sophisticated point-of-view shots that force us to participate in the murder of the prostitute, Powell has identified the camera of the *énonciation* (of the act of film-making, including the role of the director, use of camera etc.; thus the means by which we identify with story and characters) as the spectator's privileged means of access to the diegesis. The absence of the hairline cross in the 're-playing' of the opening sequence, added to the equally fundamental fact that this second sequence is in black and white whereas the first – and the rest of the film, except the films made by Mark's father – is in colour, overdetermines the ruse employed by Powell to insist on the theoretical thrust of his film. We can only conclude that our first vision of the encounter with, and the murder of, the prostitute is filtered through an act of film-making that is Michael Powell's. It is therefore the very institution of film-making that is aggressive and death-oriented, prior to any question of the subject matter of the film, a fact which at once implies the spectator and the (f)act of film-going.[3]

We can now see that it was the refusal of Powell to displace from *énonciation* onto *énoncé* ('the statement' in linguistics; thus in film the story and characters we identify with) what Christie has called 'the "normal" scopophilia of film consumption' which is hence 'inscribed and identified as the cause of the trouble', that triggered off the reactions and the ludicrous mis-readings from which the film suffered (Christie, p. 58). All the critics unconsciously recognised themselves both in the character of Mark and in Michael Powell, the extra twist coming from the latter's playing the role of Mark's father. And surely this unpalatable fact of recognising oneself in the position of a character whom, with hindsight, we can call 'a serial killer' is what is also at stake in the equally hysterical rejection of *Straw Dogs*. For what is David Sumner if not a paradigm of that well-meaning liberal intellectual opposed to violence (the reason for his leaving the States) that our politically correct critics assume themselves to be? Those who denounced *Straw Dogs* firstly recognised themselves narcissistically in their hero David (their ideal ego, constructed from imaginary identifications determining how the subject sees itself), then found themselves in the more than uncomfortable position of having to defend his own defence of his home. Unable to assume the contradictions of such a subject position, they could only reject the behaviour of David their ego ideal (the 'ideal' adult figure whose social and cultural values are assimilated by the subject and taken as natural: the liberal academic), which rejection could find only one outlet: a hysterical denunciation of the film and its 'lack of realism'. This defence mechanism, I would argue, corresponds exactly to the 'phoney cinema artifice' already referred to in the case of *Peeping Tom*. Both films reveal a sort of 'impossible Truth', to recognise which would demolish that imaginary critical distance that was precisely one of the reasons for admiring Kubrick's cynical and irresponsible film and the concomitant 'self-centred' subject position of the critics themselves.

This finds expression in another, closely related manner: the refusal within dominant discourses to pay attention to the various fissures, incoherences and tensions inherent in classical Hollywood cinema, provided these appear in a sufficiently distorted and displaced form as not to allow those painful and unwanted de-centring processes so manifestly determining the reactions evoked above. Should the displacement be massive enough, then all matters which criticism considers 'minor' – in other words, not entering into that imaginary realm of eternal themes, concerns and transcendental signifieds (concepts considered fixed for all time, outside History, hence enabling the critic to see him or herself as the source of knowledge and values, rather than as their unconscious and ideological effect) that are the stuff of so much writing on film – are duly misrecognised and shunted onto a siding. I propose to focus here on some of these details and shall try to clarify the position by referring to Hitchcock's *Vertigo* (1958).

One of the most unsettling sequences in *Vertigo* occurs when Scottie follows Madeleine to the old hotel where he knows she is wont to spend long periods of time sitting in an upstairs room gazing out of the window. I do not think there is any other film where Hitchcock shows such an understanding and control of identification techniques which he applies here literally, as we shall see. When Scottie questions the hotel proprietor about Madeleine, the woman flatly denies she is there. Scottie refuses to believe her and the audience cannot but support his reaction: the use of subjective point-of-view shots means that we see what Scottie sees and there is no possibility of deceit. We are therefore as stupefied as he is to discover that Madeleine is not in the room, thus confirming the proprietor's insistence that nobody has entered the hotel prior to Scottie as she has not moved from the reception desk.

What is happening here? The 'logical' response would be, either that the woman is lying and is Madeleine's accomplice, or that Scottie is dreaming. The film surely eliminates the former possibility inasmuch as involving her in the plot to kill Elster's wife would endanger the whole operation. The latter interpretation is valid only if Hitchcock's direction had not implicated the spectator totally in Scottie's way of seeing things. We must therefore seek the answer elsewhere. The logic of the text imposes its own solution. *Vertigo* is concerned, amongst other matters, with the way desire determines the way people see others as *images* rather than as real people: although Madeleine is meant to be suffering from an identity problem to the point of schizophrenia, it is in fact Scottie who has transformed Madeleine into an image corresponding to desires of which he is unaware. And Hitchcock's use of identification techniques (at the restaurant, in the museum, at the florist's, in the cemetery) encourages us to see what Scottie sees and to lend to characters and events the meanings he does. This, however, does not apply to the owner of the hotel who is completely outside this fantasy structure. My point is the following: Hitchcock is forcing the spectator to take everything for what the cinema is – a succession of images. From this viewpoint, applied to the letter, what enters the hotel is, for Scottie and us, literally an image and not a 'real' person, whereas Madeleine exists as a real person for the hotel owner who cannot conceive that she can signify something else. The image of Madeleine functions as a signifier of which we and Scottie are the unconscious effects, a logic from which the woman is excluded. Madeleine has not entered the hotel for the eminently sane reason that 'Madeleine' as we and Scottie *see* her *simply does not exist* for the hotel proprietor. All talk of *Vertigo* in general and this sequence in particular as supernatural is as meaningful – or trivial – as solving the problems posed by late Buñuel (such as *Le Fantôme de la Liberté*, 1974) by labelling him a 'Surrealist'.[4]

One film whose off-putting complexity could easily be put into the supernatural category is Lynch's *Lost Highway* (1996). Certainly the influence of the horror film is patent in the visuals: Balthazar Getty staggering along the corridors of the hotel with blood coming from his nose (a little detail linking him to Bill Pullman whom the policeman has punched during interrogation) recalls Oliver Reed in Fisher's *Curse of the Werewolf* (1961); and the transformation scene at the end of the film, following the love-making in the desert, is just as explicitly a reference to the werewolf tradition (and to Jekyll and Hyde). But any attempt thus to limit Lynch in general and *Lost Highway* in particular is simply another example of that critical blindness evoked up to now, serving to displace what disconcerts and decentres so as to re-centre the critics and their discourse.

Rather we should see the film as a variant on what I have just suggested concerning the hotel sequence in *Vertigo*. The opening of *Lost Highway* contains some of the most remarkable examples of point-of-view camera work since Lang and Hitchcock (and *Peeping Tom*). Thus Lynch alternates a shot of the outside of the house from Bill Pullman's point of view that we see as if we occupied his physical position, and a shot taken from across the street where we see Pullman looking out of the window. The physical placing of the camera, overdetermined by what it shows, means that the spectators are, within the 'space' of two shots, identified with a character, then forced to watch the very person they have identified with. This places us in two radically different *subject* positions and becomes a *mise en abyme* of the film's crucial moment where, as a result of a crisis in prison, Pullman 'becomes' Getty. The schizophrenia of the Pullman character thus enables Lynch to place us in the uncomfortable position of looking and being looked at, of being murderer and paranoid victim of persecution. It is surely not excessive to claim that everything that follows the prison sequence is literally a question of point of view: Pullman adopting a second subject position determined by schizophrenia in order to 'see life differently'. This means that nothing of what follows the prison scene 'really happens' and that there is no event that is not determined elsewhere: by Pullman's desire concerning his wife, her lover, etc. It does not 'really happen' except in his imagination, which gives back to the story its literal status as a series of images representing desire. Again, once one looks, desire comes into operation.

Despite the patent differences on the level of themes, characters and treatment, I would argue that Lynch is a contemporary equivalent of Lang and Hitchcock and, as such, a representative after the fact of the concerns of 'high modernism'. It is therefore both amusing and instructive to find French critics writing ecstatically about David Mamet's *The Spanish Prisoner* (1997) because they are able to compare it to Hitchcock and Lang's *Beyond a Reasonable Doubt* (1956). This comical mis-reading is due simply to the fact that both movies deal with the framing of a character.[5] The only problem is that, on the one hand, the central character of Mamet's movie is a victim, whereas the Dana Andrews character engineered his own framing; and that, on the other hand, Mamet is concerned with the theme of the 'fall-guy' in order to denounce moral dishonesty and money, whereas Lang makes of the concept of 'framing' the very cinematographic basis of his approach to the status of the image, a major concern of his throughout his career from the first *Mabuse* film in 1922 to the last in 1960. Mamet is a pessimist who feels one can trust nobody and places this in the context of the spectator's relation, not to the image, but to the characters. Rather the film is a variant on the theme of the 'treacherous woman' and as such needs to be seen in the context of classical film noir and contemporary re-writings of the genre.

All too often the postmodern interest in 'nothing being quite what it seems' reduces the matter to a question of games (a decisive rejoinder to this would be Michaël Haneke's uniquely disturbing *Funny Games*, 1997), but a notable exception would be *Suture* (David Siegel and Scott McGehee, 1993). A white businessman invites his black half-brother to Phoenix after the murder of their father. The situation is unusual but hardly impossible. What follows, however, is literally impossible, if one sticks to the story and a certain logic.

The white brother is suspected of having murdered his father and has decided to disappear, the most radical way of doing so being to die. And the black brother will die in his place so that he can live abroad comfortably. He plants his identity papers on his brother, then arranges for his car to explode while the brother is driving it. However, the brother survives, albeit in a state of total amnesia. A psychiatrist is hired to help him remember. At this point the film becomes 'impossible': the black brother is taken for the white brother. Meanwhile, the psychiatrist, whose off-screen voice discusses the case, assures us that we always know who we are, even if we forget things – an ideology the film sets out to deconstruct via a particular approach to the image.

The white brother's girlfriend has a 'home movie' showing him at a party and plays it to herself to remind herself of what he was like before the accident, which clearly articulates the functions of memory, the image and desire. During the convalescence of the victim she behaves as if a manifestly black man were the just as manifestly white man she has always known. Nor can this be put down to wishful thinking veering to psychosis: everyone takes the black man for his white brother, despite incontrovertible evidence (that of the senses) to the contrary. And photographs of the black man after the accident circulate among the close friends of the white man. At the end of the film the black man gets his memory back and tells the psychiatrist everything, including his intention to continue to be his brother (after all, he was rich, whereas the black man is poor). But the brother returns to try again, only this time he gets killed: he is shot in the face and is unrecognisable. Contrary to what the psychiatrist believes, the black brother gets away with it. The images of the 'home movie' become thus more real than the actual evidence of our eyes, which suggests that the image takes the place of memory, thus eradicating History itself. The fiancée retreats into a past that no longer exists because the normal function of the image today is, precisely, to deny the past, to fetishise the present and to encourage the ego to adapt to it, thus erasing the very concept of 'subject' in both the Marxist and psychoanalytic senses. That *Suture* is stigmatising the commercial cinema – the role of the 'home movie' and of what can only be called a 'collective hallucination' in everyone's belief that the black man is the white man (and the black-into-white reversal is what occurs when the negative is processed) – makes of the film an extension of the modernist concerns evoked above. Like another 'impossible' movie, David Cronenberg's *M Butterfly* (1993), it refuses to give spectators what they want, showing them instead that they really only see what they desire.[6] *Suture* is hardly representative of the cinema of the 1990s, but it is certainly an extraordinarily accurate representation of the current obsession with the 'autonomous' status of the image, where even the virtual can be commodified, 'once the referent seems to have disappeared, as so many people from Debord to Baudrillard always warned us it would'.[7]

Robert J. Corber has invited us to inscribe films such as *Vertigo* into the precise historical and political context of the 1950s.[8] I would suggest that a particular detail – which seems to have gone unnoticed – in Minnelli's contemporary *Some Came Running* (1958) merits interest for similar reasons.[9] The melodrama of that decade has been the subject of much attention, so I would like to de-centre the discussion somewhat. Towards the end of the film, which has presented itself as taking place at the time it was made, we are shown a banner evoking the town's celebration of its centenary: the dates '1848–1948' are offered to our gaze. So the film's action takes place a full ten years before the date of its production, a considerable discrepancy which invites us to interpret certain details anew and to foreground an aspect of the film which, up to this point, has passed itself off as a mere detail of the script, nothing more: the fact that Dave Hirsch is a soldier returning home. We do not think about it, as the film's main concerns leave no place for such interrogations. With the action set in 1948, however, things change markedly.

In this context we are justified in seeing close links between *Some Came Running* and the various examples of post-war film noir dealing with the return home of soldiers and the social problems raised.[10] This, however, does not answer the question of why this theme should suddenly return, like the repressed, years after the event. The fact that Dave Hirsch puts his considerable savings, not into his brother's bank, but that of a rival, gives us the beginning of a clue. The smug, self-satisfied atmosphere of the town in general and the Hirsch family in particular is severely criticised by the film, which would thus seem to be making a progressive critique of a society which has got fat at the expense of those who made sacrifices during the war. This, however, neglects the film's narrative structure.

On three occasions after his return Dave Hirsch is involved in scenes of violence: firstly he is attacked by the jealous boyfriend of Ginny, the young woman he has befriended; secondly, during a poker game, there ensues a fight where Bama Dillert gets stabbed in the arm; then, finally, Dave gets shot in the arm by the same boyfriend and Ginny dies saving him from certain death. His horrified elder brother has already drawn attention to the problems he has brought with him, as if they were Dave's fault and his alone. What I am suggesting by saying this is that the violence emanates from the desire of the big Other (radical otherness, the historical and social source of language and hence the empty locus from which values and ideologies circulate) whose discourse has determined the film's unconscious and its concomitant narrative structure – based on repetition – as follows: Dave Hirsch represents something that the American society of the 1950s cannot entertain – a form of collective responsibility and solidarity – and which it needs to 'forget', or, to put it in the terms of unconscious desire, *eliminate*. This scandalous dimension of History having been raised, it must be exorcised and the film's logic does so dutifully by a form of displacement both social and sexual: eliminating the *working-class woman* who represents an unacceptable 'foreign body'. Ginny is melodrama's femme fatale, but being a woman is fatal to her and not to a male victim. The abrupt change of style during the final fairground sequence, which Minnelli films as a cross between the musical, the film noir and a nightmare, suggests that, on the level of the signifier, the film is trying to express ideology reaffirming itself, while at the same time showing things going wrong.

A contemporary melodrama, *A Star is Born* (1954), is an illuminating case of a film whose script raises a problem and 'solves' it by indicating that it lies elsewhere. Such incoherence can only mean something else. Foregrounded in the film is the alcoholism of Norman Maine which everyone is powerless to combat. At one point, just prior to Maine's suicide, his producer says to the Judy Garland character that he has always known Maine to have this problem and has never fathomed it. Clearly, then, the character's alcoholism is not a *cause* but an *effect* (of something else repressed). Early in the film, during a conversation between Maine and a waiter in a night-club, we learn that Maine is obsessed by age and needs to feel he can be successful with young women. The film then proceeds to turn this masculine problem upside-down just as it has reversed cause and effect through the theme of alcoholism and to suggest that the cause of this particular problem is – a woman.

Because of his drinking Maine's career is on the rocks (unlike his whisky) and he is reduced to staying at home while his wife, Judy Garland, soars to stardom. This 'humiliating' situation is brought home to him brutally by a phone call where he is asked if he is the butler (an interesting case of going down the social ladder). Worse is yet to come: a postman brings a registered package for his wife and calls him by *her* name which he must then sign on the accompanying slip. Here, surely, we have a more coherent explanation for his drinking. Maine literally takes his wife's place, with all that implies in a masculine-dominated society where the woman depends on the man. I would argue therefore that the character has always had difficulty in accepting the precise male role imposed on him by society – as a big star he's meant to be a 'ladies' man' – but that the film, having raised this important theme, must repress it in favour of something far less dangerous. Order is then restored when Judy Garland appears in public for the first time after his suicide and presents herself to the public – who applaud thunderously – as 'Mrs Norman Maine'. The Name-of-the-Father (the Law of the dead father conferring identity on the subject, prohibiting incest and determining for the subject its sexual place in society, a place overdetermined ideologically) as an ideologically repressive apparatus is thus assumed 'freely' by the woman.

To insist on the importance of fatherhood must not, however, be seen as conservative or repressive in itself. To do so would be to turn a social question into something eternal (the old problem of essentialism) and to evacuate any possibility of using theories of ideology and psychoanalysis to pinpoint and analyse the contradictions inherent in any representation of gender: the image, by (re)activating the gaze, cannot but partake of the dimension of desire. When Slavoj Zizek, writing of *Jurassic Park* (1993), denounces critical blindness and insists on the importance of the father in the film, he does so in an attempt to analyse the unconscious effects of the signifier on the spectator.[11] This in turn enables us to grasp the cynical opportunism of *The Lost World* (1997) where the Jeff Goldblum character is given a black daughter by the script, on the one hand to be 'politically correct' (the ideology of the United Colours of Benetton, of what Jameson has called 'random difference'), and on the other hand to suddenly reveal the girl as an athlete so that she, unlike the script, can 'miraculously' get the characters out of a nasty situation (cornered by a raptor).

The necessary theoretical interest in gender has tended to neglect a detail whose ideological implications merit analysis. I shall sketch in here briefly what I have in mind by referring to two very different films: *Bringing up Baby* (1938) and, once again, *Vertigo*. Readers who have seen that frivolous documentary *The Celluloid Closet* (Rob Epstein and Jeffrey Friedman 1995) will remember that it includes the now celebrated shot where the unfortunate Cary Grant character, wearing a very feminine robe and confronted with the very masculine aunt, cries out in frustration: 'I just went gay all of a sudden'. Now everything in this fascinating movie points to David being a man who is not at ease with the specifically masculine role the discourse of the Other (represented by his rather masculine fiancée and the lawyer, symbol of the Law) imposes on him as scientist: devoted to his work, eschewing all forms of pleasure in favour of social and, crucially, economic success. If it is impossible to go into detail here, we can at least offer the following interpretation of the shot in question, namely that David desires to adopt a 'feminine' position as a form of protest against a vision of masculinity that is repressive, hidebound and destructive of any value that does not have as its ultimate aim upward mobility and a solid bank balance. Just when chaos threatens to overwhelm everything, the fiancée and the lawyer, forming a 'perfect' couple, suddenly return to impose order.

I would make the same claim for Scottie in *Vertigo*. On one level he identifies with his old school chum Elster, a fact the latter exploits in assuming Scottie will find it normal that a woman should have mental problems and, as a policeman (another representative of the Law), will find it equally normal to tail her (= the male gaze brought to bear on a woman in order to 'understand' her, then have her incarcerated as mad). Corber has rightly insisted on the way Scottie identifies unconsciously with a variety of female positions throughout the film (notably in the extraordinary nightmare sequence, one of the high spots in Hitchcock) and it is not difficult to see what Scottie is reacting against. Elster yearns for the good old days of the nineteenth century when men were 'free', in other words they had the right to use and abuse women thanks to their own social and economic status, then discard them like old clothes. Elster is the signifier of the market economy, considering that any person and any object can be exchanged for any other, reducing all and sundry to money: use value and exchange value become one as there are literally no 'values' left. Significantly, Scottie has private means like Elster. Nor is it a simple coincidence that he is 'feminised' by having to wear a *corset* as the result of his fall, a garment which functions as the signifier of his hysterical condition, brought on by the unconscious contradiction between desiring a feminine position and the fact that this is taboo, a desire which can therefore, like the Real in Lacanian psychoanalysis, never become conscious but can only exercise certain effects on the subject. Thus the nightmare sequence represents the Real (the presence of death and the death drive, a radically unconscious source of anxiety that leaves its uncanny effects without the subject knowing why) for Scottie and for us.[12]

If this is not the place to go into the question of a political aesthetics of film, we can perhaps broach the matter via a brief consideration of Oshima's *Death by Hanging* (1968). The story concerns a young Korean condemned to death for raping and murdering two young Japanese women. But the execution does not kill him: he emerges from it in a state of amnesia which, under Japanese law, means he cannot be executed again – until he recognises who he is. (And there is surely a parallel to be drawn between the authorities here and the psychiatrist in *Suture*.) We can isolate three reasons for the prison authorities wanting R (the murderer) to recognise himself as R. Firstly, if he knows who he is, confesses to rape and murder and admits he must be punished, then he alone assumes responsibility for his own death and, as it were, exonerates the authorities and Japanese law. Secondly, by so doing, he gives up any attempt to blame Japan for its treatment of Koreans and thus for his own anti-social behaviour. Thirdly, this in turn enables the prison authorities to see the post-war treatment of Korea as a logical (read: natural) outcome and extension of the war situation and thus to excuse themselves for any killings committed during the war and to exonerate themselves for the conditions in which Koreans live in contemporary Japan.

For a detailed reading of the film and its multiple implications, I refer readers to Stephen Heath's article.[13] In the context of the present essay, the central concern is that of subjectivity and subject positions. By recognising, at the end of the film, that he is indeed R but not the R that the authorities want him to be and about whom they have been talking, R shifts the question from some transcendental and ahistorical subjectivity onto that of intersubjectivity, defined as precisely the place of the subject in History. Which, albeit in a radically different context, was surely the polemical thrust behind Barr's article with which I opened this debate.

In these postmodern days, where the end of History and ideology and the exaltation of the present moment and the virtual image reign supreme, it has become urgent to keep in mind the history lessons of Oshima in *Death by Hanging* (and *The Ceremony*, 1971, where the family stands in for both the repression of History and its constant, nightmarish reminder). I shall finish therefore on a polemical note of my own by calling to my aid Spielberg's dinosaurs. At a moment when neo-liberal economists and ideologues have cast the social in general and the Bolshevik Revolution in particular into the outer darkness of pre-History, *Jurassic Park* presents us with the dinosaurs as signifiers of the archaic, returning like the repressed to remind us that History and the past insist even in such a degraded example of mass culture, however displaced and distorted these concepts are. If we keep this in mind, we shall perhaps avoid film theory being relegated to some future museum of pre-History.

Notes

1. Charles Barr, '*Straw Dogs, A Clockwork Orange* and the Critics', *Screen* vol. 13, no. 2 (Summer 1972), pp. 17–31. Further page references are cited in the text.
2. Ian Christie, 'The Scandal of *Peeping Tom*' in Ian Christie (ed.), *Powell, Pressburger and Others* (London, 1978), pp. 53–9. Further page references are cited in the text.
3. I refer readers to my article, 'Caught in the act of looking: the opening sequence of Michael Powell's *Peeping Tom*', *Caliban* no. 32 (January 1995), pp. 39–53.
4. See my article, 'Lacan and the Ostrich: Desire and Narration in Buñuel's *Le Fantôme de la Liberté*', *American Imago* vol. 52, no. 2 (Summer 1995), pp. 191–203.

5. This is symptomatic of a desire to erase History in much writing in France today and of a concomitant return to an appropriately ignorant cinephilia where any attempt to distinguish theoretically between different kinds of filmic texts, to highlight the specificity of a given film, has been equally erased. A British equivalent would be the fetishistic canonisation of someone like Kenneth Branagh who gets himself compared to Orson Welles, presumably on the grounds that they have both filmed Shakespeare.

6. The film's title should therefore be interpreted, not as a simple reference to the black man being 'put back together' surgically, but to the Lacanian notion of the subject misrecognising its status: as being constituted by desire and within discourse, by the logic of the signifier. Thus the spectators, like the characters, are the effects of a 'de-suturing'.

7. Fredric Jameson, *Postmodernism, or, the Cultural Logic of Late Capitalism* (London and New York, 1991), p. 415.

8. Robert J. Corber, *In the Name of National Security: Hitchcock, Homophobia, and the Political Construction of Gender in Postwar America* (Durham, NC and London, 1993).

9. See Robert Lang, *American Film Melodrama: Griffith, Vidor, Minnelli* (Princeton, NJ, 1989). *Some Came Running* is discussed pp. 194–209.

10. See Frank Krutnik, *In a Lonely Street: Film Noir, Genre, Masculinity* (New York and London, 1991).

11. Slavoj Zizek, *The Metastases of Enjoyment* (London and New York, 1994), pp. 180–1.

12. For a complementary view, see Slavoj Zizek's remarks on the femme fatale in *Looking Awry: An Approach to Jacques Lacan through Popular Culture* (Cambridge, MA and London, 1991), pp. 65–6. This is arguably the most important recent contribution to film theory.

13. Stephen Heath, '*Anata mo*', *Screen* vol. 17, no. 4 (Winter 1976–77), pp. 49–66.

15 *Writing about specularity and Modernity: the case of* Dancing Lady

Leighton Grist and David Lusted

I.

Writing, like all representation, is never innocent. To write about anything is, explicitly or implicitly, to delimit, uphold, expand, or challenge how it is perceived and constituted. Neither is writing ever neutral. We write from a particular position, inhabit a particular discourse, which the very act of writing itself seeks to validate. The aim of this essay is to write about, to (re)constitute, a single film from contrasting discursive/theoretical positions: cine-psychoanalysis and cultural studies, 'bodies of work which have historically been set in antagonism to each other'.[1] The dominant representations of cine-psychoanalysis and cultural studies place those discourses, respectively, as text- and context-centred, as formalist and historicist, and as offering pessimistic and more optimistic models of text–spectator relations. They are likewise seen to discuss cinema in terms of a putatively monolithic notion of the cinematic institution (an Althusserian Ideological State Apparatus if ever there were one), and a broader, more fissured (Gramscian) realm of cultural production and contestation.[2] Whereas cine-psychoanalysis enjoyed theoretical dominance within film studies during the 1970s and early 1980s, this position has been since usurped by cultural studies.[3] Nevertheless, as they here differently 'write' the selected film text, the discourses not only re-present their claims for legitimacy, but raise the seemingly paradoxical issue of the possibility, even desirability, of their reconciliation.

The MGM production *Dancing Lady* (Robert Z. Leonard 1933) was a sizeable box-office success, but within film studies it is hardly a 'canonical' text. *Dancing Lady* has been written about in terms of David O. Selznick's time as a producer at MGM, as an example of the second cycle of early film musicals, in relation to the star images and careers of Joan Crawford and Clark Gable, and as Fred Astaire's film debut (playing himself).[4] However, as a specific film text, *Dancing Lady* presents a virtually blank tablet to write on.

II.

Cine-psychoanalysis is founded upon the proposition that 'film-viewing and subject-formation' are 'reciprocal', that the cinema 'reinscribes' those 'structuring processes which form the human psyche'.[5] Implicated in this 'reinscription' is a model of cinema as an all-encompassing 'machine', a concept indebted to Jean-Louis Baudry's two articles on the cinematic apparatus and Christian Metz's account of the cinema institution as 'not just the cinema industry': it is 'also the mental machinery – another industry – which spectators "accustomed to the cinema" have internalised historically and which has adapted them to the consumption of films'.[6] For Baudry, the film viewing situation – darkness, stillness, a heightening of visual perception – induces psychic effects. The spectator–screen relation 'reconstructs the situation necessary' to the Lacanian mirror stage, enabling an illusory loss of ego, a temporary regression to the unity and plenitude of the Imaginary (Baudry, p. 45). However, as the situation thus re-plays the mirror stage, so it simultaneously reinscribes the ego, a process further heightened through the spectator's identification with characters within the diegesis. The consequent positioning of the spectator as a unified, transcendent subject is cruelly dissimulative. Like the interpellated subject of Althusserian ideology, the cinematic spectator is less subject than subjected, an effect of the cinematic apparatus. Yet, as the cinema holds out the promise of psychic plenitude, so the spectator is impelled to re-live the experience, an imperative facilitated by – and which facilitates – the cinema industry's constant stream of product.

The cine-psychoanalytic description of cinema has been criticised, like psychoanalysis itself, as being totalising and universalist. It would seem not only to reduce all cinema to the same effect and meaning, but as the spectator is invariably subjected to and positioned by the cinematic apparatus, and despite Metz's nominal adduction of history, to disregard actual differences between spectators historically and in terms of class, race and gender. The seminal feminist intervention within cine-psychoanalysis is that of Laura Mulvey, who in a massively influential article seeks explicitly to demonstrate 'the way the unconscious of patriarchal society has structured film form'.[7] In a move consistent with the heightened visual apprehension of film viewing, Mulvey centres her argument upon specularity: 'In a world ordered by sexual imbalance, pleasure in looking has been split between active/male and passive/female' (Mulvey, p. 11); the male accordingly bears the look, is subject, the female 'holds the look', is object. A like 'active/passive heterosexual division of labour' informs narrative structure (Mulvey, p. 12). The spectator is placed to identify with a 'main male protagonist' who forwards the story, makes things happen (Mulvey, p. 12). Moreover, cinema 'masculinizes' the spectator position 'regardless of the actual sex (or possible deviance) of any real live movie-goer'.[8]

The opening sequence of *Dancing Lady* enables elaboration of Mulvey's specular model. It begins with Tod Newton (Franchot Tone) buying tickets for a striptease at the 'International Burlesque House'. Cut to the theatre's interior, a site for what Mulvey describes as a characteristic 'erotic spectacle' wherein woman is coded 'for strong visual and erotic impact', 'to connote *to-be-looked-at-ness*' (Mulvey, p. 11). By the time the striptease is halted by a police raid, the performers have removed their long gowns to reveal tight, skimpy, flesh-toned two-pieces. The sequence's representation of woman as sexual image is flagged reflexively by the presence of a life-size illustration of a burlesque performer in the theatre's foyer. As one of Tod's female companions contemplates this illustration, Tod covers her bare back with her fur wrap: an act which both differentiates her from the image and draws attention to her bareness, to her sexuality.

A series of reverse shots of the burlesque's audience shows that it is comprised predominantly of men. Mulvey writes: 'Traditionally, the woman displayed has functioned on two levels: as erotic object for the characters within the screen story, and as erotic object for the spectator within the auditorium' (Mulvey, pp. 11–12). In the sequence at hand, this tension is resolved by the device common to the 'show-girl' situation, of identifying the looks of the camera and spectator with that of the diegetic audience (Mulvey,

p. 12). We also specifically share Tod's point of view, are positioned to identify with one of the film's two main male protagonists. It is a look which objectifies on stage the main female protagonist, Janie Barlow (Crawford), over whom both Tod and the spectator therefore gain 'control and possession' (Mulvey, p. 13). Compounding this sexed inequity, while Tod has so far forwarded the narrative, Janie here, as an object of erotic spectacle, acts typically 'to freeze the flow of action' (Mulvey, p. 11).

Mulvey situates these representational structures institutionally in relation to 'the monolithic system based on large capitalist investment exemplified at its best by Hollywood in the 1930s, 1940s and 1950s' (Mulvey, p. 7). This, however, is itself problematically monolithic, and returns us to cine-psychoanalysis's nominal historicity. The opening of *Dancing Lady* reflects upon, and demands to be read in terms of, the more defined context of Hollywood *circa* 1933. Generically, *Dancing Lady* is one of the spate of backstage musicals which sought to cash in on the success of Warner Brothers' *Forty-Second Street* (Lloyd Bacon 1933). It is, moreover, the backstage or show musical which formalises the secularisation of the showgirl. For Rick Altman, 'the identification of the camera/audience as male and the show as female constitutes the very foundation of the show musical's syntax' (Altman, p. 223). We need also to consider the Hollywood institution's specific historical and economic situation. The Depression hit the majors hard, and with audiences and revenues declining, the majors had quickly turned to sex. Given this situation, the secularisation of the female obtains a tangible logic.

Sexual excess provoked calls for its suppression, and Will Hays forced through a 'Reaffirmation of Objectives' of the Production Code on 5 March 1933. Still the majors bridled: the police raid on the burlesque in *Dancing Lady* can correspondingly be read as a figure for the Production Code. Hence the represented disrespect for the legal process – witness, for example, the mocking of the flustered night court judge by Janie's confidante, Rosette (Winnie Lightner), or Janie's contestation, 'I'm the victim'. Janie's explanation that if you 'hadn't eaten for a week, you'd do a striptease too', serves not only, as the first Depression reference, to justify Janie's position, but implies an economic rationale for the majors' own *risqué* practices. Indeed, just as Altman describes the musical in general 'as Hollywood's own self-justification', and 'the world's most complex and expensive publicity scheme' (Altman, p. 344), so the show musical is, in its emphasis on the problems and politics of show-making, the most consistently reflexive of its subgenres.

III.

Janie's defiance of the judge, and thus the Law, is punished by 30 days in jail. But Janie's defiant independence is reinforced when, after Tod buys her out of jail, she first refuses his offer to forward her career and then smoulders over his written advice and 'gift' of $50 to buy a dress. Tod's offer of help and $50 carry strong implications of prostitution, which compound not only the conventional connotations of the showgirl but those presented both by the reference of one of Tod's companions to the burlesque performers being 'Right off the street' and by Janie's statement in court that she had 'walked the streets' looking for a job. As though in reaction, Janie asserts that she is going uptown 'on my own', and the next day, ignoring a sign reading 'No More Girls Wanted', crashes the rehearsals for director Patch Gallagher (Gable)'s new Broadway show. In terms of, and possibly problematising, Mulvey's argument, Janie can be seen as dissident, for she forcefully assumes the narrative agency which Mulvey assigns to the male.

Janie's journey uptown is summarised by a montage largely comprising blurred fast-motion and subway station signs. Fast-motion recurs as a transition device throughout, and, in its emphasis on speed and the machine, is redolent of the emerging late modernity of 1920s and 1930s USA. Janie's assertiveness in turn invites consideration, from a cultural studies perspective, in relation to the contemporaneous phenomenon of the new woman: the increasing appearance of 'independent' femininity within the previously masculine spheres of paid work and public experience; a situation accelerated by the dislocations of the Depression. Hollywood, moreover, perceived this 'new' femininity to be a substantial audience segment, and fostered its cinematic investment through the representation of strong female figures and genres like the woman's film, as well as through the marketing and publicity surrounding stars. The early career and star image of Crawford offer suggestive parallels to the apparent rise and accepted representation of the new woman. As studio publicity sought to exploit, Janie's driven ambition in *Dancing Lady* 'tied in uncannily, almost biographically, with MGM's most driven star' (Barrios, p. 396).

The cultural transgressiveness of the new woman is implied by the montage sequence which follows Janie's ejection from the rehearsals. Dominated by shots of the characters' legs, this represents Janie pursuing Patch through the city streets. As the sequence proceeds, Janie increasingly 'invades' masculine space, and we might note that, within Freudian dream symbolism, legs figure male/ phallic potency. Janie's pursuit of Patch is stopped literally by the Law, by a police whistle which pulls her legs up short. This jars somewhat against her previous, textually validated, defiance of the Law, opening up a contradiction which points, symptomatically, to the threat Janie poses. The 'threat' is further contained when Janie accepts Tod's offer of a letter of introduction to Patch's producer, Jasper Bradley (Grant Mitchell). This circumscribes Janie as an active narrative agent: her acceptance is tacitly that of patriarchal authority, of the Law. Tod's letter eventually results in Janie landing a part in Patch's show. It is, however, a success predicated upon Janie becoming a bare-limbed object of the look, again both for the male characters and for the spectator. This specular subordination is reinforced dramatically. For while Janie proceeds to pursue Patch into and around his office, she helps him on with his jacket and displays a fawning gratitude which sits uncomfortably with her previous assertiveness. The containment of transgression within these scenes corroborates the position espoused by Raymond Bellour, who, writing within the parameters of the cine-psychoanalytic project, asserts that the structurally recurrent repetition–resolution effect which he describes as being dominant within classical Hollywood film functions inevitably to recuperate feminine desire. Further, for Bellour, 'a woman can love, accept and give a positive value to these films only from her own masochism, and from a certain sadism that she can exercise in return on the masculine subject'.[9]

Although Janie trades in burlesque for Broadway, she continues diegetically to be placed as the object of the look within an institution founded upon the peddling of female flesh. Extra-diegetic parallels with the cinematic institution remain inescapable. When Tod and Bradley are shown spying on rehearsals, their situation reflexively suggests the voyeurism which underpins cinema's specular regime. Mulvey explains that mainstream film portrays 'a hermetically sealed world which unwinds magically, indifferent to the presence of the audience, producing for them a sense of separation and playing on their voyeuristic phantasy' (Mulvey, p. 9). Moreover, as Tod and Bradley spy, the camera cranes back to reveal them looking through (at?) a rectangular, screen-like aperture. Reflexivity is also implied when Patch demands changes to his show's script: 'You got to give 'em something out of modern everyday life.... A girl who has to beat time to the city's rhythm, a girl who craves to dance.' On one hand, Patch's words can be seen as the film's self-rationale, as 'proof' of its innovation. On the other, they can be read as trumpeting the film's institutional/ideological recuperation of the challenge posed by late modernity and the new woman.

The textual objectification of Janie exceeds the context of performance. Consider her repeated, soft-focus facial close-ups, or the full shot of her swimsuited body emerging from the lake at Tod's estate. From Mulvey's cine-psychoanalytic perspective, at stake here is more than just gendered power. Lacking a penis, 'the female form', within the phallocentric, patriarchal order, 'in the last resort', 'speaks castration and nothing else' (Mulvey, p. 6). Hence the irony of cinematic specularity, that the female 'displayed for the gaze and enjoyment of men, the active controllers of the look, always threatens to evoke the anxiety it originally signified' (Mulvey, p. 13). To combat this, Mulvey describes 'two avenues of escape' for the male unconscious within narrative cinema. One is the disavowal of castration through the transformation of the female form into a fetish, 'so that it becomes reassuring rather than dangerous'. This 'builds up the physical beauty of the object, transforming it into something satisfying in itself' (Mulvey, pp. 13, 14), whether it be the female body in its entirety or in its erotic fragmentation.

We might return here to the representation of women's legs in *Dancing Lady*. Within the text's process of repetition–resolution the 'legs' montage reflects a similar montage of shots when the police raid the burlesque, although in this instance it is female legs which are pursued by male legs, by the Law. If the difference within repetition further marks Janie's pursuit of Patch as transgressive, the shots of the women's legs during the raid operate according to Mulvey's argument, as iconic, erotic fragmentation. Throughout, moreover, there is a visual and narrative emphasis on Janie's legs. In a cell after her court appearance, she is filmed in the foreground of the shot kicking her legs, while the transition to the following scene comprises a vertical wipe up her legs. Later, when Janie asserts, 'I've got good legs', Patch responds: 'Yes, so I've noticed'. Plainly, such emphasis can be related narratively to Janie's desire to dance and institutionally to the exploitation of Crawford's physical assets. However, psychoanalytic connotations not only remain insistent, but have a particularly overdetermined complexity. For the erotic emphasis on Janie's legs functions fetishistically, so it simultaneously evokes the transgressive assumption of phallic activeness which they likewise figure, reactivating castration anxiety in the very moment of its disavowal.

The other of the 'avenues of escape' from castration anxiety outlined by Mulvey centres upon the sadistic subordination of the female, on dominating the woman 'through punishment or forgiveness' (Mulvey, p. 14). Intimately linked with the voyeuristic impulse, this also 'fits in well with narrative': 'Sadism demands a story, demands on making something happen, forcing a change in another person, a battle of will and strength, victory/defeat' (Mulvey, p. 14). This sadistic strategy finds demonstration in *Dancing Lady* when Janie breaks down/is broken by Patch during a rehearsal – a punishing of Janie's ambition, energy and confidence. Again, reflexive connotations obtrude. Virginia Wright Wexman has unpacked a pungent contradiction which attends female stars. For while 'they have been held up as ideals of heterosexual romantic attraction under a regime in which the woman is understood to play a subordinate and dependent role', their 'success in embodying this ideal of feminine dependence on men has elevated them to positions of power that other women have rarely managed to attain'.[10] Consequently, 'the woman star can be said to represent a subversive force that continually threatens to erupt as an emergent discourse of female potency' (Wright Wexman, p. 134). In the 1930s Crawford undoubtedly possessed such latent power. That Crawford as Janie breaks down as she rehearses with Astaire accordingly becomes highly suggestive. Crawford displays many talents, but not that of dance. That she should thus be paired with Astaire in itself smacks of vindictive demystification, a connotation which Janie's collapse with cramp merely compounds. It is a cramp, moreover, which affects one of Janie's legs, and which is 'cured'/ painfully massaged away by Patch – 'punishment' followed by 'forgiveness'. The need to punish Janie once more bears testimony to the perceived threat posed by the character, but also to that posed by Crawford as star, and, possibly, the new woman with which both character and star can be associated. Indeed, while the specular and textual models proposed by cine-psychoanalysis would appear to ensure and (re)assert male dominance, it is an assertion predicated upon at times barely dissimulated fears. In the words of Steven Cohan and Ina Rae Hark, 'what are we to make of a masculinity that can preserve its hegemony only by confessing its anxieties at every turn?'.[11]

IV.

The triangle of Janie, Tod and Patch partakes of a generically familiar choice of partner structure. However, the opposition of Tod and Patch is massively weighted in the latter's favour. Apart from the contrasting star power of Tone and Gable, Tod embodies an early 1930s hate figure: an idle, rich playboy who pays Bradley to close Patch's show and throws 'a hundred people out of work' so that he can get Janie. Not only does Patch redress Tod's sin by putting on the show with his own money, but he shares with Janie a somewhat ambiguous, if aspirational and audience-friendly working- to middle-class status. Like Janie, Patch is a driven professional, who had a similarly rocky road to success. Also implicit in the romantic opposition of Tod and Patch are contrasting models of heterosexual relationships and marriage. Tod personifies upper-class patriarchal mores, founded upon gender inequality, capital, and the perpetuation of family. Thus while Tod repeatedly attempts to 'buy' Janie, his grandmother, Mrs Todhunter (Mary Robson), says, approvingly, upon meeting Janie: 'Looks like good healthy stock'. Patch would alternatively appear to offer Janie a companionate relationship, which emphasises the couple rather than family, and is founded upon an ideal of equality and shared interests.[12] The companionate model also historically intersects with, and has been linked to, the rise of 'independent' femininity and the new woman.[13] With regard to this, Janie significantly defers Tod's proposal of marriage because she has 'a job to go through with first'. Notably, Tod concludes his proposal with the query: 'Sold?'.

Tod's unequal representation is compounded by intimations of limited sexual potency. Capping these is Patch's jibe about guys like Tod being 'a lot of silk hats and silk socks with nothing between'. Played by Gable, Patch is clearly beyond any such imputations. Complicating this, Tod, unlike Patch, has money and power, has social autonomy, 'has' the phallus. It is noteworthy that Tod's family is free of any male rival or father-figure. His *maternal* grandmother and his sister are 'all the family there is'. By contrast, Patch is for most of the film financially dependent upon Bradley, who stands structurally as a father-figure. Moreover, as Tod puts money into Patch's show, and pays Janie during rehearsals, it is a structural position which he, too, inhabits. Extending this reading, the closing of the show by Bradley and Tod figures Patch's symbolic castration.

Janie is twice given the look in *Dancing Lady*, and each time she objectifies Patch. The first time occurs when she intrudes upon the rehearsals, and underlines her actions' transgressiveness. The second occurs when, having returned to New York from Cuba with Tod, she gazes at a drunken, slumbering Patch in a restaurant. Although, in Janie's absence, Patch has proceeded to produce his show himself, he remains, implicitly, symbolically castrated: the show is in deep financial and other trouble. In brief, Patch is 'lacking', tacitly feminised, and thus open to objectification. While an exception to the rule of male looking, Janie's look would nevertheless appear to prove the relationship between specularity and power.

Patch is also symbolically castrated in that he 'lacks' Janie. As Jacques Lacan points out, within 'the comedy' of heterosexual relationships, woman stands in for the phallus.[14] Janie's turning to Patch from Tod accordingly renders Patch 'entire'. Further, Janie specifically gets Patch upright on his feet from sitting, slumped, in a chair in his apartment by mockingly claiming that, should Patch give up on his show, 'the wiseys on Broadway'll say it wasn't Gallagher it was Bradley . . .'. That Janie's turning to Patch simultaneously saves his show conforms to the prime show musical convention that the creation of the couple is reciprocated by the successful culmination of their shared creative endeavours. Even so, the situation's psychoanalytic connotations, that the show's salvation should coincide with Patch's assumption of the phallus, and his consequent, implicit identification with/replacement of Bradley as successful producer/father-figure, places it unequivocally within what cine-psychoanalysis, but especially Bellour, discerns to be the total and unflinching Oedipal logic of classical Hollywood narrative.[15]

Janie's 'saving' of Patch follows her own temporary reanimation as a narrative agent. This repeats her earlier transgressive activeness. As before she refuses Tod, leaving him in the restaurant, and re-plays her crashing of the rehearsal by barging into Patch's apartment. It is also an activeness which is curbed and recuperated, a process which here presents a disquieting masochistic edge. When Janie refers to Bradley, Patch stands up and shapes to hit her, to which she responds: 'If that's what it takes to get you on your feet, go ahead'. In terms of repetition–resolution, this is the culmination of a series of sado-masochistic incidents which commence when Patch 'playfully' slaps her backside and she responds with a rapturous: 'Thank-you'. In turn, if Janie's masochism can be seen to operate reflexively with regard to Bellour's pathologising of the female spectator, the character's representation would likewise appear to bear out his claim that 'the American cinema is entirely dependent, as is psychoanalysis, on a system of representations in which the woman occupies a central place only to the extent that it's a place assigned to her by the logic of masculine desire' (Bergstrom, p. 93).

A similar logic informs the cultural discourses and social structures which determined and delimited the new woman, who veers away from the radicalism associated with antecedent and consequent feminisms. Her independence is instead amenable and attuned to the needs of patriarchal capitalism, as increased freedom and ability to consume. Moreover, the occupational opportunities open to the new woman were largely limited to 'the lower-paying, growth sectors of clerical and service work', while popular representations upheld the ideology 'that women could work while single, but should not pursue a career that superseded marriage and motherhood as their life goal' (Lent, p. 319). Analogous contradictions attend the companionate relationship which in practice 'was customarily interpreted as a wife who offered enlightened support to her husband's activities and values' (Wright Wexman, p. 13).

V.

The last two scenes of *Dancing Lady* confirm Janie's choice of Patch over Tod, and the film closes with Patch and Janie's kiss. The text, however, effectively climaxes with the preceding pair of numbers. The first of these is notable mainly for its timid pastiche of Busby Berkeley staging. Hence its single top shot of a circular formation, a trope evocative, within Berkeley's work, of female sexuality, and the fetishistic montage of identically posed women seated suggestively beside foaming beer glasses. The second number, 'Rhythm of the Day', functions as a *mise en abyme*: a textual passage which summarises and reflects back upon the whole. A paean to late modernity, the number begins with figures moving, via a split-screen effect, from past to present, from period to modern dress, and from a wooded fountain to an urban street set. Yet this is late modernity as appropriated by Hollywood and governed, according to the song, implicitly by patriarchy ('Faster, faster, follow master . . .'). Janie enters this modernity sitting beside a rich man in a limousine, which she promptly leaves for a roadster and a 'college boy'. As this suggests a displaced reflection of Janie's choice of Patch before Tod, so the man Janie leaves is explicitly a father-figure. Enter a group of women in flesh-toned body-suits, whose truncheons and policemen's badges and hats mark them as 'traffic cops'. In its *risqué* explicitness, the section recalls Tod's claim that 'what's a striptease on Second Avenue is art on Broadway' and reprises the text's coded contesting of the Production Code. The women's costumes likewise reopen the text's contradictory relation to the Law. Accepting this, it is a contradiction which the women's representation itself reconciles – 'mockery' is here contained by the male look, articulates an institutional challenge which remains entrenched within, and seeks not to contest, the dominant patriarchal order.

The number continues with a line of old women tottering into a beauty parlour where, in silhouette, other female figures grotesquely 'operate' on them with building tools and an oversized pair of scissors. The 'shapely' results hold themselves for the look. The reverberations of this section are acute. Not only is feminine activeness here recuperated in terms of masculine need, and late modernity represented as the site of objectifying consumption, but women are placed as masochistically complicit in their own subordination, and the sadism actioned elsewhere in the text by Patch is displaced onto other women. Objectification, sexual suggestiveness, and renewed indebtedness to Berkeley become rampant as women are shown riding and leaning back 'ecstatically' on merry-go-round horses. Interspersed with a fetishistic montage of facial close-ups, this cuts to a series of shots of women lying, motionless, in various poses, and dressed in skimpy flesh-toned costumes, on a revolving backdrop. As in many sequences directed by Berkeley, woman is reduced explicitly to erotic object. Finally, Janie herself rides across the screen on a merry-go-round horse, upon which the curtain falls and the film cuts to Tod sitting in the audience, implicitly, as at the burlesque, the bearer of the look.

VI.

In writing *Dancing Lady* from the supposedly antithetical positions of cine-psychoanalysis and cultural studies, what is perhaps surprising is the complementarity of the conclusions. True, cultural studies inclines toward foregrounding the text's potentially empowering mediation of feminine independence and changes in heterosexual relations, whereas cine-psychoanalysis tends to emphasise textual strategies which maintain the psychic economy of the patriarchal subject. Even so, Janie's narrative-cum-cultural recuperation reciprocates that effected by the text's specular and structural organisation. Similarly, the cultural discourses which define and delimit the new woman and companionate relationships give word, so to speak, to the patriarchal anxieties revealed textually via cine-psychoanalysis. In turn, it is through these anxieties that the text opens itself to radical critique. Plainly, the key to the apparent complementarity of the cultural and the psychic is their mutual historicisation. Accordingly, it might be profitable to consider psychoanalysis itself as a particular cultural discourse which emerges from a specific historical nexus. This would helpfully unhitch psychoanalysis from reductive universalism and enhance its explanatory pertinence, especially with regard to the affects and products of late modernity, including classical Hollywood cinema.

But what of the present? Miriam Hansen writes that the cine-psychoanalysis of the 1970s and 1980s ironically emerged upon, and became rendered obsolete by, 'a paradigmatic transformation of the ways films are disseminated and consumed'.[16] The economic, social and political changes wrought by postmodernity have resulted in widely discussed shifts in the production, reception and textual operation of Hollywood cinema. For Hansen the model of spectatorship proposed by cine-psychoanalysis 'no longer functions as the totalitarian norm' (Hansen, p. 199), and the look is now more extensively assumed both by women and other previously marginalised and objectified groups. Does this broader assumption of the look reflect wider social and psychic developments? Or is it a characteristically self-conscious and 'affectless' example of post-modern play? Such issues demand historically founded analyses of texts and contexts. Further, while the psychoanalytic unequivocally requires historical and cultural contextualisation, the cultural without the psychoanalytic remains 'lacking'. To return, in conclusion, to Hansen, 'even if we situate reception within a specific historical and social framework, and even as the category of the spectator has become problematic, we still need a theoretical understanding of the possible relations between films and viewers, between representation and subjectivity' (Hansen, p. 206).

Notes

1. Jackie Stacey, *Star Gazing: Hollywood Cinema and Female Spectatorship* (London, 1994), p. 47.
2. See Louis Althusser, 'Ideology and Ideological State Apparatuses (Notes Towards an Investigation)' in L. Althusser, *Lenin and Philosophy and Other Essays*, pp. 121–73, trans. Ben Brewster (London, 1971) and A. Gramsci, *Selections from the Prison Notebooks of Antonio Gramsci*, ed. and trans. Q. Hoare and G. Nowell Smith (London, 1971).
3. This chronology perhaps helps to explain the tendency of discussions of the two discourses to represent cultural studies as redeeming, or at least mitigating, the 'sins' of cine-psychoanalysis. See, for example, David Morley, 'Changing Paradigms in Audience Studies' in E. Seiter, H. Borchers, G. Kreutzner and E-M. Warth (eds), *Remote Control: Television, Audiences and Cultural Power* (London, 1989), pp. 16–43.
4. See Ronald Haver, *David O. Selznick's Hollywood* (London, 1980), David Thomson, *Showman: The Life of David O. Selznick* (London, 1993), Richard Barrios, *A Song in the Dark: The Birth of the Musical Film* (New York, 1995), and Rick Altman, *The American Film Musical* (London, 1989). Page references to the latter two books are cited in the text.
5. Robert Stam, Robert Burgoyne and Sandy Flitterman-Lewis, *New Vocabularies in Film Semiotics: Structuralism, Post-structuralism and Beyond* (London, 1992), p. 124.

6. Christian Metz, 'The Imaginary Signifier', trans. B. Brewster, *Screen* vol. 16, no. 2 (Summer 1975), pp. 18–19. Jean-Louis Baudry's articles on the cinematic apparatus are 'Ideological Effects of the Basic Cinematographic Apparatus', trans. A. Williams, *Film Quarterly* vol. 28, no. 2 (Winter 1974–75), pp. 39–47 (page references to this essay are cited in the text), and 'The Apparatus', trans. J. Andrews and B. Augst, *camera obscura* no. 1 (Fall 1976), pp. 104–26.

7. Laura Mulvey, 'Visual Pleasure and Narrative Cinema', *Screen* vol. 16, no. 3 (Autumn 1975), p. 6. Further page references are cited in the text.

8. Laura Mulvey, 'Afterthoughts on "Visual Pleasure and Narrative Cinema" inspired by *Duel in the Sun* (King Vidor, 1946)', *Framework* 15–16–17 (Summer 1981), p. 12.

9. Janet Bergstrom, 'Alternation, Segmentation, Hypnosis: Interview with Raymond Bellour', trans. Susan Suleiman, *camera obscura* nos 3–4 (Summer 1979), p. 97. Further page references are cited in the text.

10. Virginia Wright Wexman, *Creating the Couple: Love, Marriage, and Hollywood Performance* (Princeton, NJ, 1993), pp. 133–4. Further page references are cited in the text.

11. Steven Cohan and Ina Rae Hark, 'Introduction', in S. Cohan and I. Rae Hark (eds), *Screening the Male : Exploring Masculinities in Hollywood Cinema* (London, 1993), pp. 1–8 (p. 2).

12. See Wright Wexman, *Creating the Couple*, pp. 3–36 and 133–59.

13. See Tina Olsin Lent, 'Romantic Love and Friendship: The Redefinition of Gender Relations in Screwball Comedy' in K. Brunovska Karnick and H. Jenkins (eds), *Classical Hollywood Comedy* (New York, 1995), p. 315. Further page references are cited in the text.

14. Jacques Lacan, 'The Signification of the Phallus' in J. Lacan, *Écrits: A Selection*, trans. A. Sheridan (London, 1977), p. 289.

15. With regard to Bellour and the Oedipal trajectory of classical Hollywood narrative, see his discussion of *The Westerner* (William Wyler 1940) in Bergstrom, 'Alternation, Segmentation, Hypnosis', pp. 87–93.

16. Miriam Hansen, 'Early Cinema, Late Cinema: Permutations of the Public Sphere', *Screen* vol. 34, no. 3 (Autumn 1993), pp. 197–210. Page references are cited in the text.

Part Five
Audio-visual Resources

1. 'Whose stories you tell': writing 'Ken Loach'

Ladybird, Ladybird was written by Rona Munro and directed by Ken Loach for Parallax Pictures and Film on Four. The film premièred in September 1994 and is now available on video. Rona Munro has written for theatre, television and radio as well as film, and has worked in youth and community theatre.

Ken Loach first became known for his work directing British television drama for the BBC in the 1960s, often in collaboration with the producer Tony Garnett. Loach's cinema films before *Ladybird, Ladybird* include *Up the Junction* (1967), *Kes* (1969), *Fatherland* (1986), *Hidden Agenda* (1990), *Riff-Raff* (1990), *Raining Stones* (1993). He has since directed *Land and Freedom* (1995) and *My Name is Joe* (1998). The films made in 1990 and after are available on video, as is *Kes*.

Rona Munro's television writing includes the plays *Bumping the Odds* (BBC 1997), *Men of the Month* (BBC 1994), *Biting the Hands* (BBC 1989) and *Hardware* (Scottish TV 1983 and Channel 4 1984). She wrote three episodes of *Dr Who* (BBC 1989), and an episode of *Casualty* titled 'Say it with Flowers' (BBC 1990). She is currently adapting *Mary Barton* by Elizabeth Gaskell for BBC television.

2. Questions of authorship: Samuel Beckett and *Film*

Access to *Film* and the television plays written by Beckett is difficult. *Film* can be obtained on 16mm film from the British Film Institute, and some of the television works can be obtained on videotape from the same source. Archives of Beckett material, like the Samuel Beckett Archive at the University of Reading, hold videotape copies of some or all of the film and television works based on Beckett texts. These can be viewed by researchers. The written texts on which *Film* and the television plays are based are published in Samuel Beckett, *The Collected Shorter Plays of Samuel Beckett* (London: Faber 1984), and the single edition, Samuel Beckett, *Film* (London: Faber 1972, first published New York: Grove Press, 1969) includes stills from the production of the 1964 version.

The first version of *Film*, directed by Alan Schneider, produced by Evergreen Theatre Inc., was released in 1964. This is the version discussed in the essay. A second version directed by David Clark, produced by the British Film Institute, was released in 1979.

It is interesting to compare *Film* with the plays by Beckett written for television. *Eh Joe* was directed by Alan Gibson for BBC television and broadcast in 1966. The play was then directed by Walter Asmus for Süddeutscher Rundfunk in Stuttgart and transmitted in Germany in 1988. *Ghost Trio* was directed by Beckett and produced by Süddeutscher Rundfunk in Stuttgart, transmitted in Germany in 1977 as *Geister Trio*. Also in 1977 the play was directed by Beckett assisted by Donald McWhinnie, for the first UK broadcast on BBC2. *... but the clouds ...* was directed by Beckett and produced by Süddeutscher Rundfunk in Stuttgart, transmitted in Germany in 1977 as *Nur noch Gewölk*. Also in 1977 the play was directed by Beckett assisted by Donald McWhinnie, for the first UK broadcast on BBC2. *Quad* was directed by Beckett and produced by Süddeutscher Rundfunk in Stuttgart, transmitted in Germany in 1981 as *Quad I & II*. The first UK transmission was on BBC2 in 1982. *Nacht und Traüme* was directed by Beckett and produced by Süddeutscher Rundfunk in Stuttgart in 1982, transmitted in Germany in 1983.

3. Publicists – distribution workers in the pleasure economy of the film industry

Of the films mentioned in the essay, all but the most recent are available on videotape: *You Were Never Lovelier* (Seiter 1942), *William Shakespeare's Romeo and Juliet* (Luhrmann 1996), *Hamlet* (Branagh 1996) and *Donnie Brasco* (Newell 1997). At the time of writing, *Shooting Fish* (1997), *Keep the Aspidistra Flying* (1997), *Waking Ned* (1998) and *Titanic* (1998) were yet to appear, but are now available.

The 'publicity personality' of films can often be gauged from the trailers shown in cinemas and on television, and, later, in the collection of trailers and ads which appear on videotape copies of other films. Occasionally the construction of a publicity personality is part of a film story itself. For example, the first minutes of *The Player* (1992), a wryly comic narrative focusing on the Hollywood film business, show ideas for future films being 'pitched' to studio executives, mainly by indicating the publicity personality of the proposed film.

4. Preliminaries for a taxonomy and rhetoric of on-screen writing

The following films, referred to in the essay, are all available on videotape unless otherwise stated.

Blade Runner (Ridley Scott 1982): SF noir with an interesting use of on-screen writing in the title sequence.

Clive of India (Richard Boleslawski 1934): Unavailable on video. A typical historical biopic, but interesting for its extreme dependence on titles to supply narrative information and coherence.

Le Crime de M. Lange (Jean Renoir 1936): Popular Front drama whose subtitling on recently released UK print offers an opportunity to study the relative autonomy of subtitles from the production process.

Dune (David Lynch 1984): Adaptation of sprawling SF epic with interesting use of faux-computer screens to supply backstory and orientation.

Gone With the Wind (Victor Fleming et al. 1939): The Selznick mega-production, whose title sequence is as overblown as the rest of the film.

La Hora de los Hornos (*Hour of the Furnaces*) (Fernando Solanas and Octavio Gettino 1966–68): Aggressive and propagandistic Third Cinema documentary using graphics as part of its intellectual armory.

Intolerance (D.W. Griffith 1916): Griffith's silent epic uses complex symbolic codes to decorate intertitles, suggesting a universal visual language.

I Was a Male War Bride (Howard Hawks 1943): Cross-dressing comedy with a classical title sequence.

Man with a Movie Camera (Dziga Vertov 1928): Surprisingly, unavailable on video in the UK, where the available 16mm print does not have the original dynamic Russian intertitles, which bring the montage principle to the clash of typographics and photography.

The Peacemaker (Mimi Leder 1997): Awaiting video release at the time of writing. First feature from SKG Dreamworks and ER helmer Leder. Opening sequence in Russian with English subtitles.

Pulp Fiction (Quentin Tarantino 1992): Uses titles to break up the 'chapters' of the narrative.

sex, lies and videotape (Steven Soderbergh 1989): Self-reflexive Canadian independent feature, referenced for its unusual use of lower case in the title.

Starship Troopers (Paul Verhoeven 1997): Awaiting video release at the time of writing. Overdone militaristic SF epic, extremely reliant on pseudo-internet screens to provide not only information but moral guidance.

Star Wars (George Lucas 1977): All versions share the angled scrolling of the pre-credit narrative.

5. Writing, cinema and the avant-garde: Michael Snow and *So Is This*

Avant-garde films are very much less likely to find their way onto video, even if their makers would agree to this 'translation' from one medium to another – and since film-makers are often concerned with the specificity of the film medium they might well not agree to it. However, most of Michael Snow's films mentioned in the essay, including *So Is This* (1982), are available to rent on 16mm film from the London Film-Makers' Co-operative, The Lux Centre, 2–4 Hoxton Square, London N1 6NU, as are Paul Sharits's *Word Movie* (1972) and Martha Haslanger's *Syntax* (1974). The London Film-Makers' Co-operative is the major UK distributor of avant-garde film. Snow's *Wavelength* (1966–67), certainly his best-known film, is also available on 16mm from British Film Institute Film and Video Library, 21 Stephen Street, London W1P 2LN.

Jean-Luc Godard's and Dusan Makavejev's work is much better represented on video, as befits films which circulate more or less within the 'art film' constituency. Although *Vivre sa vie* (1962), *Le Gai savoir* and *Vent d'Est* (both 1969) are not available on video, most of Godard' s films are, including those others mentioned in the text: *Pierrot le fou* (1965), *Masculin féminin* and *Deux ou trois choses que je sais d'elle* (both 1966) and *Tout va bien* (1972). Makavejev's *Switchboard Operator/Love Dossier, or the Tragedy of a Switchboard Operator* (1967) and *WR – Mysteries of the Organism* (1971) are both available on video, as are his *Man is Not a Bird* (1966) and *Innocence Unprotected* (1968).

The availability of silent cinema on video is hit-and-miss, but *Broken Blossoms* (1919) is available, as are other features by D.W. Griffith, such as *Birth of a Nation* (1915), and many of the important Soviet films of the 1920s are also available, though the experimental work in France in the 1920s is not. Laserdisk availability of Griffith's work, both features and earlier short films, and of Soviet 1920s work is generally good. The British Film Institute Film and Video Library (see above) is the major UK distributor of silent cinema (and much else) on 16mm film.

6. Inscription in *The Piano*

Jane Campion is a New Zealander, who has directed *Sweetie* (1989), which she also co-wrote, *An Angel at My Table* (1990), based on the autobiography of Janet Frame, and *The Piano* (1993), for which she also wrote the screenplay. *The Piano* won an Academy Award for Campion's screenwriting, and an Academy Award nomination for her direction of the film. All three films are available on videotape, and also on laserdisk.

Deaf and mute characters have featured in a variety of films, including *Johnny Belinda* (Jean Negulesco 1948), available in US videotape format only, *Mandy* (Alexander Mackendrick 1952), *The Miracle Worker* (Arthur Penn 1962), and *The Heart is a Lonely Hunter* (Robert Ellis Miller 1968), each of which are on video. Deaf characters who communicate in Deaf Sign Language are represented in *Children of a Lesser God* (Randa Haines 1986) and *Four Weddings and a Funeral* (Mike Newell 1994). Both films are available on both videotape and laserdisk.

7. The mutinies on HMS *Bounty*

The 1935 *Mutiny on the Bounty*, directed by Frank Lloyd for MGM, stars Charles Laughton and Clark Gable. There is no current videotape version, though the film is available on laserdisk. The 1962 version of *Mutiny on the Bounty* was directed by Lewis Milestone, again for MGM, and stars Trevor Howard and Marlon Brando. Its is available both on videotape and laserdisk. *The Bounty*, released in 1984, is a Dino di Laurentis production, directed by Roger Donaldson, starring Anthony Hopkins and Mel Gibson. The film is available on video and laserdisk, and the soundtrack was released on CD. The audio tape mentioned in the essay, *Mutiny on the Bounty*, is a BBC Radio 4 dramatisation based on the Charles Nordhoff and James Hall novels, adapted by Bert Coules, and directed by Adrian Bean. The production features Oliver Reed and Linus Roache in the roles of Bligh and Christian, and was released by Mr Punch (Audio) Limited.

8. Three *Madame Bovarys*: Renoir, Minnelli, Chabrol

Renoir's *Madame Bovary* (1934) does not seem to be available on videotape currently, which is very curious, but Minnelli's *Madame Bovary* (1949) and Chabrol's (1991) are both on video, and laserdisk as well. Each of these directors has a distinguished pedigree, and has made numerous films. Rather than making an invidious selection from the work of these directors, it may be more useful for comparative work to provide details of films discussed in the essay which feature dance sequences. These films are *The Leopard* (*Il Gattopardo*, Visconti 1963), *The Conformist* (*Il Conformista*, Bertolucci 1971), *Last Tango in Paris* (Bertolucci 1973), *1900* (*Novecento*, Bertolucci 1976), *Age of Innocence* (Scorsese 1994) and *Stealing Beauty* (Bertolucci 1995). At the time of writing *The Leopard* is not available on video, while *The Conformist* is on video in the USA but not the UK, and can also be obtained on laserdisk.

9. The fiction is already there: writing and film in Blair's Britain

The English Patient was directed by Anthony Minghella, with a screenplay by Anthony Minghella, and was produced by Saul Zaentz for Tiger Moth Productions. It was released in 1996 for cinema exhibition, and a videotape version is widely available.

Fever Pitch was directed by David Evans, with a screenplay by Nick Hornby, and was produced by Amanda Posey for Channel Four Films/Wildgaze Films Production. The film was released in 1997, and is widely available on videotape.

Crash was directed and produced by David Cronenberg, who also wrote the screenplay. The film was an Alliance Communications Production, released in 1996. As discussed in the essay, its release on videotape was a controversial issue in Britain, though it was granted video classification (the precondition for its release on videotape) in 1998.

10. Public spaces and private narratives – the plays and films of David Hare

Wetherby (directed by Hare and produced by Simon Relph) was made in 1985 by Greenpoint Films, and is available on video in US format only. *Paris by Night* (directed by Hare and produced by Patrick Cassavetti) was made by Greenpoint Films in conjunction with Pressman Productions in 1988, and is not available on videotape. *Strapless* (directed by Hare and produced by Rick MacCallum) was made in 1989 by Strapless Films for Granada International, and is on video and laserdisk. *The Secret Rapture* (directed by Howard Davies, who also directed the first stage production, and produced by Simon Relph) was made by Greenpoint Films in association with British Screen for Channel 4, 1993, and is available on video and laserdisk. The screenplays of all the films written by David Hare discussed in the essay are published by Faber. *Wetherby* is available as a single edition (published in association with Greenpoint Films and containing stills) and in a collection with *Heading Home* and *Dreams of Leaving*. *Paris by Night* and *Strapless* are published in single editions. Both *Knuckle* and *Plenty* are published by Faber and can be found in *Plays: One*. A useful selection of Hare's key writings on both plays and films can be found in *Writing Left-Handed* (Faber).

11. Preserving machines: recentering the decentered subject in *Blade Runner* and *Johnny Mnemonic*

Johnny Mnemonic (Robert Longo 1995), *Blade Runner* and *Blade Runner: The Director's Cut* (Ridley Scott 1991) are all currently available on video, the latter in a letterbox format. But you've not seen cyberpunk cinema (whatever that means) until you've seen *Videodrome* (David Cronenberg 1983), *The Adventures of Buckaroo Banzai Across the Eighth Dimension* (W.D. Richter 1984), *Tetsuo: The Iron Man* (Shinya Tsukamoto 1989), *Tetsuo 2: The Body Hammer* (Shinya Tsukamoto 1991) *Wax or the Discovery of Television Among the Bees* (David Blair 1991), and, less obviously, *Tokyo Fist* (Shinya Tsukamoto 1996), though the latter two films are not currently available on videotape.

12. From SF to sci-fi: Paul Verhoeven's *Starship Troopers*

Starship Troopers (1997) is available on videotape. Paul Verhoeven's earlier Dutch films are *Wat Zien Ik* (*Business is Business*, 1971) which is not available on video, *Turks Fruit* (*Turkish Delight*, 1973) and *Keetje Tippel* (*Cathy Tippel*, 1975) which are on videotape, *Soldaat van Oranje* (*Soldier of Orange*, 1977) which is not on video, *Spetters* (1980) and *Die Vierde Man* (*The Fourth Man*, 1983) which are available on video in the USA only. His later American films *Flesh + Blood* (1985), *RoboCop* (1987), *Total Recall* (1990), *Basic Instinct* (1992) and *Showgirls* (1995) are available on videotape and laserdisk. Most of the science fiction films listed in the essay are also available on video.

13. Writing and reputation: *The Searchers* 1956–1976

Ford's development and changing representations both of white American society and of the hero can be traced in a series of remarkable Westerns from *Stagecoach* (1939) to *Cheyenne Autumn* (1964), among the most significant of which are *My Darling Clementine* (1946), the cavalry 'trilogy', *Fort Apache* (1948), *She Wore a Yellow Ribbon* (1950) and, *Rio Grande* (1950), and *The Man Who Shot Liberty Valance* (1962). Most of these (and *The Searchers* (1956)) are readily available on video, but it is worth trying to find the widescreen version of *The Searchers*, the excellent visual quality of which gives some sense of what the film originally looked like in VistaVision. Other Westerns which made important contributions to the increasingly disturbing hero in the post-war period were *Red River* (Howard Hawks 1948) and *Winchester 73* (Anthony Mann 1950), both of which are available on video. All Anthony Mann's Westerns (including, for instance, *The Naked Spur* (1952), *Bend of the River* (1952), and *Man of the West* (1958)) are worth watching out for on television, but most have not been released on video. Westerns from the late 1960s and early 1970s that give a clear sense of what was happening to the genre at the time that *The Searchers* was being re-evaluated include *The Wild Bunch* (Sam Peckinpah 1969), *Little Big Man* (Arthur Penn 1970), *High Plains Drifter* (Clint Eastwood 1972) and *Ulzana's Raid* (Robert Aldrich 1972) (all available on video). *Taxi Driver* (Martin Scorsese

1976) is readily available on video, but as with *The Searchers* it is worth looking for a widescreen version.

14. Writing on film: practical propositions

Questions of voyeurism and point of view can be explored in *Vertigo* (Hitchcock 1958) and *Peeping Tom* (Powell 1960). *Vertigo* also opens up avenues of approach to the audience's relation to the image, as do *Beyond a Reasonable Doubt* (Lang 1956), *Suture* (Siegel and McGehee 1993) and *Lost Highway* (Lynch 1996). Each of these films is available on videotape.

Gender can be approached in numerous ways: in its relation to genre and history (*Some Came Running*, Minnelli 1958); as a problem involving the relationship between two people (*Bringing up Baby*, Hawks 1938; *A Star is Born*, Cukor 1954; *M Butterfly*, Cronenberg 1993); in its relation to fatherhood (*Jurassic Park*, Spielberg 1993). Each of these films is available on videotape.

Politics and history are represented in particularly complex and very different ways in *Death by Hanging* (Oshima 1968), *The Ceremony* (Oshima 1971) and *Le Fantôme de la Liberté* (Buñuel 1974), though only Buñuel's film is currently on video.

The representation of violence as a social and political problem is central to *Straw Dogs* (Peckinpah 1971), available on video but not in the UK, and *Funny Games* (Michaël Haneke 1997), not yet available on video. The question is aestheticised and duly trivialised in *A Clockwork Orange* (Kubrick 1971), available on video but not in the UK.

15. Writing about specularity and Modernity: the case of *Dancing Lady*

Complementary to *Dancing Lady* (1932) in their relation to issues of specularity and modernity are a slate of contemporaneous Warner Brothers' musicals: *Forty-Second Street* (Lloyd Bacon 1933), *Footlight Parade* (Bacon 1933), *Gold Diggers of 1933* (Mervyn Le Roy 1933) and *Dames* (Ray Enright 1934). All of these films feature numbers choreographed by Busby Berkeley. For examples of MGM's elaboration of the 1930s backstage/show musical, see *Born to Dance* (Roy Del Ruth 1936), *The Great Ziegfeld* (Robert

Z. Leonard 1936) and *Broadway Melody of 1938* (Del Ruth 1937). Unfortunately, the only two of the films presently available on video are *Footlight Parade* and *Broadway Melody of 1938*. The Warner Brothers' musicals in particular, however, have enjoyed comparatively frequent screening on both terrestrial and satellite television channels.

Selected bibliography

Writing for cinema

Botan, C., and V. Hazleton (eds), *Public Relations Theory* (Hove: Lawrence Erlbaum Associates, 1989).

Corliss, Richard, *Talking Pictures: Screenwriters in the American Cinema* (New York: Viking, 1973).

Dale, Martin, *The Movie Game* (London: Cassell, 1997).

Durie, John, *The Film Marketing Handbook* (London: British Film Institute, 1993).

Francke, Lizzie, *Script Girls: Women Screenwriters in Hollywood* (London: British Film Institute, 1994).

Gaines, J., *Contested Culture: The Image, The Voice and The Law* (London, British Film Institute, 1992).

Goldman, William, *Adventures in the Screen Trade: A Personal View of Hollywood and Screenwriting* (London: Futura, 1985).

Hill, John, Martin McLoone, and Paul Hainsworth (eds), *Border Crossing: Film in Ireland, Britain and Europe* (London: British Film Institute, 1994).

Hill, John, and Martin McLoone, *Big Picture, Small Screen: The Relations Between Film and Television* (Luton: University of Luton Press, 1996).

Ilott, Terry, *Budgets and Markets: A Study of the Budgeting and Marketing of European Films* (London: Routledge, 1996).

Jones, Chris, and Genevieve Jolliffe, *The Guerilla Filmmaker's Handbook and Producer's Toolkit* (London: Cassell 1996).

Litivik, L., *Reel Power* (New York: William Murrow, 1986).

McKnight, George (ed.), *Agent of Challenge and Defiance: The Films of Ken Loach* (Trowbridge: Flicks Books, 1997).

Moran, A. (ed.), *Film Policy* (London: Routledge, 1996).

Nash, Constance, and Virginia Oakley, *The Screenwriters' Handbook (Writing for the Movies)* (New York: Barnes and Noble, 1978).

Parker, Philip, *The Art and Science of Screenwriting* (Exeter: Intellect Books, 1997).

Petrie, Duncan (ed.), *Inside Stories: Diaries of British Filmmakers at Work* (London: British Film Institute, 1996).

Postman, Neil, *Amusing Ourselves to Death: Public Discourse in the Age of Show Business* (New York: Viking, 1985).

Root, William, *Writing the Script* (New York: Holt, Rinehart and Winston, 1980).

Short, K.R.M., *Screening the Propaganda of British Air Power* (Trowbridge: Flicks Books, 1997).

Swain, Dwight, *Film Scriptwriting* (New York: Hastings House, 1977).

Ward, Sue, *Getting the Message Across: Public Relations, Publicity, and Working with the Media* (London: Pluto, 1992).

Writing in cinema

Abel, Richard, *Silent Film* (London: Athlone, 1996).

Brunette, Peter, and David Wills, *Screen/Play: Derrida and Film Theory* (Princeton, NJ: Princeton University Press, 1989).

Conley, Tom, *Film Hieroglyphs: Ruptures in Classical Cinema* (Minneapolis: University of Minnesota Press, 1991).

Elsaesser, Thomas, *Early Cinema: Space, Frame, Narrative* (London: British Film Institute, 1990).

Gidal, Peter (ed.), *Structural Film Anthology* (London: British Film Institute, 1976).

Hansen, Miriam, *Babel and Babylon: Spectatorship in American Silent Cinema* (Cambridge, MA: Harvard University Press, 1991).

McLuhan, Marshall, *Understanding Media: The Extensions of Man* (London: Routledge and Kegan Paul, 1969).

Ong, Walter, *Orality and Literacy: The Technologizing of the Word* (London: Methuen, 1982).

Peterson, James, *Dreams of Chaos, Visions of Order: Understanding the American Avant-Garde Cinema* (Detroit, MI: Wayne State University Press, 1994).

Rees, A.L., *A History of Experimental Film and Video* (London: British Film Institute, 1998).

Sitney, P. Adams, *Visionary Film: The American Avant Garde 1943–1978* (2nd edn, Oxford and New York: Oxford University Press, 1979).

Sitney, P. Adams, *Modernist Montage: The Obscurity of Vision in Cinema and Literature* (New York and Oxford: Columbia University Press, 1990).

Snyder, Ilana (ed.), *Page to Screen: Taking Literacy into the Electronic Era* (London: Routledge, 1998).

Winston Dixon, Wheeler, *The Films of Jean-Luc Godard* (Albany: State University of New York Press, 1997).

Writing into cinema

Aldgate, Anthony, *Censorship and the Permissive Society: British Cinema and Theatre, 1955–1965* (Oxford: Clarendon, 1995).

Beja, Morris, *Film and Literature* (New York: Longman, 1976).

Bluestone, George, *Novel into Film* (Berkeley and Los Angeles: University of California Press, 1957).

Boose, Lynda E., and Richard Burt (eds), *Shakespeare, The Movie: Popularizing the Plays on Film, TV and Video* (London: Routledge, 1997).

Bordwell, David, *Making Meaning: Inference and Rhetoric in the Interpretation of Cinema* (London: Harvard University Press, 1991).

Bordwell, David, *On the History of Film Style* (London: Harvard University Press, 1998).

Braendlin, Bonnie, and Hans Braendlin (eds), *Authority and Transgression in Literature and Film* (Miami: University Press of Florida, 1996).

Brewster, Robert B., *Theatre to Cinema: Stage Pictorialism and the Early Feature Film* (Oxford: Clarendon, 1997).

Cancalon, Elaine, and Antoine Spacagna, *Intertextuality in Literature and Film* (Miami: University Press of Florida, 1994).

Cartmell, Deborah, I.Q. Hunter, Heidi Kaye, and Imelda Whelehan (eds), *Pulping Fictions: Consuming Culture across the Literature/Media Divide* (London: Pluto, 1996).

Cartmell, Deborah, I.Q. Hunter, Heidi Kaye and Imelda Whelehan (eds), *Trash Aesthetics: Popular Culture and its Audience* (London: Pluto, 1997).

Cartmell, Deborah, I.Q. Hunter, Heidi Kaye, and Imelda Whelehan (eds), *Sisterhoods Across the Literature/Media Divide* (London: Pluto 1998).

Chatman, Seymour, *Story and Discourse: Narrative Structure in Fiction and Film* (Ithaca, NY: Cornell University Press, 1978).

Cohen, Keith, *Film and Literature: The Dynamics of Exchange* (New Haven: Yale University Press, 1979).

Esslin, Martin, *The Field of Drama* (London: Methuen, 1987).

Fitzsimmons, Linda, and Sarah Street (eds), *Moving Performance: British Stage and Screen, 1890s–1920s* (Trowbridge: Flicks Books, 1998).

Gelder, Ken, *Reading the Vampire* (London: Routledge, 1994).

Giddings, Robert, Keith Selby, and Chris Wensley, *Screening the Novel: The Theory and Practice of Literary Dramatization* (London: Macmillan, 1990).

Gifford, Denis, *Books and Plays in Films 1896–1915: Literary, Theatrical and Artistic Sources of the First Twenty Years of Motion Pictures* (London: Cassell, 1993).

Harrington, J. (ed.), *Film and/as Literature* (Englewood Cliffs, NJ: Prentice-Hall, 1977).

Hawkins, Harriet, *Classics and Trash: Traditions and Taboos in High Literature and Popular Modern Genres* (Hemel Hempstead: Harvester, 1990).

Jinks, William, *The Celluloid Literature* (London: Glencoe, 1971).

Klein, Michael, and Gillian Parker (eds), *The English Novel and the Movies* (New York: Ungar, 1981).

Luhr, William, and Peter Lehman, *Authorship and Narrative in the Cinema* (New York: Putnam, 1977).

Marcus, Fred H. (ed.), *Film and Literature: Contrasts in Media* (New York: Chandler, 1971).

McFarlane, Brian, *Words and Images* (London: Secker and Warburg, 1987).

McFarlane, Brian, *Novel to Film: An Introduction to the Theory of Adaptation* (Oxford: Clarendon, 1996).

Miller, Jonathan, *Subsequent Performances* (London: Faber, 1986).

Morissette, Bruce, *Novel and Film* (Chicago: University of Illinois Press, 1985).

Peary, G., and R. Shatzkin (eds), *The Classic American Novel and the Movies* (New York: Ungar, 1977).

Reynolds, Peter (ed.), *Novel Images: Literature in Performance* (London: Routledge, 1993).

Sinyard, Neil, *Filming Literature: The Art of Screen Adaptation* (Beckenham: Croom Helm, 1986).

Wagner, Geoffrey, *The Novel and the Cinema* (Rutherford, NJ: Farleigh Dickinson University Press, 1975).

Writing about cinema

Abel, Richard, *Silent Film* (London: Athlone, 1996).

Altman, Rick, *The American Film Musical* (London: British Film Institute, 1989).

Andrew, Dudley, *Concepts in Film Theory* (Oxford: Oxford University Press, 1984).

Baudry, Leo, *Narrative, Apparatus, Ideology*, ed. P. Rosen (New York: Columbia University Press, 1986).

Baxter, John, *Science Fiction in the Cinema, 1895–1970* (London: Tantivy Press, 1970).

Bazin, André, *What is Cinema*, vol. 1, ed. Hugh Gray (Berkeley and Los Angeles: University of California Press, 1967).

Belton, John (ed.), *Movies and Mass Culture* (London: Athlone, 1996).

Bennett, Tony, Susan Boyd-Bowman, Colin Mercer, and Janet Woollacott (eds), *Popular Television and Film* (London: British Film Institute, 1981).

Bignell, Jonathan, *Media Semiotics: An Introduction* (Manchester: Manchester University Press, 1997).

Bordwell, David, *Narration in the Fiction Film* (London: Routledge, 1986).

Bordwell, David, *Making Meaning: Inference and Rhetoric in the Interpretation of Cinema* (Cambridge, MA: Harvard University Press, 1989).

Bordwell, David, *On the History of Film Style* (London: Harvard University Press, 1998).

Branigan, Ed, *Narrative Comprehension in Film* (London: Routledge, 1992).

Brosnan, John, *The Primal Screen: A History of the Science Fiction Film* (London: Orbit, 1991).

Brunette, Peter, and David Wills, *Screen/Play: Derrida and Film Theory* (Princeton, NJ: Princeton University Press, 1989).

Brunovska Karnick, Kristine, and Henry Jenkins (eds), *Classical Hollywood Comedy* (New York: Routledge, 1995).

Buscombe, Ed, and Roberta Pearson (eds), *Back in the Saddle Again: New Essays on the Western* (London: British Film Institute, 1998).

Cameron, Ian (ed.), *The Book of Film Noir* (New York: Continuum, 1992).

Cameron, Ian, and Douglas Pye (eds), *The Movie Book of the Western* (London: Studio Vista, 1996).

Caughie, John (ed.), *Theories of Authorship* (London: Routledge and Kegan Paul/British Film Institute, 1981).

Clarke, David (ed.), *The Cinematic City* (London: Routledge, 1997).

Cohan, Steven, and Ina Rae Hark (eds), *Screening the Male: Exploring Masculinities in Hollywood Cinema* (London: Routledge, 1993).

Collins, Jim, Hilary Radner, and Ava Preacher Collins (eds), *Film Theory Goes to the Movies: Cultural Analysis of Contemporary Film* (London: Routledge, 1993).

Conley, Tom, *Film Hieroglyphs: Ruptures in Classical Cinema* (Minneapolis: University of Minnesota Press, 1991).

Cook, David, *A History of Narrative Film* (4th edn, New York: Norton, 1996).

Corber, Robert J., *In the Name of National Security: Hitchcock, Homophobia, and the Political Construction of Gender in Postwar America* (Durham, NC and London: Duke University Press, 1993).

Daiwara, Manthia, *Black American Cinema* (London: Routledge, 1993).

De Lauretis, Teresa, and Stephen Heath (eds), *The Cinematic Apparatus* (New York: St Martin's Press, 1980).

De Lauretis, Teresa, *Alice Doesn't: Feminism Semiotics Cinema* (Bloomington: Indiana University Press, 1984).

Denzin, Norman, *Images of Postmodern Society: Social Theory and Contemporary Media* (London: Sage, 1991).

Denzin, Norman, *The Cinematic Society: The Voyeur's Gaze* (London: Sage, 1995).

Dyer, Richard, *Stars* (rev. edn, London: British Film Institute, 1998).

Elsaesser, Thomas, *Early Cinema: Space, Frame, Narrative* (London: British Film Institute, 1990).

Feuer, Jane, *The Hollywood Musical* (2nd edn, London: Macmillan, 1992).

Gaines, Jane (ed.), *Classical Hollywood Narrative: The Paradigm Wars* (Durham, NC: Duke University Press, 1992).

Gledhill, Christine (ed.), *Stardom: Industry of Desire* (London: Routledge, 1991).

Groden, Torbal, *Moving Pictures: A New Theory of Film Genres, Feelings and Cognition* (Oxford: Clarendon, 1997).

Hansen, Miriam, *Babel and Babylon: Spectatorship in American Silent Cinema* (Cambridge, MA: Harvard University Press, 1991).

Harwood, Sarah, *Family Fictions: Representations of the Family in 1980s Hollywood Cinema* (London: Macmillan, 1997).

Hayward, Philip (ed.), *Culture, Technology and Creativity* (London: John Libbey, 1990).

Hayward, Philip, and Tana Wollen (eds), *Future Visions: New Technologies of the Screen* (London: British Film Institute, 1993).

Heath, Stephen, *Questions of Cinema* (London: Macmillan, 1981).

Higson, Andrew (ed.), *Dissolving Views: Key Writings on British Cinema* (London: Cassell, 1996).

Higson, Andrew, *Waving the Flag: Constructing a National Cinema in Britain* (Oxford: Clarendon, 1997).

Hill, John, *Sex, Class and Realism: British Cinema 1956–63* (London: British Film Institute, 1986).

Hill, John, Martin McLoone, and Paul Hainsworth (eds), *Border Crossing: Film in Ireland, Britain and Europe* (London: British Film Institute, 1994).

Hill, John, and Martin McLoone, *Big Picture, Small Screen: The Relations Between Film and Television* (Luton: University of Luton Press, 1996).

Hillier, Jim, *The New Hollywood* (London: Studio Vista, 1992).

Hillier, Jim, and Nick Browne (eds), *Cahiers du Cinéma* (3 vols, London: Routledge, 1996).

hooks, bell, *Reel to Real: Race, Sex and Class at the Movies* (London: Routledge, 1997).

Jameson, Fredric, *Postmodernism or, the Cultural Logic of Late Capitalism* (London: Verso, 1991).

Jameson, Fredric, *The Geopolitical Aesthetic: Cinema and Space in the World System* (London: British Film Institute, 1992).

Jancovich, Mark, *Rational Fears: American Horror in the 1950s* (Manchester: Manchester University Press, 1996).

Kaplan, E. Ann (ed.), *Psychoanalysis and Cinema* (London: Routledge 1990).

Krutnik, Frank, *In a Lonely Street: Film Noir, Genre, Masculinity* (New York and London: Routledge, 1991).

Kuhn, Annette (ed.), *Alien Zone: Cultural Theory and Contemporary Science Fiction Cinema* (London: Verso, 1990).

Lang, Robert, *American Film Melodrama: Griffith, Vidor, Minnelli* (Princeton, NJ: Princeton University Press, 1989).

Mast, Gerald, Marshall Cohen, and Leo Braudy (eds), *Film Theory and Criticism* (4th edn, New York and Oxford: Oxford University Press, 1992).

Mayne, Judith, *Cinema and Spectatorship* (London: Routledge, 1993).

McKnight, George (ed.), *Agent of Challenge and Defiance: The Films of Ken Loach* (Trowbridge: Flicks Books, 1997).

Monaco, James, *How to Read a Film: The World of Movies, Media, and Multimedia Art: Technology, Language, History, Theory* (3rd edn, Oxford: Oxford University Press, 1998).

Mulvey, Laura, *Visual and Other Pleasures* (London: Macmillan, 1989).

Neale, Stephen, *Genre* (London: British Film Institute, 1980).

Neale, Stephen, and Frank Krutnik, *Popular Film and Television Comedy* (London: Routledge, 1990).

Nichols, Bill (ed.), *Movies and Methods*, vol. 1 (Berkeley and Los Angeles: University of California Press, 1976).

Nowell-Smith, Geoffrey (ed.), *The Oxford History of World Cinema* (Oxford: Oxford University Press, 1996).

Sayles, John, *Thinking in Pictures* (Boston: Houghton Mifflin Company, 1987).

Silver, Alan, and James Ursini (eds), *Film Noir Reader* (New York: Limelight, 1996).

Slusser, George E., and Eric S. Rabkin (eds), *Shadows of the Magic Lamp: Fantasy and Science Fiction Film* (Carbondale, IL: Southern Illinois University Press 1985).

Sobchack, Vivian, *Screening Space: The American Science Fiction Film* (New York: Ungar, 1991).

Springer, Claudia, *Electronic Eros: Bodies and Desire in the Postindustrial Age* (London: Athlone, 1996).

Stacey, Jackie, *Star Gazing: Hollywood Cinema and Female Spectatorship* (London: Routledge, 1993).

Stam, Robert, Robert Burgoyne, and Sandy Flitterman-Lewis, *New Vocabularies in Film Semiotics: Structuralism, Post-Structuralism and Beyond* (London: Routledge, 1992).

Street, Sarah, *British National Cinema* (London: Routledge, 1997).

Tasker, Yvonne, *Spectacular Bodies: Gender, Genre and the Action Cinema* (London: Routledge, 1993).

Tasker, Yvonne, *Working Girls: Gender and Sexuality in Popular Cinema* (London: Routledge, 1998).

Telotte, J.P., *Replications: A Robotic History of the Science Fiction Film* (Urbana and Chicago, IL: University of Illinois Press, 1995).

Thornham, Sue, *Passionate Detachments: An Introduction to Feminist Film Theory* (London: Arnold, 1997).

Williams, Linda (ed.), *Viewing Positions: Ways of Seeing Film* (London: Athlone, 1995).

Winston Dixon, Wheeler, *The Films of Jean-Luc Godard* (Albany: State University of New York Press, 1997).

Wollen, Peter, *Signs and Meaning in the Cinema* (London: Secker and Warburg, 1969).

Wollen, Peter, *Readings and Writings* (London: Verso, 1982).

Wright Wexman, Virginia, *Creating the Couple: Love, Marriage, and Hollywood Performance* (Princeton, NJ: Princeton University Press, 1993).

Young, Lola, *Fear of the Dark: 'Race', Gender and Sexuality in the Cinema* (London: Routledge, 1995).

Zizek, Slavoj, *Looking Awry: An Approach to Jacques Lacan through Popular Culture* (Cambridge, MA and London, 1991).

Zizek, Slavoj, *Enjoy Your Symptom!: Jacques Lacan in Hollywood and Out* (London and New York: Routledge, 1992).

Zizek, Slavoj, *The Metastases of Enjoyment* (London and New York: Verso, 1994).

Index

Material in the *Audio-visual resources* section is not included in the Index